Bookvan

CHILDFREE BY CHOICE

CHILDFREE
by CHOICE

The Movement Redefining
Family and Creating a
New Age of Independence

DR. AMY BLACKSTONE

AFTERWORD BY
LANCE BLACKSTONE

DUTTON

DUTTON

An imprint of Penguin Random House LLC
penguinrandomhouse.com

Copyright © 2019 by Amy Blackstone
Afterword copyright © 2019 by Lance Blackstone

LIBRARY OF CONGRESS CATALOGING-IN-PUBLICATION DATA

Names: Blackstone, Amy, author.
Title: Childfree by choice : the movement redefining family and creating a new age of independence / Dr. Amy Blackstone.
Description: First edition. | New York, New York : Dutton, [2019] | Includes bibliographical references.
Identifiers: LCCN 2018039378| ISBN 9781524744090 (hardcover) | ISBN 9781524744106 (ebook)
Subjects: LCSH: Childfree choice.
Classification: LCC HQ755.8 B583 2019 | DDC 306.874—dc23
LC record available at https://lccn.loc.gov/2018039378

Printed in the United States of America
1 3 5 7 9 10 8 6 4 2

BOOK DESIGN BY KRISTIN DEL ROSARIO

For the trailblazers
who made my own choice possible

CONTENTS

CONTENTS

We threw the party for J's first birthday. When it came time for cake, our guest of honor, the smallest person in the room by a long shot, fittingly selected the largest slice. It sat undisturbed on his high chair tray for just a few seconds.

Soon J, his chair, the floor, and, as we like to retell it, the ceiling were covered in cake. By some miracle, J's pudgy arms had the reach of the construction cranes he would later become obsessed with as a toddler.

It was a mess. Encouraged by our laughter, J massaged the frosting into his face. We were happy to egg him on. Post–J cleanup wasn't our problem. That was his parents' job.

As my nephew J's nanny for the first few months of his life, I brought a good deal of experience to the role. A certified babysitter since age eleven, I had prior experience as a nanny and a stint in high school as perhaps the youngest church nursery head of all time. All roads pointed toward the inevitability of parenthood for me. My husband, Lance, was sure of it.

Never mind that we'd already agreed we weren't having kids. Never mind that Lance had no plans to change his mind. He knew, one day, I would change mine. My biological clock would tick on.

My maternal instinct would kick in. When the time came, Lance would silently mourn his freedom, accept it, and move on.

While Lance counted the days remaining until I changed my mind, I waited for the world to catch on to a simple truth: that not having kids is a perfectly acceptable life choice.

We hadn't fully "come out" as childfree yet, but we'd told a few people we weren't planning to have kids. The "oh, you'll change your minds" were a dime a dozen. No one took us seriously.

It wasn't really a surprise, then, when my sister chirped, "So when are you two going to give J a cousin?" My impassioned retort brought the room to a halt: "Never!"

The last glob of frosting clinging to J's flailing paws hit the floor with a thud. The news was out. We were {not} having a baby!

While we knew that our decision not to have kids fell outside the path that others had envisioned for us, Lance and I had no idea when we made the choice that we'd find ourselves discussing it on the set of Katie Couric's talk show years later. Lance, one of very few publicly vocal childfree men, joined the audience. I took my seat on the stage along with Katie. I was there to be interviewed in my capacity as Dr. Amy Blackstone, professor of sociology at the University of Maine and a nationally recognized expert on the childfree choice. When I suggested during the interview that the notion of maternal instinct is a myth, Katie's response—"This is blasphemy!"—made clear just how sacred a conviction I had challenged. But I hadn't just challenged a deeply rooted conviction, I'd made visible a choice that for many, and even for myself for many years, had remained largely unseen.

AN INVISIBLE CHOICE

Sociologist of gender Judith Lorber once observed, "Talking about gender for most people is the equivalent of fish talking about water."[1] Much the same can be said of talking about the choice to parent—or not. Parenthood is so much a part of our everyday lives, from how we arrange our families to what we see on TV and in magazines to what we learn in church and hear from our politicians, that we often take it for granted. But while everyone has at least two biological parents (sometimes more, thanks to a "three-parent" technique that in 2016 resulted in the birth of the first baby to be born with DNA from the eggs of two different females and sperm from one male[2]), not everyone becomes a parent.

In launching my research on the childfree, my goal was to better understand and make visible the experiences of people whose circumstances I did—and do—share. At the time that I decided I wanted to study the childfree, I had just submitted my tenure portfolio and felt confident that the response would be positive. Upon reaching this milestone in my career, many of my friends were reaching a significant milestone in their own lives—they were, to use the common vernacular, starting their families. Even friends I once thought were sure to be part of our lifelong childfree sister- and brotherhood were having kids.

One friend, who'd declared at her bridal shower years earlier (much to the chagrin of her mother and grandmothers) that she was never, *ever* having kids, called to tell me that she was—quite intentionally and very happily—pregnant. Shortly thereafter, a friend from grad school, who had been on the fence about kids, shared her own good news. And though I am in no way superstitious, my friends' pregnancies always seem to come in threes. A week after my grad school friend shared that she was expecting, a friend from work who I knew had been leaning toward not having kids, shared with me the news of her own pending bundle of joy. In all three cases, I was happy for my friends, genuinely so, because in spite of their earlier hesitation, I knew they'd made the choice they wanted to make. This isn't always the case for parents—something I'll explore more in the following pages.

As someone without kids but who felt that I *had* started a family—I'd already built a life on my own as an adult with a household, a career, a cat, and a companion—I was struck by the notion that my family didn't seem to count and that our friends, with whom Lance and I had once had so much in common, were disappearing. I also wondered what was wrong with me and where the batteries to my own biological clock had gone. Why wasn't I feeling the same pull toward motherhood that so many of the women around me seemed to be feeling?

So, as a newly tenured professor who was seeing less of her friends as they made the transition to parenthood and who now had a job from which I could not easily be fired, I decided to shift the focus of my research agenda to include a set of questions that I had a personal investment in, questions surrounding the childfree choice and the experience of being childfree. I launched what has become my decade-long study of the childfree after receiving a grant from the National Council on Family Relations' section on Feminism and Family Studies. As a sociologist of gender at heart and by training, I focused the grant on discovering how gender and the childfree choice might be connected. Did women and men reach the decision in the same way? Did they think about their choice similarly? How did others respond? Were the consequences of their choice the same regardless of gender?

The fifty childfree women and twenty childfree men I've formally interviewed since embarking on my research taught me that there is more to their stories than gender, though gender certainly plays a big role in shaping their experiences as childfree and how others respond to their choice. They also think about and form families in new and inspiring ways, they face workplace challenges because of their status as childfree, some are deeply involved in the lives of children who are not their own, they lead full and fascinating lives, they're involved in their communities, and they're happy with the choice they've made.

I've also learned from my students' research on the subject, including a survey of over seven hundred childfree women and men, which found that women experience the stigma of their choice more deeply than other childfree people.[3] And of course I've learned from the decades of social scientific research on the childfree choice that precedes my own, starting with the work of trailblazers Leta Hollingsworth in the early twentieth century and Jean Veevers and Sharon Houseknecht in the 1970s, to research by my contemporaries, including Kristin Park, Tonya Koropeckyj-Cox, Rosemary Gillespie, and Kimya Dennis, to emerging research by newer scholars that include Shelly Volsche, Brooke Long, Gillian Ayers, Braelin Settle, Andrea Laurent-Simpson, and Jenna Healey—to name just a few.[4]

Writers, filmmakers, and activists outside of academe have also informed my work. Laura Carroll has been spreading the word about the childfree choice since the publication of her first book nearly two decades ago.[5] Laura Scott, author and filmmaker, welcomed Lance and me with open arms to the childfree blogosphere.[6] Childfree pioneer and author Marcia Drut-Davis has been a source of inspiration for us.[7] And with filmmakers Maxine Trump and Therese Shechter I've found camaraderie and friendship and discovered ways of celebrating the childfree choice and critiquing the motherhood mandate that are touching, hilarious, and creative.[8]

All of these writers, researchers, filmmakers, and activists—and many more—have played a role in making more visible the choice not to have children. And they've inspired Lance and me in our own efforts toward that end.

WE'RE {NOT} HAVING A BABY!

As many positive role models Lance and I spoke with, however, we also had another inspiration to begin speaking out on the childfree choice ourselves: We'd seen the letters to advice columnists lamenting the pressure to give parents grandchildren, heard the cries of "You'll regret it!" from well-meaning friends, seen the name-calling ("Selfish!" "Stupid!" "Shallow!") from anonymous observers online. We knew what people thought of us, the childfree. Fueled by this fury, we began writing our blog, *we're {not} having a baby!*, together on April 1, 2013—and since then have had the rewarding experience of learning from the thousands of childfree people we've met through the blog, though it didn't start out so smoothly.

We launched the blog with the fanfare normally reserved for launch announcements of a different sort. "Special delivery!" we wrote on that very first post. "We're having a . . . BLOG!" We even included a tongue-in-cheek "birth" announcement with a photo of the two of us snuggled on the couch, staring lovingly at a computer in our laps, the opening screen of our new blog displayed. Along with the photo came the requisite sap ("With much love and hope for the future, we proudly announce *we're {not} having a baby!*") and stats (Born April 1, 2013; Weight: n/a; Height: n/a).

The significance of announcing that we were *not* having a baby on April Fools' Day, no less with a pretend "birth" announcement, didn't dawn on us until a few friends called to congratulate us on finally taking the leap by saying yes to parenthood. We were joking, right? Earlier claims that we weren't having kids must have been just talk. They knew we'd change our minds one day! Joy of joys, we really *were* having a baby! We couldn't undo our poorly timed launch, so we soldiered on and used the mishap as an opportunity to confirm with friends and family that we really, truly were *not* having a baby.

Once we all recovered from the initial confusion, the response to our plans for the blog—to document our experiences as a childfree couple and share what we'd learned about the childfree choice from my research on the topic—varied. Some thought it was a great idea, saying they couldn't wait to read it. One childfree friend was quick to offer her support and congratulations on social media: "Awesome! We *so* need this!!" Others were less enthusiastic, even confused. One relative, not yet a mother herself but soon would be, shared this reaction on Facebook: "LOL. An entire blog just to talk about how you don't want kids? What's the point?" To her credit, she changed her tone once we explained what we had in mind for the blog, but she wasn't the only person to express wonder over the need for such a thing.

We created the blog to have a space where we could celebrate our choice. We sought the sort of camaraderie that comes from knowing you've made the same life choice as those around you. Living in a small town where most people our age were parents, creating a virtual community seemed like a good option. Offering readers the chance to share their own stories, the blog also provided a space for us to learn from those who'd made the same choice but whose circumstances differed from our own. From our readers' stories we learned what it was like for other childfree people to come out as childfree and how their experiences varied by location, age, family circumstance, gender, and so many other factors.

As the blog developed, so too did my research on the topic and the public's interest in the childfree choice. I started getting calls from reporters wanting to understand who makes the choice and why. Grad students interested in writing dissertations on the topic e-mailed me for advice. Childfree people and those who love them wrote to ask for resources. Soon, I came to understand that this cultural moment isn't just a moment. It is part of a larger conversation about how we make choices about our reproductive lives, our families, our work, our free time, and how we'll age. It is about how we navigate the public consequences of our personal choices, who controls those choices, and how scientific discovery and new options for how we form bonds and plan for our futures shape our lives. I realized that this "moment" is so much more than a moment, and so much bigger than our own announcement that we weren't having a baby ourselves.

THE PERSONAL, THE PUBLIC, AND THE POLITICAL

What became the rallying cry of the second-wave feminist movement—"The personal is political"—is as relevant today as ever. What at first glance appears to be the very personal question of whether or not to have kids has become a matter of public concern and political debate. Policy makers, media commentators, and parents worried they might never experience the joys of grandchildren want to better understand the trend. What's been missing from much of the discussion to date is a perspective grounded in history, drawn from decades of scientific inquiry, and in dialogue with broader political and cultural questions about how we organize our lives and our communities.

In this book, I set out to shed light on what the childfree choice is, how the lives of those who make it are arranged, and why they've opted out of parenthood. I also explore the consequences of the choice for those who make it. Though cultural lore suggests regret is a likely consequence, more common is an awareness of the stigma of choosing the path less traveled, an acceptance that not everyone will understand, and also the joy of arranging one's life in the way that feels most right. In the context of an ever-growing global population and the simultaneous shrinking population in many Western nations, I consider what more people on earth means for all of us and what fewer people in some nations means for how we think about family, aging, and community. Both trends have consequences for city, state, national, and global policy and planning.

As more people make the choice not to have kids, a new market segment has also emerged. Though, in the words of public relations executive Adrianna Bevilaqua, "the majority of marketing talks to adult women like they are all moms or want to be mothers."[9] Communications trailblazers like Melanie Notkin, who founded the lifestyle brand Savvy Auntie, and Karen Malone Wright, founder of The NotMom Summit, are working to shift this pattern. Women without kids spend 35 percent more per person on groceries and 60 percent more days abroad per year than mothers.[10] They spend nearly twice as much on hair and beauty products. As Wright told *The New York Times*, non-mothers "have money and are beginning to get a little ticked off no one is noticing them."[11]

While marketers may not notice the childfree, others certainly do. Conservative pundits determined to keep as many women as possible out of the public sphere and at home are especially ardent in their targeting of childfree women. But the vitriol is not limited to conservatives. During the 2013 New York City mayoral race, Chirlane McCray claimed that her husband Bill de Blasio's rival, Christine Quinn, would be unable to effectively advocate for childcare issues because she wasn't a mother herself. In 2016, U.S. Green Party presidential candidate Jill Stein wrote that she wants our next president "to reflect the values that are part of being a mom," defining those values as "taking care of others and being compassionate, starting with our children."[12] Across the pond, 2016 British prime minister contender Andrea Leadsom was quoted as saying "that being a mum means you have a real stake in the future of our country, a tangible stake."[13] The implication about non-mothers is clear.

In 1976, the U.S. Census Bureau began tracking women's lifetime childlessness. For the first time ever, we could see—publicly, with data!—what women were doing in their private lives and whether and when they would make the very personal decision to become mothers. Also for the first time, we began to see that increasing numbers of women were opting out of motherhood entirely. Today, one in six women will end her childbearing years without ever giving birth. Half of millennials don't yet have children and it remains to be seen how many will.

Women are judged whatever choice they make about children. Too many and you're selfish—not enough time for each kid! Just one and you're selfish—children need siblings to thrive! None and you're selfish—why don't you care about children? Whatever choice we make, it seems we just can't win. And let's face it, the pressure to realize their supposed "natural instincts" is much higher on women—but men are not entirely off the hook. We didn't get here by accident—an intertwining of reproductive, family, medical, and gender history brought us here. Exploring that rich history helps us see that the current moment isn't just comments and opinions from friends, family, or media; it is grounded in our past and built into our very society. It also varies across cultures and geographical borders.

This book is for everyone, whether you have children or not. Who controls our fertility and which reproductive choices are available to us shape all our experiences. How we age, and who takes care of us when we're old, are questions we all face. How we balance work and life, and who is responsible for ensuring that such balance is possible, are questions we've all asked. While rates of childlessness have nearly doubled since the advent of reliable birth control in the 1960s, our cultural norms, values, and beliefs haven't caught up to this reality. Today, the childfree are at the center of these conversations, but the questions touch us all.

ONE

CHILDFREE:
THE BIRTH OF A MOVEMENT

OBITUARY: MOTHERHOOD. Died, as a symbol, a life role, a sacred institution, sometime in the early nineteen-seventies. Causes of death: concern for overpopulation; and the desire of many to live as free individuals, not nurturers of young.

—ELLEN PECK, *THE NEW YORK TIMES*[1]

n 1972, Ellen Peck's *New York Times* editorial pronounced the death of motherhood. Though birth rates in many Western nations are lower today than they were then, our growing global population suggests the pronouncement was premature. The institution of motherhood has certainly changed since the 1970s, but it is still very much alive and kicking. Peck, co-founder of the National Organization for Non-Parents, was part of a new movement dedicated to raising awareness about parenthood as a choice and in particular about nonparenthood as a reasonable and viable alternative that adults could—and should—consider making.

Emerging during the "contested realm of reproductive politics in the 1970s," childfree activism represented the "nexus of identity politics and environmental activism."[2] The childfree movement called into question the assumption that life without children lacked purpose. As birth control options expanded and improved, more and more women were free to choose whether, when, how, and to how many children they would become mothers. This new freedom created a consciousness about parenthood as a choice rather than destiny. With that new consciousness came the emergence of a childfree movement, a grassroots effort to educate the public about nonparenthood as a legitimate life choice, raise awareness about the problems associated with overpopulation, and advocate for those who made the choice to be childfree.

When the National Organization for Non-Parents (NON) launched in 1972, authors in *Time* wrote with disdain about its founding, dismissing its "frequently childish espousal of childless-ness" as "rather juvenile."[3] The magazine has since changed its tune. In its 2013 cover story about the childfree life, "None Is Enough," author Lauren Sandler wrote that childfree women are "inventing a new female archetype, one for whom having it all doesn't mean having a baby."[4] But while that may be the case, and we may be more accepting of the choice now than in the past, not having a baby still often means being dismissed as childish and juvenile. Women in particular are told that parenthood is their destiny; motherhood their most important role. And women and men both are told that a primary—if not *the* primary—purpose of their unions is to procreate. Ellen Peck's obituary for motherhood came at a time when many people and movements were questioning existing social arrangements and power structures. But to question motherhood was to attack a noble institution, one whose purpose was to rear and protect the most precious of blessings.

BLESSED ARE THE CHILDREN

Religion is among the strongest forces driving us to believe it is both our purpose and our duty to reproduce. Encouraging the proliferation of loyal followers ensures the continuation of the church. In the Catholic faith in particular, followers are taught that marriage is "primarily procreative."[5] But the tenet that followers should be fruitful and multiply can be found across a wide set of religious traditions and beliefs.[6] Sociologist Tanya Koropeckyj-Cox and colleagues found that the more conservative a person's beliefs about the Bible, in particular the more one views the Bible as the literal word of

God, the greater the likelihood that person will report a low approval of childlessness. Among the religious categories Koropeckyj-Cox examined (Baptist, Catholic, Jewish, fundamentalist Protestant, no religion, and other Protestants), Baptists and those of Jewish faith were least likely to accept childlessness.

Contraception and abortion are taboo in most religious traditions, as is sexual intercourse that is not considered unitive and procreative.[7] This is likely the reason that childfree people who report that religion is important to them are significantly more likely than the nonreligious to report feeling stigmatized for their choice not to have kids.[8] In the words of the United States Conference of Catholic Bishops, "When couples readily treat, as separate choices, the decisions to get married and to have children [t]his indicates a mentality in which children are seen not as integral to a marriage but as optional."[9]

Other religious organizations, too, assert that the purpose of marriage is children, though with varying degrees of tolerance for the possibility that sex may not always be procreative. As sociologist Mary Hunt observed, "The Evangelical mindset differs from the Catholics in that sexual acts within a heterosexual marriage which are pleasurable yet without the goal of procreation are permissible as long as the couple is willing to accept the 'potential fruit of their love,' meaning they must 'be open to the possibility' of children."[10] Theologian Cristina Richie traces these teachings back to Augustinian sexual ethics, in which children are the ultimate goal of marriage, and intercourse is deemed sinful if it is engaged in for pleasure rather than procreation.[11]

Whatever the position of religious institutions on sex—for procreation only or for procreation *and* pleasure—religious studies scholar Dawn Llewllyn notes that the "maternal expectation" in religious traditions confuses, silences, and hurts women whose faith identities do not align with their plans regarding motherhood.[12] As one childfree woman Llewllyn interviewed told her, "I have some-times wondered whether the fact that I ended up single was a kind of punishment for not wanting children or for choosing not to have children. That God was saying, 'Well, if you're not open to life then you don't deserve a partner.'" Another woman Llewllyn interviewed, a childfree married Methodist minister, said Christian sources had provoked "shame, a level of guilt" in her. She went on to share that "anything Christian I might have looked at and certainly if I looked at anything Catholic . . . [tells me] it is not an appropriate choice to make."

For heterosexual couples who don't resist the religious mandate to procreate, what becomes of all that fruit produced by their unions? Historically, this has varied. Though children today occupy a re-vered status (if not in deed, at least in word), this hasn't always been the case. As historian Steven Mintz put it, "The notion of a long childhood, devoted to education and free from adult responsibilities, is a very recent invention, and one that became a reality for a major-ity of children only after World War II."[13] It seems children became priceless at the very moment that they lost their economic value. Children were at one time essential to the economic survival of their families. In colonial times, American children labored on family farms, in home workshops, and as domestic help in their own or others' homes. As the Industrial Revolution took off, children went to work in factories. Prior to the 1920s, children were considered assets of the family head, so divorced fathers had no legal child-support obligations because once they left the home, they no longer had access to their children's wages.[14] Historian Stephanie Coontz notes that among skilled and unskilled laborers in particular, "whose earning power had often peaked by the end of their teens, it could be an advantage to marry and have children early, because after only a short period of dependence, the children could enter the labor force and increase total household income."[15] Eventually, child labor came to be seen as abusive. The Fair Labor Standards Act of 1938 instituted the first federally mandated minimum ages of employment and regulated hours of work for children.

By the 1940s, children had moved out of factories, and women moved into them, as men left for war. With less need for children to work the land at home, and regulations in place to protect them from work outside the home, kids spent an increasing amount of time at school. Between 1870 and 1988, the time children spent in school quadrupled, from 11 to 43 percent of days each year.[16] Sociologist Donald J. Hernandez credits both the decline in child labor and the increase in formal schooling to "the shift from farming to industrial jobs requiring stronger, more experienced workers; the enactment of child labor and compulsory education laws; and the rising level of affluence that made it possible for families to survive without child labor," plus the increase in occupations "characterized by high incomes and high prestige, [which] increasingly required advanced knowledge and skills that could be obtained only through formal schooling."

After World War II, we began to think differently about children's role in the family. Rather than economic contributors, they became precious blessings, representing the deepest kind of commitment and love between a man and woman. In the 1950s, men returned from war to the factories and other employment at home while women moved out of factories and back into the home. Marriage rates soared in this era, as did birth rates, going up from just 79.5 births per 1,000 women in the United States in 1940 to 123 per 1,000 women in 1957.[17] As historian Stephanie Coontz notes, we're inclined to forget that the 1950s was just one period in our vast history. The idea that a "normal" family constitutes a heterosexual married couple with (at least) two or (at most) three children along with a male breadwinner and a mom at home took hold in the fifties and has entrenched itself in our cultural memory as the "traditional" way. During "the long decade," as historians refer to the 1950s, "every magazine, every marriage manual, every advertisement . . . assumed the family was based on the . . . male wage-earner and the child-rearing, home-managing housewife."[18]

While the shift away from child labor and placing such heavy burdens on children is obviously a good thing, the pendulum seems to have swung just as far in the other direction. Today it's all about helicopter parenting, and those who don't position the role of parent as the center of their universe are chastised for being selfish and uncaring. The shift toward helicopter parenting did not arise in a vacuum, though, and is a development I explore in more depth in the chapters to come. One thing that's clear is that how we think of children, and upon whom and how we direct responsibility for raising them, is not a given and has changed over time.

"RACE DEATH"

As notions about children and their purpose shifted, so too did beliefs about who should have children and who should not. In 1883, English scientist Sir Francis Galton, inspired by the work of his distant cousin Charles Darwin, coined the term *eugenics*—from the Greek root meaning "good in birth"—to express the idea that we should give "the more suitable races or strains of blood a better chance of prevailing" by increasing reproduction of select classes of men and women.[19] While Galton primarily advocated in favor of "positive eugenics"—encouraging the breeding of native-born, white, and middle- and upper-class citizens whose families were free from "defects"—other eugenicists promoted "negative eugenics"—efforts to prevent "socially undesirable" people, such as nonwhites (including eastern and southern European immigrants) and those perceived to hold "destructive traits," from having children.[20]

Scholar and social justice advocate Dorothy Roberts notes that racist ideology "provided fertile soil for eugenic theories to take root and flourish" not just in Galton's home country but abroad as well. In the United States, the eugenics movement of the early twentieth century was a systemic, large-scale effort that, in the words of historian Elaine Tyler May, "resulted in political, institutional, medical, and legislative measures that encouraged some Americans to become parents but prevented others from doing so."[21]

In the early 1900s, University of Chicago biologist Charles Davenport received funding from the Carnegie Institute and railroad heiress Mrs. E. H. Harriman to conduct an investigation of evolution in Cold Spring Harbor, New York. Davenport led a team of researchers in the ancestral charting of families in the area believed to carry defective genes. In his 1911 report of findings, Davenport concluded that behavioral characteristics such as criminality, mental retardation and low intelligence, eroticism, and pauperism were determined by heredity and that particular traits could be attributed to different groups—for example, Italians were seen as prone to personal violence, Poles to clannishness, and Swedes to tidiness. Davenport recommended that the reproduction of "bad stock" be prevented through state-enforced sterilization and selective marriages and immigration.

President Theodore Roosevelt fueled the efforts of eugenicists in his 1903 address to Congress: "When home ties are loosened; when men and women cease to regard a worthy family life . . . as the life best worth living; then evil days for the commonwealth are at hand. . . . Surely it should need no demonstration to show that wilful [sic] sterility is, from the standpoint of the nation, from the standpoint of the human race, the one sin for which the penalty is national death, race death; a sin for which there is no atonement; a sin which is the more dreadful exactly in proportion as the men and women guilty thereof are in other respects, in character, and bodily and mental powers, those whom for the sake of the state it would be well to see the fathers and mothers of many healthy children, well brought up in homes made happy by their presence. No man, no woman, can shirk the primary duties of life, whether for love of ease and pleasure, or for any other cause, and retain his or her self-respect."[22]

Many white Americans heeded Roosevelt's admonishment. Inspired by Davenport's research, new organizations such as the American Eugenics Society cropped up to promote the study of eugenics. American colleges offered courses on eugenics. In 1921, after the Second International Eugenics Congress was held at the American Museum of Natural History, eugenicist Henry Fairfield Osborn wrote with glee, "On every side there is evidence that the eugenics propaganda has taken a firm root in this country."[23] Indeed, by that point the American Eugenics Society had established a foothold in both popular culture and policy making with "committees that focused on cooperation with clergymen, religious sermon contests, crime prevention, popular and formal education, and selective immigration."[24] And newspaper headlines such as "Eugenics First in the Ghetto" and "New Aristocracy Will Be Human Thoroughbreds" were common.[25]

In 1908, using the principles of eugenics as its foundation, former schoolteacher Mary de Garmo established the first "Better Babies" competition at the Louisiana State Fair.[26] The idea took off and in 1914 *Women's Home Companion* noted that all but three states—West Virginia, New Hampshire, and Utah—had hosted Better Babies contests.[27] Billed as a public health effort, babies were judged on mental and physical development. Family history, considered an estimate of babies' moral capacity and development, also played into babies' scores. The contests excluded black children and "promoted the idea that only White babies could achieve perfection."[28] As public health nurse Ida Williams put it at the time, "There is no corner of the country too remote, too unprogressive to respond to this new clarion call for a better race."[29] Eugenics fieldworkers submitted competition results, "a ready-made template for eugenic information on children and their parents," to Charles Davenport's Eugenics Record Office.[30]

Soon a new kind of contest grew out of the Better Babies competitions—this one focused on families. The Fitter Families competitions of the 1920s, according to education policy scholar Steven Selden, reveal a transition from a primary focus on child development to a more clearly eugenics discourse.[31] Families judged as having superior heredity received medals like one from the 1928 Third Race Betterment Conference in Battle Creek, Michigan, which carried the Psalms inscription "Yea, I have a goodly heritage." Mary Watts, credited with bringing Better Babies contests to Iowa shortly after Mary de Garmo's first such competition in Louisiana, later came to help lead the development of Fitter Family competitions in Kansas. When asked to describe these new contests, Watts explained, "While the stock judges are testing Holsteins, Jerseys, and Whitefaces in the pavilion, we are judging the Joneses, Smiths, and Johnsons, and nearly every one [who learns of this] replies: 'I think it is about time people had a little of the attention that is given to animals.'"[32]

As Theodore Roosevelt's comments and the eugenics movement make clear, panic over variable fertility rates within one's borders is nothing new; and while the composition of panic may vary across time and place, its existence has not subsided. Never mind that our global population reached 7 billion in 2011 and is increasing at a rate of 200,000 people each day.[33] This fact is forgotten or overlooked in much of the contemporary discussion about changing fertility rates. Indeed, the project of pronatalism—the political, ideological, and religious system designed to encourage childbearing and retain high birth rates within nation-states—is designed to get us to be concerned only with populating the earth with people who share our national, cultural, and racial identities. As a result, many nations and states worry that "their people" are not repopulating "their territory" at acceptable rates even though the global territory we share is already overburdened with too many of us.

Of course, pronatalist and eugenics policies and ideology do not apply to all women in the same way, nor have they ever. White women, even those who were childless by circumstance rather than by choice, were not immune from attack—all white women of middle or higher classes without children were suspect, either for willfully disobeying their duty or for making poor decisions resulting in sterility presumably caused by sexually transmitted disease or by choosing the wrong husband. Among the first to recognize that some childless marriages were voluntarily so, eugenicist Paul Popenoe referred to these unions, and those in them, as "infantile, self-indulgent, [and] frequently neurotic."[34] But as sociologist Rosemary Gillespie put it, "Paradoxically, while 'suitable' white, middle-class women have struggled to gain the right to avoid, terminate, or limit pregnancies, the rights to motherhood of Native American, Black, and Latina women have been compromised through their disproportional and nonconsensual sterilization."[35] Eugenicists had two primary targets: childless white women, who were accused of shirking their patriotic duty to the nation, and immigrants and other women of color, who eugenicists worried were on their way toward outnumbering white Americans.

The systemic abuse of black women's bodies in particular is not limited to the eugenics period; black women were being sterilized against their will in the United States as late as the 1970s, and even into the 1980s.[36] As just one example, in 1971, workers at an Office of Economic Opportunity–sponsored family planning agency in Montgomery, Alabama, began administering the contraceptive injection Depo-Provera, under clinical trials, to fourteen-year-old Katie Relf without her consent. Katie lived with her parents and her two younger sisters in public housing. Workers at the agency concluded, without any evidence to suggest so, that because Katie and her sisters were "poor and black, they would engage in unprotected sexual activity and bear illegitimate children, whom they would ask the state to support."[37] The two younger Relf girls were later sterilized, without their consent, after the Food and Drug Administration terminated clinical trials of Depo-Provera.

Margaret Sanger herself, champion of the birth control pill and founder of Planned Parenthood, "appropriated eugenic rationales" in her advocacy for birth control in order to gain the support of physicians who believed it was their role—and their right—to determine which women were fit and which were unfit for motherhood.[38] Sanger's role in the reproductive rights movement is a contradictory one. On the one hand, she "honored and exalted motherhood," calling for better health care and a reduction in maternal mortality. She also advocated in favor of sexual pleasure for its own sake, separate from reproduction.[39] But historian Rebecca Kluchin argues that Sanger's efforts compromised the feminist ideals that originally drove the birth control movement, and her collaboration with eugenicists ultimately undermined women's ability to control their own reproduction.

Details about trials of the female birth control pill also complicate narratives about Sanger as a champion of reproductive justice. The trials were launched in the 1950s in Puerto Rico, first among American female medical students at the University of Puerto Rico School of Medicine. Students were pressured to participate and those who did not comply with the procedures were threatened with academic failure. In the end, the results from the trial on students were tossed, in part because of the small sample of participants and in part because the students were "regarded as too sophisticated for demonstrating how well women with less education could deal with the contraceptive."[40]

Eventually, researchers expanded the trials in Puerto Rico, Haiti, and Mexico, targeting impoverished women, a group that researchers and birth control advocates such as Sanger viewed as in need of population control. It was assumed that if women who were "semi-literate or illiterate" could be taught to take a pill daily, the pill's likelihood of marketability and success in other regions of the world would be high.[41] Researchers brushed aside participants' complaints about side effects. Although the pill has since been linked to circulatory disorders, one woman's death from congestive heart failure and another's development of pulmonary tuberculosis were thought to be independent of their participation in the clinical trial. And writer and former UN consultant Betsy Hartmann notes that one study at the time "even blamed most occurrences of side effects such as nausea, vomiting, and dizziness on psychological factors."[42]

Also happening was the coerced sterilization of women throughout Puerto Rico. With other forms of contraception either unavailable or prohibitively expensive, women—an important source of cheap labor in an increasingly industrialized workforce—were offered sterilization at little or no cost. They were not, however, offered complete information about the permanence of the procedure. By 1968, approximately one-third of Puerto Rican women of childbearing age had been sterilized, making them ten times more likely to be sterilized than women in the United States.[43] A 1982 film, *La operación*, documents the experiences of women who were sterilized during this period, some of whom regretted having received the procedure, others who felt they hadn't had a choice, and others who felt unclear about what had happened to them.[44]

These abhorrent practices and the racist ideology that drove them are not limited to our distant past. In 2013, the Center for Investigative Reporting found that 148 female inmates in California's prison system had been sterilized between 2006 and 2010.[45]

The women had been signed up for tubal ligation surgery while pregnant. At least one woman told reporter Corey G. Johnson that she was happy to have had the surgery, but others said they were pressured to do so. African American inmate Kimberly Jeffrey said she was pressured to say yes to sterilization while strapped to an operating table and under sedation as doctors prepared to deliver her baby via C-section.

While many states and nations have moved to outlaw eugenic practices, including the 1978 Federal Sterilization Regulations in the United States, complete reproductive freedom remains beyond the reach of many women. Debates today over Planned Parenthood funding, access to contraception, and the availability of and access to abortion make clear that many people, both women and men—representing a range of institutions and belief systems—claim some stake in the right to make decisions about individual women's reproductive autonomy. Yet without complete access to the range of reproductive choices and the right to make those choices for themselves, whether they choose to have children or not, we can never claim that women enjoy complete freedom.

FRUITFUL WOMBS

As some women faced coerced sterilization, others have been effectively coerced into parenthood. Those who advocated "positive eugenics" shamed women perceived to be of good stock into procreating. But even as the eugenics movement waned, the push toward parenthood did not decline for these women. During the Second World War, parenthood became patriotic.[46] White, middle-class women were urged to focus on their families and, in response to fears that their foray into work outside the home during the war might have discouraged them from returning home, FBI director J. Edgar Hoover referred to American housewives in 1956 as "career women" because, as he put it, "I feel there are no careers so important as those of homemaker and mother."[47]

Mothering, women were told, was the best way they could contribute to the fight against communism. And along with the push toward procreation came attention to infertility and efforts to solve it. While Planned Parenthood (previously known as the American Birth Control League) in its early days focused on developing and distributing birth control, its mission expanded to include encouraging childbearing among couples deemed good candidates for parenthood and fighting infertility. In 1944, Harvard physician John Rock and his lab technician, Miriam Menkin, were the first to fertilize human eggs outside the body, a feat met with mixed reactions from their peers and journalists, one of whom compared them to cattle breeders.[48] The Rock and Menkin experiments would "ultimately shake the foundations of contemporary reproductive medicine and raise profound ethical and moral questions."[49]

Nevertheless, fertility research and treatment continued, fueled by the postwar baby boom and an interest in technological innovation. Louise Joy Brown, the first "test tube baby" conceived through in vitro fertilization, was born in 1978. But just a few years earlier, Nobel molecular biologist James Watson decried the procedure, telling a congressional subcommittee in 1974, "All hell will break loose, politically and morally, all over the world," if embryo transplants were allowed to occur.[50] Though news of Louise Joy Brown's 1978 birth is said to have thrown millions of people into moral panic at the time, in vitro fertilization is widely accepted today. Between 1964 and 1984, office visits for infertility nearly tripled.[51] Today more than six million babies have been born through IVF, a fact celebrated in a UK Science Museum exhibit in 2018.[52]

These days, it is questions about "designer babies" that occupy geneticists, ethicists, and the public. While our ability to avert serious conditions like cystic fibrosis, Tay-Sachs, and Down syndrome is mostly considered positive, some doctors assist patients who wish to choose the gender and even the eye color of their babies. One such physician, dubbed "the Benjamin Moore of the laboratory," offers parents a "choice of 30 shades of blue eyes."[53] And in discussions that teeter dangerously close to those from the eugenics period of the early twentieth century, recent news focused on findings from controversial evolutionary biologist Satoshi Kanazawa that the higher a woman's IQ, the lower her likelihood of having children suggests that we haven't moved past the idea that some babies are better, some families fitter, than others.[54]

YOU SAY YOU WANT A REVOLUTION

Stop. Before you even think *of having a baby, you must read this book. It could keep you from making the biggest mistake of your life!*

The dust jacket on the 1971 book *The Baby Trap* did not mince words.[55] Author Ellen Peck had a habit of challenging taken-for-granted notions about the way the world worked, observing that the mystique we've built up around motherhood "verges on the hysterical." Peck begins *The Baby Trap* by asserting, "To the extent that babies are emphasized, adults are de-emphasized. To the extent that a woman is regarded as a means to an end (propagating the species) she is not seen as beautiful, vibrant, valuable, in and of herself. To the extent that a man is seen as a mere provider, he may be seen as less of a person." Her critiques were scathing, radical, and totally feminist-sounding for their time. When it came to talking about parenthood, sex, relationships, and living a "creative, full, and free life," Ellen Peck was unorthodox.

But Peck didn't reject the constrictions of femininity or challenge gender relations in the way we might expect of someone known for her critique of compulsory parenthood. In one moment, Peck takes the seemingly feminist stance that women should enjoy their sexuality, and in the next she asserts that women without children are prettier and better able to keep their husbands happy than are mothers. As historian Jenna Healey put it in her 2016 piece on the history of the National Organization for Non-Parents, "Early childfree writings were more inspired by the sexual revolution than by any feminist impulse. . . . Childfree activists took aim at mandatory parenthood while leaving the rest of the domestic infrastructure—heterosexuality, monogamy, and marriage—largely intact."[56] And in a move that historian Rebecca Kluchin calls neo-eugenic, Peck also targeted poor mothers, accusing them of having children for the government benefits, and criticized welfare and housing policies she viewed as encouraging poor women to reproduce.[57]

Even with a generous reading within its historical context, it is clear that Peck was not seeking to mobilize a diverse array of allies. As *The Tonight Show* host Johnny Carson said of Peck's appearance on his show in 1971, "I thought the audience was going to lynch her . . . it was like [she was] against motherhood, against the American flag, Kate Smith, and Lassie combined."[58] Peck did not, it seemed, critique the institution of parenthood with the interests or concerns of parents in mind, some of whom might have been sympathetic to her cause. She did, however, found NON together with parent and environmental activist Shirley Radl in the year following *The Baby Trap*'s release and her efforts signaled the start of the childfree choice going from personal matter to social movement. At first only a grassroots movement, childfree activists organized so well that they eventually had in NON a "professionalized activist organization" representing the cause.[59]

Much like the woman who birthed it, the childfree movement itself embodies contradictions, some of which may serve the very useful purpose of drawing in a diverse range of supporters while others make the movement vulnerable to criticism. On the one hand, those who critique compulsory parenthood and the culture of intensive parenting, or who at least live by the notion that not everyone must become a parent, are as diverse a group as any. Think nuns, priests, atheists, environmentalists, and mothers fed up with too many PTA meetings. On the other hand, there are days when a quick scan of the childfree Reddit page, or a close read of Peck's book, could confirm the worst. While I personally don't endorse the name-calling that sometimes occurs in these forums, I think I understand where at least some of the vitriol—a sometimes equally hostile treatment of the childfree choice and those who make it—comes from, and why using it might feel cathartic at times. Responding in kind may not always be effective in the long run, but it can be empowering to push back against critics.

For the most part, the childfree choice today is about inclusivity, both within the movement and as one facet of a larger goal, for all women, of all races and socioeconomic statuses, to be supported in the choices they make about parenthood or lack thereof. But that support is not always given back. One time at a friend's birthday party, while chatting with a woman whose company I'd been enjoying and who I thought might become a new friend, The Question came: "So how many kids do you guys have?"

"None," I said as neutrally as I could, knowing that too gleeful a reply could make me look like a jerk but any tone of apology or sorrow would not only be a misrepresentation of my circumstances but could make her feel bad for asking. "It's just me and Lance. We had an awesomely terrible cat for fifteen years, too, but he's no longer with us." Sometimes the joke about our difficult, high-needs cat helps move the conversation along. I would have volleyed the "how many kids" question back her way but I already knew the answer because she'd just been talking about her "three adorable rug rats." My cat quip didn't work this time. Instead, her response: "Oh." Then she turned and walked away. She avoided me for the rest of the evening.

While the woman I met that evening certainly doesn't represent all or even most mothers, the "how many kids do you have" question is so common that developing a plan for how to respond to it was the focus in one part of a workshop I attended at the 2017 NotMom Summit. Because the summit includes women who are "NotMoms" by choice and by chance, I learned that while such questions can get old for those of us who chose not to have kids, they can be more than a nuisance—in fact, incredibly painful—for women whose nonparenthood was not a choice. That such invasive questioning is so often the go-to icebreaker tells us something about how routine it is to assume that all women of a certain age are mothers. I discuss how and why motherhood is so inextricably linked with womanhood in the following chapter.

Another time, a friend who works in an office where vacation time is planned well in advance so that it can be coordinated among all employees—and who happens to be a parent—observed that she thought parents should be first in the queue for requesting time off since "it doesn't matter when people without kids take vacations." I pointed out that people who teach, myself included, had the same limitations on availability for vacations as the students in their classes, and that some of us have partners who might need to coordinate their vacation schedules with their own colleagues. My friend wasn't convinced. And I'm not alone in this experience. The women and men I interviewed shared similar accounts. I take up the theme of work-life balance in the chapters that follow.

Childfree people also face pushback from doctors and other medical professionals from whom they seek help for solutions to avoid pregnancy. Throughout my thirties, annual exams always came with the advice that I consider adding a prenatal vitamin to my daily regimen, in case I "became pregnant or decided to become pregnant." Every year, I'd remind the doctor that motherhood was not on my agenda—ever—to which she'd reply, "Well, you never know" or "You might change your mind." After years of this routine, I finally requested a tubal ligation the year I turned forty. Despite a decade-long record of my unwavering position that I did not want to become a mom, I still got put through the obstacle course of questioning that so many of my research participants and other childfree women have described. To feel so unheard for so many years, to be treated like a child who doesn't know her own mind, and to be doubted by the very people who should be your advocates is demoralizing and exhausting. This, too, is a pattern I explore in more depth in the coming chapters.

Experiences such as these have inspired the childfree of today to speak out and to speak up. But choosing not to have children is not a new phenomenon, and the extent to which it is a socially accepted choice varies across time and space. To quote sociologist Rosemary Gillespie, "Being childfree has always been socially sanctioned for some groups, such as spinsters, widows, nuns, and nannies . . . [and] there have always been individual women who sought to prevent conception, aborted unwanted fetuses, and abandoned or killed a newborn child. What is new is both the increasing numbers of women who eschew motherhood and that increasingly they are able to articulate their rejection in ways not generally available to previous generations of women."[60]

The "new spinsters" of the early twentieth century understood that life without a husband or children meant a kind of social and economic independence that most women of the time did not enjoy.[61] As women in that period gained collective consciousness about their conditions by way of the first-wave feminist movement, more of them rejected motherhood. Today, self-proclaimed spinsters have much of the same awareness about the freedom of staying unhitched—and similar motivations for their choice—as the voluntarily single and childless women of one hundred years ago.[62]

Some ways of opting out of parenthood, such as the priesthood and the convent, have been socially sanctioned for a long time. Others, including abortion, use of contraception, and not participating in a heterosexual union, have seen varying degrees of cultural acceptance at different times and in different locations. Though there have been childfree people for perhaps as long as there have been people, the extent to which nonparenthood has been available as a choice has increased substantially in the last half century.

Social scientists credit several macro-level, cultural events when seeking to explain the changes in fertility over the past fifty years. The zero population growth movement and the publication of Paul Ehrlich's book *The Population Bomb* are both credited for raising awareness about the environmental consequences of overpopulation in the 1960s. And thanks to the second-wave feminist movement of the 1960s and '70s, women began to have more choices about what sort of life they would live as adults.[63] Betty Friedan's observation in her 1963 game changer, *The Feminine Mystique*, was dead-on: "Chosen motherhood is the real liberation. The choice to have a child makes the whole experience of motherhood different, and the choice to be generative in other ways can at last be made, and is being made by many women now, without guilt."[64] But while the second-wave feminist movement is often credited—or blamed, depending on your perspective—for providing entrée for women to a childfree life, research in the 1970s showed that most women opting out of parenthood at that time were not aware of the women's movement until after they'd made their choice about motherhood.[65]

Over the last half century, women have practiced unprecedented control over their own fertility, thanks in large part to the first federally approved oral contraceptive in 1963 and the *Roe v. Wade*

Supreme Court decision, which legalized abortion in 1973. In this period, college attendance among women increased significantly—from 38 percent of female high school graduates in 1960 to around half by 1975[66]—and women gained better access to and opportunity in the workplace. Though women had enjoyed similar rates of representation in national politics in the preceding two decades, a "third generation" of thirty-nine women—including Shirley Chisholm, our first black woman representative, elected in 1968—were elected to Congress between 1955 and 1976. Distinguishing themselves from their predecessors, the congresswomen elected in this period rejected the notion that they should have to conform to male expectations, and they challenged gender-based inequalities.[67] These shifts in medicine, culture, and politics brought us to a new historical moment, one unlike any we'd seen before. Women were making choices that best fit the lives they wanted to live. And not everyone loved it.

Recognizing the shift that was occurring, the feminist backlash of the 1980s was no accident.[68] Conservative pundits and policy makers who observed the changes of the 1960s and '70s understood what those changes could mean for their beloved 1950s notion of family. In 1980, antiabortion activists gained control of the Republican platform committee and added the position that "the unborn child has a fundamental right to life" to the party's official platform.[69] In 1986, a *Newsweek* cover story warned single forty-year-old women that they had a better chance of being killed by a terrorist than of finding a husband (though this "fact" was later debunked by scholars and ultimately retracted by the magazine).[70] Nevertheless, as the eighties progressed, fewer women had children; the percentage of women who remained childless at age forty went from 10 percent in 1980 to 16 percent by 1990.[71]

Over the years, efforts to keep women at home and having babies have been hindered not only by a heightened feminist consciousness but also by economic recession. Most recently, the recession between 2007 and 2009 caused a dip in fertility that garnered lots of attention. Data from the National Center for Health Statistics show that states that were hit hardest by the recession—such as Arizona, where unemployment grew by 165 percent—saw the greatest declines in birth rates. States like North Dakota and Alaska, where the booming oil and gas industry protected many residents from the recession, saw the lowest decline.[72] In my own home state of Maine, and in similar states, fertility has been on the decline for the last decade since the Great Recession. Though part of this can be attributed to the steep drop in the teen birth rate (thanks to the fact that teenagers are having less sex, using more effective contraception, and receiving more information about pregnancy prevention),[73] demographers also credit Maine's high rate of underemployment for the dip. It seems that highly skilled workers employed in particularly low-paying and low-skill jobs—as well as part-time workers who would prefer to be working full-time—either aren't in the mood or don't feel they're in a position to be making babies.

Feminist gains and economic loss drive increases in voluntary childlessness but also in the involuntary. Better opportunities for careers lead some women to choose to pursue fulfillment in ways outside of parenting, while for others, a career means delaying—but not deciding against—childbirth. Though the extent to which women's choice to work "caused" involuntary childlessness has been overstated by critics who'd prefer to see women at home, childlessness by circumstance is one outcome of expanding opportunities for women outside the home. And because we know that fertility rates decline in times of economic hardship, it's likely that the dip seen during the Great Recession was due at least in part to women who would have otherwise had children but delayed for financial reasons. Some of these delays may have ultimately resulted in childlessness that was not planned. For some, this outcome is disappointing, even heartbreaking; for others, it turns out to be a welcome—if unintended—consequence of delay.

THE REAL MEANING IN LIFE

This isn't just my story. It's a story for anyone who has ever given more than a moment's thought to what their adult life might look like and with whom they would spend it, to how they wanted their family to be and what they hope to leave behind when they're gone. It is as much about the moment we're in as it is about how we got here. It is about where and how we derive our sense of meaning and purpose. It's about making this life meaningful, in whatever way feels most right and true.

In recent years, it seems nearly everyone is weighing in on what they think of folks like us, the childfree. People are opting out of parenthood at unprecedented rates, and talking about it in increasingly visible ways. As the *Katie* show producers explained when they called to invite me to the show, Ms. Couric had seen writer Lauren Sandler's 2013 *Time* cover story about the childfree life on newsstands that summer and wanted to explore the question of what drives people to make the choice and to understand how others respond to the choice.

The variety of reactions to Sandler's *Time* article was telling. Though Couric's treatment—and that of many others—was empathetic, inquisitive, and balanced, some were less, shall we say, fair and balanced. *Fox and Friends*' Sunday morning panel came out swinging, asking if Sandler's piece was "sending the wrong message." On that program, Mike Huckabee observed—erroneously—that "it's a good thing the author [of the *Time* article] didn't have kids." Tucker Carlson's reply was characteristically vicious: "But having children means less time for vacations and spin class, where the real meaning in life resides, right? I mean, have you ever seen anything more selfish, decadent, and stupid?" The Fox News position on the childfree choice was clear. Others were less vitriolic but equally dumbfounded that anyone would choose not to be a parent.

Jonathan Last, a writer for the conservative opinion magazine *The Weekly Standard* and who earlier in 2013 published *What to Expect When No One's Expecting: America's Coming Demographic Disaster*, took offense as well. He called Lauren Sandler's discussion of his book in *Time* not only "a tortured reading" but "plain wrong."[74] Last objected particularly to Sandler's characterization that he "scolds" the childfree and "blame[s] their selfishness for America's problems." Lauren Sandler may not have summarized Jonathan Last's position on the childfree choice as Last would have preferred, but if Sandler got his position wrong, so too did noted demographer David Coleman. In his review of *What to Expect When No One's Expecting*, Coleman called Last's conclusions "perverse," placing the book in the genre of "a moralizing apocalyptic tradition of popular American 'disaster demography.'"[75] Whoever had it right, it was clear that these writers, academics, and other public figures were weighing in on something about which everybody seemed to have an opinion.

Disaster demography, to borrow Coleman's term, perpetuates a number of myths about fertility trends, their consequences, and the childfree choice. In *What to Expect*, Jonathan Last argues that concerns about the "looming danger of overpopulation" are "all bunk" (a conclusion David Coleman calls "inappropriate"). A closer read of Last's excited claims shows that for him, America's coming demographic disaster has to do with the increase in single-child families and the "alarming number of upscale professionals [who] don't even go that far—they have dogs, not kids." Fertility rates across the globe and our growing world population are less a concern for Last than is the fact that a particular group—middle-class and "upscale professionals"—are soon to be, if not already, outnumbered.

Whether upscale professionals have all replaced kids with dogs aside, other provocative claims about who the childfree are, how we live, and why we've opted out of parenthood abound as well. To borrow from writer Meghan Daum's popular anthology, we're perceived as "selfish, shallow, and self-absorbed." Women in particular are believed to be naturally inclined toward motherhood and those who are not mothers are either pitied or reviled.

Even celebrity doesn't save non-mothers from scrutiny. When their real-life roles don't include parenthood, well-known actresses are especially popular targets of tabloid observers. In 2016, when actor, producer, and director Jennifer Aniston had finally had enough of the rumors and speculation over the state of her uterus, she published a piece, "For the Record," in *Huffington Post*.[76] "For the record," Aniston shared, "I am *not* pregnant. What I am is *fed up*." Tackling the myth that women aren't real women unless or until they become mothers, Aniston goes on to say, "We don't need to be married or mothers to be complete. We get to determine our own 'happily ever after' for ourselves."

Childfree people—those who have made the explicit and intentional choice not to have kids—are not incomplete and they're not missing out, at least not any more than any person who chooses not to do something they have no interest in doing. Having children is not the same as, say, tasting a new food or agreeing to sit through two and a half hours of *Star Wars* for the sake of your spouse. Taking the chance that you might *not* turn out to regret it—even though you're almost certain you will—comes with vastly different consequences in the former case. As childfree Rachel, who shared her story on our blog, put it, "I know that I'm not going to wake up tomorrow and want to be a mother the same way I know I'm not going to wake up tomorrow and want to be an astronaut. To me they are both jobs. Jobs that I am ill-suited for, jobs that would make me unhappy, jobs that require the ability to let go of all the things on earth you used to know."

Childfree people are not, to borrow Tucker Carlson's words, any more—or less—selfish, decadent, or stupid than anyone else. The single criterion of nonparenthood does not cause us to stand out particularly on any of these variables. In fact, we have more in common with parents than perhaps either group realizes. In the following pages, I explore those commonalities along with our differences and consider how we might shift the conversation to focus less on how or where our experiences and perspectives diverge and instead on offering support of one another's choices and urging folks to follow whatever path that best suits them, be it parenthood or childfree.

TWO

BAD FOR AMERICA:
REPRODUCTIVE CHOICES AND A NATION OF FREE WOMEN

More and more Americans are childless by choice.
But what makes sense for the individual may spell disaster
for the country as a whole.

—HARRY SIEGEL, *NEWSWEEK*

n 2013, writer Harry Siegel told a nation of *Newsweek* readers that the choice to be childless was bad for America.[1] If Siegel was to be believed, it would seem we were finally paying the price for the freedom for which women had so valiantly fought since first-wave feminists brought us birth control clinics and the right to vote, and their second-wave sisters ushered in legal access to abortion and better opportunities in the workplace. Thanks to both waves of the women's movement, increasing numbers of women had emerged from the privacy of their homes to the public sphere, free from the surety that marriage or an active sex life meant eventual parenthood. Sex without procreative consequences had consequences nonetheless, and mostly male pundits like Siegel and others claimed the nation was bearing the costs of our choices.

Women who opt out of parenthood have quickly become one of America's favorite scapegoats. Declines in fertility came with our being credited for a decline in family values, an aging workforce, a lack of global competitiveness, overdependence on the state, and a culture of selfish young adults and depressed, lonely old folks. Our demands for reproductive autonomy along with insistence on equal access to education and work led—we were told—not only to our own detriment but to that of our fellow Americans. As Siegel put it, our "lack of productive screwing could further be screwing the screwed generation."

Surely these are not the outcomes Planned Parenthood founder Margaret Sanger had in mind when she observed that no woman can call herself free who does not own and control her own body. Reproductive freedom and access to the public sphere were meant to improve women's lives and, in turn, the fate of our nation. And while they have in many ways done just that, we wouldn't know it from the speeches of our religious leaders, the cries of our politicians, or the lamentations of conservative media hosts.

It isn't just that some people forgo parenthood that inspires contempt, it is who does so and what their choice could mean for our social institutions and life as we know it. Who makes the childfree choice—today and in the past—and what does it mean for families, our economy, our communities, for how we age, and for how we live?

THE UNICORNS OF SOCIETY

Writers Rhiannon Lucy Cosslett and Holly Baxter once dubbed happily childless women the "unicorns of society."[2] If that's so, then unicorns are the new ground squirrel, given our ubiquity across the United States. Census numbers from 2014 show that 47.6 percent of women between the ages fifteen and forty-four were childless in that year. This figure was the highest we've seen it since the Census Bureau began tracking women's lifetime childlessness in 1976.

While some of today's childless women will eventually become mothers, it seems they are in no hurry to do so. In the summer of 2017, the Centers for Disease Control and Prevention released data showing that for the first time since the numbers were first officially tracked four decades ago, women in their thirties were having more babies than younger women.[3] Birth rates for women between the ages of thirty and thirty-four increased from 101.5 babies per 1,000 women in 2015 to 102.6 in 2016. For women ages twenty-five to twenty-nine, rates declined from 104.3 in 2015 to 101.9 in 2016.

These changes may seem small, but they reflect significant cultural and economic shifts. Increasingly, to the joy of some parents and the chagrin of others, young people are delaying the transition to adulthood.[4] As Jenna Healey, professor in the history of medicine at Queen's University, notes, "The postwar tendency towards early childbearing, which we now imagine to be the product of some kind of biological inevitability, was actually a cultural aberration."[5] While women once married much earlier—on average, at age twenty-two in 1890 and age twenty in 1960—today, women's average age at first marriage is twenty-seven.[6] While one does not need to be married to have a child, it is true that spending fewer of their fertile years married means fewer babies being born. Even more, from 1880 until 2014, the most common living arrangement for adults between the ages of eighteen and thirty-four was to share a home with a spouse or partner.[7] Sixty-two percent did so in the 1960s; today just 31.6 percent do. Slightly more than that, 32.1 percent, live in their parents' homes.

These changes are due in part to shifts in the way people parent their kids—parents are much more intensively involved in their kids' lives than they were in the past—but the changes can also be explained by changes in the economy.[8] As noted in the previous chapter, the economic recession in 2008, for example, was followed by a dip in fertility that garnered lots of attention and, in some cases, near panic.[9] Some explained the dip as a result of economic insecurity. Others, including columnist Ross Douthat, blamed the decline on a "decadence . . . that privileges the present over the future."[10]

Despite the scare tactics of some pundits and news outlets, research shows that children, and possibly even mothers, are better off when motherhood begins later in life. One study of Danish children born to older mothers found that, independent of other demographic and socioeconomic characteristics, children ages seven and eleven with older mothers had fewer behavioral, social, and emotional problems.[11] Another study, of 551 families in the United States and Denmark, found that women who had their last child after age thirty-three had significantly higher odds of surviving to an unusually old age compared with women who had their last child by age twenty-nine.[12]

The shift toward later childbearing could also be reflective of several positive cultural changes. Millennials, half of whom are childless today, say they don't want to become parents until they are ready, certainly a position any child advocate would support.[13] Teen birth rates have also plummeted over the past decade.[14] Between 2007 and 2015, the teen birth rate declined by 46 percent. A study from the Pew Research Center points to a number of reasons for this change.[15] Far fewer women in their teens report that they have ever had sex when compared to those in the 1980s: from 51 percent in 1988 to 44 percent in 2011–2013. And, though the rate at which teens report using contraception hasn't changed (79 percent of teen women and 84 percent of teen men use contraception the first time they have sex), they are using more highly effective forms these days. In 2002, just 8 percent of sexually active teen women reported having used emergency contraception; by 2011–2013, that figure had risen to 22 percent. Use of long-acting reversible contraceptives such as IUDs and implants is also more common, going from 0.4 percent in 2005 to 7.1 percent in 2013. In addition, as is true of birth rates for women of all ages, the economic struggles we've seen over the last decade have also brought teen birth rates down.[16]

Perhaps most surprising of all, reality TV appears to have helped drive down teen birth rates as well. Say what you will about shows like MTV's *16 and Pregnant* and *Teen Mom*, but a 2015 report by Brookings Fellows Melissa Kearney and Phillip Levine found that these shows account for around one-third of the overall decline in teen births. As the researchers note, the shows seem to have an effect by "showing that being a pregnant teen and new mother is hard—it strains relationships with friends, parents, and the baby's father, and means physical discomfort, potential health problems, and sleep deprivation."[17] And while the Christian right will tell us that more teens must be having more abortions, the abortion rate among young women ages fifteen to nineteen has actually fallen, from 43.5 per 1,000 female teens in 1988 to 16.3 in 2009.[18]

At the same time that we celebrate the decline in teen birth rates, newspapers and pundits warn us that waiting too long to have kids could be to women's own—and, the more likely concern of public commentators, our country's—detriment. A 2018 *New York Times* column warned, "Forecasts show many millennial women won't fulfill their wishes on family size."[19] Author Lyman Stone, frequent contributor on the right-wing Institute for Family Studies blog and self-described husband, Lutheran, and Kentuckian, notes that "the gap between the number of children that women say they want to have (2.7) and the number of children they will probably actually have (1.8) has risen to the highest level in 40 years." He blames the gap on delayed marriage, later age at first birth, cell phones, and pornography (the latter two of which he says contribute to less sex).

What Lyman neglects to consider is where the reported desired number of children comes from (I'd argue pronatalism) and why on earth we would want young people to become parents before they know they're ready, able, and willing to do it. We're also led to believe that the family size a person purports to be ideal early in life remains constant throughout their life. If my own plans had worked out as I'd envisioned early in life, I'd have become a mom at age twenty. As a kid, I'd landed on twenty as the ideal age to "start my family" because I noticed that my friends who had the coolest moms also had the youngest moms. What I didn't realize until later was that these young moms struggled to make ends meet more than my own parents did and that they themselves might have preferred to settle into their relationships and careers before embarking on parenthood. That's not to say it didn't work out for them, only that the lens through which I saw their lives and imagined my own was more narrowly focused than it became as I matured. And I'm grateful not to be on the hook for those early plans I made.

The particular historical moment we find ourselves in today shows recent increases in childlessness across birth cohorts, but the moment is just that—a single moment and part of a broader pattern that should be considered before we get too concerned about the possibility that we're un-breeding ourselves out of existence. Rates of childlessness have been higher in some periods and lower in others. In mid-nineteenth-century America, around 15 percent of women were still childless by the time they reached their forty-fifth birthday.[20] This figure peaked just after the turn of the century, reaching 25 percent in 1920. Birth rates then took off, and the postwar baby boom saw the lowest rates of childlessness we'd seen in decades, with just 8 percent of women in 1944 still childless by age forty-five.

While rates of childlessness have long fluctuated up and down, one thing that appears to be changing is a recognition and, among some circles at least, an acceptance that not everyone will or must become a parent. Never having children may be the road less taken, but those of us who aren't parents do have company. Data from the CIA's 2015 *World Factbook* show that, globally, women today have an average of 2.42 births each. The lowest birth rate, representing the average number of children born per woman if all women lived to the end of their childbearing years, is found in Singapore, where women have an average of 0.81 births each. The highest rate, 6.76 births per woman, is in Niger.

In the United States, the estimated 2015 fertility rate was 1.87

children born per woman. This placed us at the eighty-third lowest rate among 224 countries listed. In fact, fertility rates here have been below the population replacement rate of 2.1 births per woman since 1972.[21] And while fertility rates vary by race and ethnicity—in 2013, rates were 1.75 for white women, 1.88 for black women, and 2.15 for women of Hispanic/Latin American descent—the gap between groups in the United States is shrinking.[22] Fertility rates are highest among women who themselves were born outside the country, a trend that has nationalist groups worried to no end.

One of the figures most commonly cited in today's media reports about childlessness is the percentage of women who have never given birth by the time they reach their fortieth birthday. While there are exceptions—adoption, stepparenthood, and childbirth after forty, for example—it is true that most of these women will remain childless for their lifetimes. And although adoption is a possible pathway into parenthood, we know that only about 1 percent of women and 2 percent of men choose this path.[23] Stepparenthood is another way to be involved in children's lives. Analysis from the Pew Research Center shows that 13 percent of adults in the United States have a stepchild.[24] Some of these, of course, were already parents to their own children before the addition of stepchildren to their families and, as our community of blog followers can attest, not all stepparents identify as parents themselves.

One recent exploratory study suggests that not identifying as a stepparent to the children of one's partner may be especially common among lesbian couples. Psychologist Victoria Clarke and colleagues conclude from their interviews with five childfree lesbians that the pressures on lesbian childfree women to engage in the lives of the children of their partners are lower than pressures on heterosexual stepparents.[25] Clarke and colleagues cite the "relational ethic of 'co-independence'" in lesbian relationships as explanation for this finding. As one interview participant told them, "There was no pressure or expectation for her to develop a relationship with the child or see this child as part of her family."

In the United States, rates of childlessness have increased fairly steadily since the 1970s. In 2006, 20 percent of women ages forty to forty-four had never had a child.[26] Thirty years earlier, half that many in the same age group had never had kids.[27] Rates of childlessness among younger cohorts and among men have also increased over this period.[28]

It should be noted that much of what we know about people who don't have children comes from studies that don't differentiate voluntary childlessness from that which is not chosen.[29] From these studies we do know, however, that nonparents are more heavily concentrated in professional and managerial occupations and they are, on average, more highly educated than parents.[30] We're also more likely to find nonparents residing in urban areas (satirical diatribes about the scourge of urban strollers—like the *Reductress* piece "If You Wanted to Use the Sidewalk, You Should Have Had Two Babies Like Me"—notwithstanding).[31]

Among those for whom nonparenthood was a choice, less traditional views on gender and lower religiosity are common when compared to parents and the involuntarily childless.[32] In a national survey of 708 voluntarily childless adults, Mary Hunt found that just 6 percent of respondents identified as religious, while 23 percent described themselves as agnostic and 38 percent atheist.[33] It is perhaps this fact that makes childfree people a favorite target of Pope Francis and other religious leaders and followers. Within the U.S. population as a whole, just 4 percent of people say they're agnostic, and 3 percent claim an atheist identity.[34] And among religious groups, atheists remain one of the least liked in America, with respondents to a Pew poll rating their feelings of warmth toward atheists—on a scale of 0 to 100—a cool to neutral 50, just two points above Muslims, the lowest-rated group.[35]

People who opt out of parenthood cite a variety of motives for their choice, which I explore in more depth in the coming chapters. At the top of the list, though, are reasons such as interest in maintaining a sense of autonomy, prioritizing one's marriage over other relationships, and environmental concerns. The financial cost of rearing children also comes up as one rationale for not having them, and for good reason. In the United States, the U.S. Department of Agriculture estimates that for kids born in 2013, parents spend an average of $245,340 to raise a child to the age of eighteen.[36] This figure doesn't even include college or the years of early adulthood that often come with funding from dear old Mom and Dad as well.

In my own research, the cost of rearing children came up as a reason not to have them more often for men than it did for women.[37] Some of these men said they didn't want the financial pressure that adding children to their families would create. In an earlier study focused exclusively on childfree men, Patricia Lunneborg found that while none of the men she interviewed said they were childfree because of money, the freedom to change jobs and a desire to retire early were in their top ten reasons.[38] It is possible, given historical patterns and our culturally constructed gender roles, that the pressure to serve as a breadwinner weighs more heavily on men than women and that this pressure therefore serves as a motivator for men who opt out of parenthood more often than it does for women who make the same choice.

This idea aligns with research on what draws men *toward* parenthood as well. In her study of men's parenting decisions, sociologist Kathleen Gerson found that among men who choose to be especially involved fathers, disillusionment with their careers played a role in their choice. These men deemphasized the importance of the breadwinner role in favor of becoming involved fathers but were nevertheless acutely aware of the pressure on them to serve as breadwinners.[39] In both cases, whether they turn toward fatherhood or away from it, pressure on men to provide financially for their families plays a role in their decision. While the desire to develop meaningful careers is often linked to the choice not to parent for women, among men, relevant variables are more directly financial and include the high cost of rearing children and a desire for financial flexibility.

For other childfree people, the choice is far less complex: They simply don't want them and don't feel there are strongly compelling reasons to have them. As Bob, a married childfree man in his late thirties said when I interviewed him, "It's not that I decided *not* to have kids, it's that I haven't. I can't find a good reason to do it. Sure, it would make my family happy and my partner and I do feel that pressure. But these are modest reasons to have kids. And so why haven't I made this decision? It's because there hasn't been enough to push me to make a decision in the opposite direction. There just isn't anything that tells me that having kids is really the right thing to do. And I really don't want them." A well-received POPSUGAR piece from 2017 makes this very point. In it, writer Mary White cites the "one simple reason" she decided not to have kids: "I just don't want them."

One thing that sometimes gets overlooked in media reports about childlessness is that the percentage of women who reach their forties without having had a child has actually gone down over the last few years. In the first decade of the 2000s, this number peaked at nearly 20 percent. Today, around 15 percent of women reach their fortieth birthday without having given birth.[40] The decline in childlessness among women over forty can be explained in large part by increases in fertility rates among the most highly educated women in the United States; those with a PhD or an MD have experienced the most dramatic change. In 1994, 35 percent of these women had not had children by age forty; twenty years later, that figure had gone down to just 20 percent. Despite the uptick in highly educated women's fertility rates, research shows that childfree men and women differ with regard to educational attainment; higher education increases women's chances of being childfree but it does not for men.

The recent increase in fertility among the United States' most highly educated women can be explained at least in part by women's increasing roles as leaders in the workplace. In 1968, just 30.6 percent of managerial and professional positions were occupied by women. By 2013, that number had risen to over 50 percent. Yahoo CEO Marissa Mayer—who famously took just two weeks off after the birth of her son in 2012—notwithstanding, women leaders are likely to have impacted employers' awareness of the value of work-life balance policies for employees and expanded opportunities for women to maintain their careers and have children. It isn't just that more women are in the workplace but that more of them are in positions of power to influence workplace policies that make balancing work and children more feasible.

THE MOTHERHOOD MANDATE

The idea that all women will, or at least must aspire to, become mothers one day permeates our collective conscience. Suggestions to the contrary don't seem to register or even seep in. Psychologist Nancy Felipe Russo calls this the "motherhood mandate," noting the centrality of motherhood to the definition of adult womanhood.[41] Russo's articulation of the mandate specifies not only that women must raise children—and raise them well—but also that they must raise at least two of them. As Lauren Sandler demonstrates in her book *One and Only: The Freedom of Having an Only Child, and the Joy of Being One*, having a single child is almost as unforgivable as having none.[42] Though mothers of onlies are not stigmatized in all or exactly the same ways as childfree women, there are plenty of parallels. The "ideal woman" must be a mother, and preferably a mother to exactly two children; fewer than that and she's selfish, more than that and she's crazy. This ideal holds even though only about a third of women in the U.S. actually have two children.[43] It seems the other two-thirds of us, whether we have kids or not, remain disappointing failures.

Motherhood itself is a relatively new invention, historically speaking.[44] Though "the word mother is one of the oldest found in languages around the world," motherhood, as an identity and a role in itself, did not appear in writing prior to the 1597 version of the *Oxford English Dictionary*.[45] Four-hundred-some years ago may sound like a long time but it's relatively brief in the span of human history. While caregiving for the young to ensure survival may be a universal across most times and places, the idea that the individual who happens to give birth to a newborn is solely or primarily responsible for said new person's survival and socialization is not universal, nor is it necessary. The Shakers, in fact, prohibited sex, establishing celibate communities where children were brought in by way of adoption.[46] In the eleventh and twelfth centuries, the use of wet nurses, who took their employers' newborns into their own homes to feed and care for them while they nursed, was widespread and believed to be the best approach among the European aristocracy.[47]

Today, new research raises questions about the utility of efforts like the U.S. government's well-financed "Breast Is Best" campaign, which compel birth mothers to halt everything—work, home, friendships, and other social connections—in favor of always having a breast available for their nursing children.[48] Campaigns built from the belief that mothers, above all others, are best equipped to care for children promote the idea that motherhood comes naturally to women, and that motherhood is all but synonymous with womanhood. Despite the progress our feminist predecessors made over the last century, we just can't seem to shake the notion that if you are a woman, you must become a mother, and that if you are not a mother, you must not be a real woman.[49] It isn't just government campaigns like "Breast Is Best" where these ideas arise. As psychologist Gilla Shapiro notes, "The construction of womanhood as motherhood has been established through social, political, medical, and religious institutions."[50] What Shapiro describes is the project of pronatalism.[51]

Pronatalism doesn't just prescribe that women bear children or that we are best suited to rear them. We must also bear enough children. As in Lauren Sandler's *One and Only*, psychologist Sara Holton and colleagues argue that "it is not motherhood status per se which is associated with attitudes toward women and motherhood but the actual number of children a woman wants and has."[52] Wanting only one may raise eyebrows, but wanting none raises pitchforks. In response to both, nationalist policies are created to rescue nations at risk of having certain portions of their populations decline, a result of having given (some) women free will to decide for themselves when, whether, and how they wish to have kids. In 2009, forty-three countries had policies designed to increase fertility among their populace.[53] These policies are most heavily concentrated in Europe, where fertility rates have dipped below population replacement levels in many nations. While the U.S. does not have such a policy, declining birth rates among (some) American women has been the focus of much hand-wringing and popular news articles and stories.[54]

In Italy, where birth rates are lower than anywhere else in the European Union, the Ministry of Health introduced a campaign in 2016 to try to increase fertility. The campaign went viral—but not in the way health officials had hoped. One campaign poster, depicting a beautiful young woman holding an hourglass in hand at the end of her outstretched arm—as though shoving it in the face of the reader—comes with a dire warning: "Beauty has no age. Fertility does." It also comes with its own, signature hashtag: #fertilityday.

Another poster reminds women that their fertility is not their own. In it, the image of a dripping water faucet accompanies the text, "Fertility is a public good." Perhaps unsurprisingly, the posters were quickly denounced and the entire campaign was withdrawn within days of its launching, but the fact that they were created in the first place points to the necessity of having more open discussions about who gets a voice in how or whether women use their bodies to bear children.

In 2014, the Danish travel company Spies Rejser launched a better-received "Do It for Denmark" campaign, urging couples to take a romantic holiday and get busy populating their nation. The company even offered an "ovulation discount" and couples who could prove that they had conceived during their trip were promised three years of baby supplies and a free child-friendly holiday. That campaign was followed two years later by Spies Rejser's "Do It for Mom" campaign. The television ad from the "Do It for Mom" campaign is a two-and-a-half-minute mini comedy-drama featuring two mothers of adult sons who worry they might never become grandmothers. The ad begins with dire proclamations about the pressure under which the Danish welfare system finds itself, thanks to the nation's low birth rates. It then urges these potential grandmothers to purchase a romantic getaway vacation package from Spies for their sons, showing data that such vacations encourage sex. The ad ends by asking the women to "join forces [with Spies] and give the world more grandchildren. If they won't do it for their country, surely they will do it for their mother."

As Denmark's campaign shows, contemporary pronatalist efforts take a different tack from the eugenics movement of the early twentieth century and from Hitler's horrific nationalist pronatalist campaign in the middle of that century.[55] And while the Danish commercials are admittedly funny, their subtext is anything but: Only native Danish babies are desirable, and women cannot be trusted to make their own decisions about when and whether children are right for them. Though the campaign takes a different tack than its more blatantly racist predecessors, it reflects, in at least some ways, what sociologist Leslie King calls "ethno-nationalist ideologies," which emphasize women's roles as "biological reproducers of the nation" and a shared race/ethnicity, language, and religion. Sociologist Leta Hong Fincher says the same of China's birth policies.[56] Though the 2015 easing of its decades-long one-child policy was heralded as a win for reproductive rights, Hong Fincher notes that it was "only the right sort" of women who were urged to reproduce for China, those who were married.

More common today, says King, are the campaigns of countries like France, Romania, Singapore, and Israel, which she calls "civic/cultural nationalist visions." Singapore, for example, abandoned its ethnonationalist "Graduate Mothers Program" of the 1980s in favor of policies that do not differentiate on the grounds of race/ethnicity or education. The old program provided fertility incentives (in the form of tax incentives and school choice for children) to the nation's most highly educated citizens of Chinese descent, and disincentives (in the form of cash for sterilization) to Malays and Indians of lower educational status. Today, all citizens—regardless of racial or ethnic background—are encouraged to have children through tax incentives, childcare subsidies, maternity leave, housing priorities for families with three or more children, and even state-sponsored dating services. And rather than casting women as mere biological reproducers, pronatalist policies in Singapore now emphasize women's roles as working mothers.

In these examples, says King, we don't see specific targeting of particular racial/ethnic groups nor do we see an overtly narrow vision of women's purpose and roles. Yet there are additional things we don't see that are more troublesome. We don't see attention to our rising global population or to the social, economic, and environmental consequences—such as depletion of fresh water and other natural resources, species extinction, various health crises, and rising cost of living, to name just a few—that are associated with an overpopulated planet. And, with the exception of nations such as Canada, we don't see attention to solutions like immigration or multicultural policies (as opposed to assimilation policies) that could bring new citizens to nations concerned about population within their borders. Not to mention we don't see whether these women *want* to have kids or not.

A THOUGHTFUL CHOICE

It may seem a decision deserving of further contemplation than whether to have pizza or Indian for dinner. But more than one in three couples agree not to have children after just one conversation, research shows.

—JOURNALIST DOMINIC YEATMAN

When the research, finding that many couples who don't want children reach the decision after just one conversation, emerged in 2014, reporters had a field day.[57] Dismayed, they called it a "snap choice" and referred to couples' limited discussions about the matter as "strange."

Lance and I were also surprised. It didn't reflect our own experience as a childfree couple, nor was it consistent with what other childfree couples had shared in my interviews with them. Digging into the coverage a bit further, we learned that the hubbub was based on responses to a single question answered by sixty-three women who had been recruited through the researcher's social media networks and word of mouth. Just over a third of these women, twenty-three of the sixty-three surveyed, reported that they'd decided against parenthood after one conversation with their partner. From these twenty-three responses, media reports cast childfree couples as careless and shallow.

Observant readers of the original press release might note that the survey in question was not statistically representative of child-free women across the board.[58] The researcher herself carefully made this point but her caution was lost in coverage of the finding. Even more, media reports did not consider that the twenty-three respondents might have reached their decisions not to have kids prior to meeting their mates, perhaps even after a great deal of soul-searching. If you know that you don't want the life required to operate a ranch, foster dogs that need a home, or work as a full-time musician, it's likely that you don't require much discussion once you've made up your mind.

Though these pursuits differ—in significant ways—from rearing children, they all imply a particular set of activities and way of life. If you feel strongly enough about how you'd like your life to unfold, finding a partner who feels the same way is probably a priority. It isn't surprising, then, that couples who don't want kids end up together. If two individuals who've made the decision on their own happen to meet and there's a love connection, why would they require lengthy discussion about something they've each already considered?

The confusion over whether any—and how much—thought goes into people's parenthood status may be due in part to confusion over the distinction between childlessness that is the result of choice and that is the result of happenstance. In neither case should a person's status be relegated to the strange or thoughtless, and both groups have much in common, but there are also important differences between the two.

As parenthood became increasingly viewed as a choice rather than destiny, the term *childfree* emerged to differentiate those who had chosen nonparenthood from those for whom childlessness was not a choice. When social scientists began studying people who had chosen not to have kids in the early 1970s, they used the term *childless* to refer to them. Over time, they came to recognize the differences between voluntary and involuntary childlessness, using these terms to refer to the two groups. *Voluntarily childless* and *involuntarily childless* certainly better describe the differences between these two groups, but they're also a mouthful. And for some in the "voluntary" category, the "less" part of childless doesn't feel representative of their experience. As actress and voluntarily childless woman Kim Cattrall once remarked in an interview with BBC, "It's the '*less*' that is offensive." Thus, the term *childfree* emerged to try to distinguish nonparenthood as a choice from nonparenthood as a circumstance.[59]

The term *childfree* is not without its critics. In her study of women's "intentional childlessness," social worker Carolyn Morell says, "For me, this term [*childfree*] has a presumptuous ring to it. It suggests that women who do not have children of their own want to be rid of children, as in those who promote a 'union-free' or 'smoke-free' environment."[60] More recently, one of my own favorite writers and cultural critics (and, as it happens, woman-without-children-by-choice), Meghan Daum, has taken issue with the term as well. In Daum's words, "Why should children fall into the same category as smoke or gluten?"[61] A fair point. At the same time, it is clear that those of us who have chosen not to have kids do not belong in a category that emphasizes our lack of something we never wanted in the first place.

My own stance on *childfree* differs from that of its critics. I use it not to suggest that the world should be free of children. That I even have to say so tells us something about the assumptions we make about those who know that parenthood isn't for them. In my view, *childfree* should be taken in the positive light—and perhaps with a dash of good-natured sass—that's intended. It's an affirmative take on a contested identity. It may be a bit on the nose, but to those who take offense, I'd say simply and with the kindest of intentions, it isn't about you. It's about joyfully claiming our own life choices. It's about embracing the conscious and intentional choice that those of us who've opted out of parenthood have made. Overwrought assumptions that it means anything else are exactly what motivated me to write this book.

As much as this might seem like a fruitless exercise in semantics, the terms we use are important. Having different terms for different circumstances allows us to better understand the particulars of each experience. In one case, a person is living the life they've chosen for themselves and in the other, they are not. Indeed, research shows that childless women feel more distress over their status as nonparents than do women who are childfree.[62] It's also true that our cultural stereotypes of each group are quite different. If we look to images in popular media, such as *Time*'s 2013 cover displaying "the childfree life," we might think all childfree people are white, heterosexual vacationers who "have it all."[63] And that we all love the beach. While a good share of those things happen to be true for me personally, they certainly aren't true of all childfree people.

Stereotypes of the childless are not any better. A search for creative common images using the term *childless* on the photo-sharing website Flickr yields a black-and-white image of a woman sitting alone on a carpeted floor in an empty room, looking down with head in hands, next to her vacuum. I don't know any woman—parent or not, happy about it or not—who would say that sitting alone with her vacuum cleaner is either the most accurate representation of her life or how she'd choose to be represented if given the choice.

Some of the studies I consider in the following pages do not distinguish childless from childfree, and only make a distinction between parents and nonparents. When discussing research findings of this sort, I use the term *nonparents* to refer to childless and childfree people as a group. Other work does recognize the differences between not having children by choice and not having them due to circumstances one wishes she could change, and these studies do examine the two groups as distinct. When discussing this work, I'll be clear about to whom the findings in question refer. My own research, which includes interviews with seventy women and men and a survey of over seven hundred, is limited to only those who have made the explicit and intentional choice not to have kids. Any quotes I share from my research participants or patterns I describe from across the study are therefore about only the childfree experience.

The differences between childless and childfree—in both experience and in our cultural mythology—are not insignificant. Nevertheless, all of us without children live in a culture where having children is the norm. The patterns of our everyday lives do not include picking Johnny and Susie up from school, taking them to soccer practice, attending PTSA meetings, or scheduling pediatric exams. And while inquiries and looks of pity from strangers when they find out we don't have kids may be experienced differently, that we face these inquisitions is the same.

Karen Malone Wright, founder of thenotmom.com who hosts the biennial NotMom Summit, argues that we're more alike than we are different. In many ways, she's right; Elaine Tyler May found that the values of childless and childfree people are "remarkably similar," noting that in her own study, both groups ultimately express a desire for the same things: "intimacy, happiness, and fulfillment in private life."[64] And parents want these things, too. We all want the autonomy to pursue the life of our choosing, to spend our time as we choose, and to make choices for our fertility that are best for us as individuals.

From the earliest days of the childfree movement, there have been times when parents, the childless, and the childfree worked together to challenge myths about parenthood, nonparenthood, and choice. The National Organization for Non-Parents included parents from the very beginning. Whatever critiques some might have had of Ellen Peck's *The Baby Trap*, it is notable that half of the original officers and board members of the NON were parents themselves. Though they may not have always agreed, they did manage to find common ground—concern about overpopulation, conviction that parenthood is a role best performed if chosen—to build a movement around their shared values. We'd all be better off if we better understood how those without children make meaning in a world where parenthood is presumed to be the singular most meaningful experience a person can have. We might be surprised by what we discover.

THREE

A SELFISH CHOICE:
FINDING FULFILLMENT AND LEAVING A LEGACY

The retreat from child rearing is, at some level, a symptom
of late-modern exhaustion—a decadence that first arose in the
West but now haunts rich societies around the globe.
It's a spirit that privileges the present over the future, chooses
stagnation over innovation, prefers what already exists over
what might be. It embraces the comforts and pleasures
of modernity, while shrugging off the basic sacrifices that
built our civilization in the first place.

—ROSS DOUTHAT, *THE NEW YORK TIMES*

Columnist Ross Douthat calls it like he sees it. And how he sees it is that the thing America most had going for it, until recently, was that we had "more babies than the competition."[1] The plunge in fertility rates that followed the Great Recession, says Douthat, is thanks in no small part to a cultural shift "away from a child-centric understanding of romance and marriage." And Douthat claims that shift is tied to our preference for the decadent, the easy path, the present. If that's not a thinly veiled proclamation to the childfree—"You're selfish!"—I don't know what is.

Douthat isn't alone in this sentiment. In a 2012 op-ed I wrote summarizing findings from my research on the childfree, one reader left this comment: "Way to rationalize your own narcissistic, 'it's all about me' attitude."[2] While a couple of readers noted that my findings described their own experiences as childfree and one mother offered her support, other comments ranged from confusion about why anyone would make the choice not to have kids to outright hostility toward those who do so. Pope Francis, known for welcoming diversity and encouraging open-mindedness on issues about which the Catholic Church has historically been decidedly closed, is not a fan of the childfree either. In remarks given in Vatican City in 2015, Francis made the following observation: "A society with a greedy generation, that doesn't want to surround itself with children, that considers them above all, worrisome, a weight, a risk, is a depressed society. The choice to not have children is selfish."

Condemnation is a state the childfree know well. A 2017 study by psychologist Leslie Ashburn-Nardo confirmed it: The decision not to have kids inspires moral outrage in others.[3] Ashburn-Nardo's survey of 197 respondents, undergraduate students who don't identify as childfree themselves, say that parenthood is a moral imperative and people who don't opt in are morally corrupt. Perhaps in some ways, as the commenter responding to my op-ed suggested, the reasons we provide for our choice are rationalizations in response to these hostilities. But the rationalizations most childfree people offer—they want to make an impact on the world in ways other than parenthood or they don't want to contribute further to overpopulation or they prefer to focus on their existing intimate relationships or they knew they wouldn't make good parents—are generally provided with the aim of deflecting criticism, not drawing it.

Any life choice closely examined could appear selfish. Ask a parent why they decided to have kids and chances are that at least some portion of their rationale will have to do with the life they envisioned for themselves. They may like the idea of having a busy and bustling home. Perhaps they can't imagine Christmas mornings without the pitter-patter of tiny (human) feet. Or they might be counting on children to take care of them in their old age. The childfree, too, decide about parenthood based on their vision of a fulfilling life. They want the freedom to find fulfillment in a way that is not conducive to child-rearing. They want spontaneity. Some enjoy quiet and solitude. Others, a busy and bustling home, but where the pitter-patter comes from furry feet. Parent or not, individuals' own interests, needs, and desires are bound to shape the path they choose.

WHY {NOT} HAVE KIDS?

Studies show there are a host of reasons people choose not to have kids, just as there are many reasons people have them. Like others I've interviewed, I grew up believing—and learning from those around me—that we should have children to fulfill our destinies as humans (especially if we're women), to carry on the species, for the good of the world, because our kid might be the one to cure cancer, or because our god decreed it. In reality, parents have kids for a much different set of reasons. One study asking a sample of young, unmarried college students why they wanted to become parents found that "the majority of respondents seem most concerned about themselves."[4] These respondents reported that they were interested in having children because they thought it would be personally fulfilling, they wanted to have a little person like themselves, they thought they'd benefit from it, they wanted someone to love, and that it would give them something to do.

In another study, women expressed that they have children to relieve themselves of a difficult personal situation or household setting and for the potential emotional connection and relational intimacy offered by parenthood.[5] In another, men said they had kids after becoming disillusioned with their careers, seeking the intrinsic rewards they believed parenthood would provide.[6] Analysts at the Pew Research Center found that the most common response parents give to the question of why they had their first child was "the joy of having children."[7] Eighty-seven percent of parents responded in this way, and men and women were equally likely to choose this response. For people who were not yet parents but planned to be, the joy of having children held even stronger appeal. Ninety-five percent of childless people who plan to become parents one day said this was an important factor in their decision to have kids. In short, some people are drawn to parenthood by individual motives such as personal fulfillment, the draw of possible emotional connection with a child, or an interest in changing their existing household arrangements. In other cases, parenthood's appeal rests in factors external to the individual, such as a change in the economy or fewer opportunities in the workforce.

Just as the reasons for parenthood are a mix of internal and external motivations, so too are the reasons for nonparenthood.[8] In terms of factors that lie outside the individual, researchers point to concern about the environment, concern about the current state of world affairs, and concern for the children who are already here as factors driving nonparenthood. For Jan, a childfree forty-three-year-old engineer, "it's wrapped up in environmental issues; you know, the population point. If we ask are there enough resources to support people around the world in the lifestyle that we're accustomed to, the answer is definitely not. And are we in developed nations prepared to give up what we have? I doubt it. And in the developing world, there are so many children that are born and they're just assigned to an early death and it just seems wrong. Our environment can't support our population."

Jan's claim is certainly supported by the available evidence. Studies link an increasing population to the spread of disease, malnutrition, extreme weather, and crop decline.[9] In the simplest terms, "current populations and lifestyles are exhausting non-renewable resources like fossil fuels; creating shortages of renewable resources such as fresh water, fisheries, and forests; and generating accumulating levels of pollution, particularly hazardous wastes."[10] As Jan notes, the problem isn't simply that there are too many of us but also that those of us in the global north consume far more of the earth's resources and that we have been, to date, unwilling to scale back our ecological footprint. One estimate shows that we consume two to thirty times the bioproductive resources as those in poorer nations.[11]

So it isn't that "babies are the enemy of the human race," as bio-chemist and science fiction writer Isaac Asimov once proclaimed about overpopulation, it is that our lifestyles demand a dispropor-tionate share of the earth's resources.

For some childfree people, concern about our world isn't limited to concern about the state of our environment. Jessica, who at twenty-five hails from a generation younger than Jan, has similar worries but expressed them more generally. "Why I am choosing not to have kids is more of a political and social reason," Jessica told me. "I'm really just concerned about our world. Diving more deeply in the social issues, I really think that the world is against the child right now. At this time in our social structure, there's not a good way to bring up children healthfully."

Beyond more global concerns like those expressed by Jan and Jessica, we know that childfree people also have individual or inter-nal motives for their choice. Some of the more common personal reasons people give include their desire for autonomy, an interest in spontaneity, and a preference to nurture relationships with partners and other adults in one's life. Steve, an engineer in his early thirties, told me, "I want to be able to travel. I want to be able to do things that I would not be able to do if I had kids." Kate, in a long-term partnership and in her late thirties, shared, "I'm a free spirit and I found that, when I thought about having children I was thinking 'I don't know if I want to be anchored down.'" Janet, a partnered thirty-one-year-old working in real estate, said simply, "I don't want to give up my healthy sex life."

In the case of both the parents and the childfree, personal ful-fillment and an interest in nurturing meaningful relationships are at the top of the list of reasons for their chosen path. If we accept that the childfree are selfish for their choice, then we must accept the same of parents. Or we can reject the notion for both. In either case, it doesn't make sense to ascribe selfishness to one but not the other when both groups make their choice for a very similar set of reasons. What's important is that parents and the childfree make the choice that's right for them.

While reflecting on the selfish question, Sarah, a psychiatrist in her mid-thirties, told me, "If you have kids, there's gonna be a constant constraint on how freely you can move. So I think that's a selfish decision [not to have them] but I think some of the reasons why people have children are also as selfish—like they want company in the future or they see the child as an elongation of one's self." According to Bob, a married professor in his mid-thirties, the motivations in both cases "are entirely selfishness and fear." Bob explained, "If I wanted to have kids, it would be to enjoy seeing them grow up, seeing how they might be like me or my partner. And I would enjoy having young adults around while I'm retired. The reasons for not having kids are how will this affect my free time, it's gonna cost a lot of money, it's gonna take a lot of energy. All of those things, on both accounts, I feel are pretty selfish."

SELFISH IS AS SELFISH DOES

Reasons for our choices aside, some argue that the childfree are more selfish than parents in their everyday lives and behaviors. Though claims about childfree people's selfishness are common, sociologist Robert Reed points out that prior to his 2012 dissertation examining the topic, "no existing empirical studies have compared parents and nonparents on selfishness."[12] In his own study, Reed found no difference between parents and nonparents on a measure of self-reported selfishness. Reed's respondents were asked to identify on a 5-point scale how well the phrase "a selfish person" described themselves. Forty-two percent of nonparents said this was not a good description at all of themselves; 44 percent of parents said the same. And parents and nonparents responded identically at the other end of the scale; just 3 percent in each category said selfish was a good or a very good description of themselves.

Though media reports suggest that at least some childfree people freely describe themselves as selfish,[13] self-reports may not be the most reliable measure of what is generally considered to be an undesirable trait. An alternative way of assessing the extent to which a group's behaviors are selfish is to examine how they spend their time. Many of the childfree people I spoke with said that wanting to preserve time for involvement in their communities was an important reason for not having kids. As forty-five-year-old teacher Michelle put it, she opted to remain childfree because she wanted "plenty of free time to volunteer."

In a survey of over seven hundred childfree women and men, led by one of my students, we found that one-third of respondents were actively involved in civic life.[14] These respondents were involved in a variety of organizations and efforts, including animal welfare groups, human rights and environmental organizations, volunteer and charity groups, hobby and sports clubs, and political and religious groups. These sorts of involvement are not unique to the childfree, of course. Parents are also engaged in volunteer groups, clubs, and community organizations. The U.S. Department of Labor found that in 2015, 31.3 percent of parents with children under eighteen volunteer, most typically in activities associated with children, such as coaching, refereeing, or tutoring.[15] These similar rates of civic engagement suggest that status as parent, or not, may have very little to do with one's likelihood of being involved in their community.

Community involvement was common among the childfree women and men I interviewed. Barb, a thirty-three-year-old working in an animal welfare nonprofit, came to her decision about not having kids as a result of her activism. She describes her move into the animal rights movement in her twenties as "a really pivotal thing for me. I felt like I found my calling. It was like finding a religion.

This was a cause that needed me, that I believed in with every cell in my being." Barb went on to explain, "Within the animal rights movement, there's a large number of people who deliberately decide not to have children and I definitely fall into that category. It's a kind of philosophical/political decision. I became really deeply concerned about world overpopulation. We're at six billion now and I've heard it's going to be eight billion by 2050 and meanwhile we're in an age of mass extinction. Animals and plants are dying at alarming rates. There's something like three hundred right whales left and only a few hundred mountain gorillas left in Rwanda. There's maybe a thousand tigers left in India. . . . When I think about that, I just grieve. I deeply grieve. Meanwhile people are populating and populating and populating. We are creating extinction because there's just way, way too many of us."

Thirty-one-year-old Lauren spends much of her free time volunteering with homeless and immigrant populations in her community. She says she feels "particularly called to people who don't have families, whether that is widowed people, orphaned, the homeless, the marginalized, refugees, whoever that is. I strongly believe that my imperative is to take care of those who are kind of lost and forgotten, those who are marginalized. My calling is to take care of those people. It's my heart and my passion."

The calling to take care of others extends into older age, too. Susan, who is fifty-three, told me, "I give to charity. I'm more generous with my nieces and nephews than their other aunts and uncles. I enjoy giving to my friends, and so on. I feel very good about that." And sixty-two-year-old Terrie St. Claire told the *Bangor Daily News* that being childfree means she and her husband are able to sustain their strong commitment to supporting the arts and other charitable efforts in their community.[16]

Speaking from the perspective of a couple of mid-fortysomethings, Lance and I enjoy our involvement on a variety of organizational boards and volunteering at events in our community as well. And we engage in these activities alongside many parents. For us, as I'm sure for the parents whose company we share, involvement provides a sense of meaning, purpose, and belonging. Research on older adults does show, however, that while parents and nonparents are equally likely to perform volunteer work, nonparents are more intensively involved in their volunteer work.[17] This makes sense, as parents who give to their communities must still carve out time to give to their kids, too.

Though I don't believe most childfree people are involved in their communities because they expect to get anything other than a sense of joy or personal fulfillment from it, it has occurred to me that giving to one's community may not have the same likely "return on investment" as devoting oneself to offspring. There are no guarantees that our community will return the favor of our time, energy, and investment and allow us to rely on it should we find ourselves in need in our old age. Indeed, research examining nonparents in older age finds that while the support networks they *rely on* may be somewhat weaker than those of parents, the support *they offer* their communities is stronger. But as I discuss in chapter 6, it doesn't always turn out that kids are there for their elderly parents in the ways we might expect them to be. Neither path—parenthood nor nonparenthood—offers absolute certainty for the future. And in both cases, giving with the expectation of getting something in return probably qualifies as selfish.

Perhaps one return on the investment of their more intensive civic engagement is the more active social lives older childfree people enjoy when compared to those of older parents.[18] While it makes sense that young parents might be less socially engaged given the demands of rearing young children, that this pattern continues into older age is striking. Maintaining social activity is critical not just for emotional well-being but also for longer-term health. One study found that older adults who regularly engage in visits with friends and family, volunteering, and participation in clubs and other programs have fewer physical and cognitive health problems.[19] It is important to acknowledge, however, that childfree people's more active social lives do not necessarily translate into a roster of closer friendships. Research shows that older parents are as likely to sustain close friendships as older nonparents.[20]

If we assume that selfish people are inactive in their communities and lack close friendships, we cannot claim that the childfree fall into this category. Even if selfishness is measured extremely narrowly as lacking interest in children's well-being, most childfree cannot be cast in this light. A survey of 1,000 non-mothers inspired by Melanie Notkin's memoir, *Otherhood*, found that children play an active role in the lives of 80 percent of women who don't have children of their own.[21] Notkin's joint study on the power of the PANK (Professional Aunt No Kids) found that it's common for aunts to spend money on the children in their lives and assist kids' parents financially.[22] My own interviews show that childfree adults—including both aunts and uncles—serve as mentors and friends to children and work with them as teachers, social workers, doctors, and counselors. The essays in Meghan Daum's edited volume *Selfish, Shallow, and Self-Absorbed* further attest that childfree women and men invest significant emotional and other resources advocating for children's well-being.[23]

Daum's own story, as described in her 2014 piece in *The New Yorker*, "Difference Maker," recounts her own impassioned advocacy for children, first as a "big sister" with Big Brothers Big Sisters and later as a court-appointed advocate for kids in the foster care system.[24] It is telling that Daum and several of the childfree writers in her edited volume go to great lengths to make clear that they really do care about children. While I have no reason to doubt that this is true, insisting too adamantly that we don't hate kids doesn't always sit well with childfree audiences. I explore this in more depth in chapter 5 but for now I'll leave it at the claim that in today's culture, not making children the center of one's universe, or at least not asserting that children are or should be the center of the universe, leaves one open to criticism. It's tantamount to admitting to kicking puppies, or worse. Even parents are not immune.

ALL FOR THE CHILDREN

Unless they always make everything they do about their kids, parents also risk being accused of selfishness. As Steve observed, "One of the things that I think people who have kids are not allowed to say is that kids are not the best thing that ever happened to them. It's like admitting that kids make their life harder is equivalent to saying they wish they'd never had kids. And they don't have any room to wiggle. It's only every once in a while you get into these interesting conversations with parents and they'll say something like 'you know, if we had known what this was gonna be like, we might not have done it.'"

In 2014, an American Greetings video showing candidates interviewing for the "world's toughest job" quickly went viral.[25] Job requirements included working while standing 135 to unlimited hours per week, no breaks, no vacations, and, ideally, degrees in medicine, finance, and the culinary arts. The punch line? Candidates learned they'd applied for the job of Mom. The aim of the video was to sell Mother's Day cards but it provides an opportunity to think more deeply about where our expectations of mothers come from and what effect they have on us all. The unrealistic expectations we place on moms hurt everyone: mothers, fathers, kids, and even the childfree lose when intensive and helicopter parenting are held up as ideals.

In the late 1990s, sociologist Sharon Hays observed that the predominant view of parenting is that it should be "child centered, expert-guided, emotionally absorbing, labor-intensive, and financially expensive."[26] It is also thought to be primarily a mother's responsibility. This means that mothers who wish to be viewed as "good" must be constantly available—emotionally, mentally, and physically—for their kids. They are expected to tote little Susie and Johnny from school to soccer to Scouts, all with a supportive smile, a dedicated ear, and a homemade gluten-free, sugar-free, dairy-free, antibiotic-free, GMO-free snack. As Hays puts it, "If you are a good mother, you *must* be an intensive one."

Childfree Kate watched helplessly when, as she describes it, she lost a friend—and, Kate says, her friend lost herself—to the pressures of intensive motherhood. "A friend of mine has two kids, they're ten and twelve. She's basically given her life to them. Everything revolves around her kids. It's all about the kids but on the other hand she has all these other things going on in her life that she doesn't want to give up but the kids always come first and everything just kind of piles up. Just watching her live her life, I'm exhausted. We had a candid discussion a couple of weeks ago and she said she was taking antidepressants because she doesn't want to give up all of these different things. She'd rather take a pill. There's no joy for her in all this chaos. She's trying to make sure that the kids are having the best possible life they could have and I'm just like 'Whoa, what about *you*?'"

The pressure on mothers hasn't declined but it has expanded to include fathers. Moms and dads dedicate more of their time to their kids these days than in any previous era. Between 1965 and 2003, men's time with their kids tripled; women's doubled.[27] And helicopter parenting often doesn't stop when kids reach adulthood. A 2014 survey of eighteen- to twenty-year-olds found that parents of young adults are taking an increasingly active role in their children's job searches, some going so far as to accompany children on their job interviews or writing thank-you notes after interviews.[28] Another survey, this one of senior managers, found that parents have taken charge in salary negotiations for their adult children, disguised themselves as previous employers so they could serve as references, and even delivered cake to employers to convince them to hire their adult child.[29]

The pressures of intensive mothering and burdens of helicopter parenting are not good for anyone. For mothers, the culture of intensive parenting comes with the heavy burden of unrealistic and unhealthy expectations. A 2013 study by a team of University of Mary Washington psychologists found that "aspects of intensive mothering beliefs are detrimental to women's mental health."[30] The pressure to intensively parent is not good for couples either. Psychologist Joshua Coleman notes that "the increase in parenting hours on the part of both husbands and wives may pose some threats to the couple relationship since many couples have increased their time with their children by eliminating or greatly reducing time for romance."[31] When couples make time for each other through date nights and other kinds of targeted just-them time, marital quality goes up and risk of divorce goes down.

While parents of only children may be more able to make time for each other than parents of multiple kids, they—like the childfree—are susceptible to accusations of selfishness. In their case, even having a child isn't enough to free one from being perceived as selfish. As Lauren Sandler notes in *One and Only*, parents of "onlies" know well the stereotypes attached to choosing to rear just one: They're selfish, narcissistic, maladjusted, and not *really* committed to family.[32] Sounds familiar.

Lance and I had the chance to meet Ms. Sandler when she and I shared the stage on Katie Couric's talk show for an episode on the childfree. Sandler was there to discuss her *Time* article on the childfree choice,[33] but when we got to talking with her, we were shocked to discover just how many parallels there are between the experiences of the parents of onlies and the childfree. As Sandler put it when Lance interviewed her for our blog, "There are great similarities [between the childfree and parents of onlies]. We are the selfish ones. We are the ones who are asked to explain ourselves. We are the ones who are presumed not to love children, to put our own needs first at all times, to be egregiously committed to careers, or superficial desires. And like the stereotypes of childfree women, the myths about parents of only children simply don't bear up. And yet these myths seem eternal."[34]

Thus, it isn't always all for the children—it must also be all for the right number of children. While the ideal number of kids was once higher—3.6 in the 1930s—today half of Americans report that the ideal number of children is two.[35] And accusations of selfishness don't end with the childfree and the parents of onlies. One must be a parent of enough children—but not *too many*. In 1999, Karla Mueller and Janice Yoder found that childfree women, single-child mothers, and "supernormative mothers" of four or more children all experience stigmatization and pressure from outsiders to stay within "normative parameters" of two or three children each.[36]

While extreme examples like the Duggar family of *19 Kids and Counting* make headlines, any family of more than a few kids can raise eyebrows. A recent conversation with a new colleague drove this home for me. After responding to her query about whether I had kids, I returned the question. She looked at me sheepishly. "Yes," she said, "we have five." This was followed with a quick, "All planned! All loved! I swear!" It hadn't occurred to me to wonder whether she had planned her kids or loved them, but in the conversation that followed, I learned that sharing you have five children can be as anxiety-producing as sharing you have none. My colleague shared that she worries people will think she's not feminist, not well educated, that her children are not well cared for. These are not worries I share when I first tell someone I don't have kids but then she added, "And people think we're selfish." To that I could relate.

I tried to imagine how the pressures of intensive parenting must have felt for my colleague, to be being all things at all times for all of her children. The exercise made me grateful for the choice I'd made and also even more aware of the importance of challenging the idea that helicopter parenting should be the standard to which all parents aspire. It isn't just parents—whether they have one child or ten—who are hurt when the pressures of intensive parenting prevail. A study of the impact of helicopter parenting found that the children of parents who hover are more likely than children of non-hoverers to use prescription drugs for anxiety and depression and more likely to use pain pills recreationally. They also don't fare as well emotionally.[37] The culture of intensive parenting harms the childfree as well. Positing that adults' exclusive focus should be children ignores the variety of ways that childfree people find meaning in their lives and contribute to their communities. Historian and journalist Elinor Burkett, author of *Baby Boon: How Family-Friendly America Cheats the Childless*, says that this culture also sends the message that childfree people's time is less valuable than that of parents'.[38] Parents, as individuals, are not to blame for these problems. If any finger-pointing occurs, it should be in the direction of the larger culture of intensive parenting; and we're all responsible for pushing back against it.

IT'S ALL ABOUT BALANCE

There is perhaps no place where it is clearer that parents' lives are supposed to be all about their children than in debates and hand-wringing over work-life balance. It is also in these discussions that accusations about childfree people's presumed selfishness often appear. The childfree are accused of being selfish when they ask for—or worse, expect—a reasonable balance between work and their lives outside of work. Parents report that the way we think about work-life balance isn't doing them any favors either and mothers are among the biggest losers in the work-life balance wars.

While men see a boost to their incomes after becoming parents,[39] women who opt in to parenthood are penalized with lower salaries[40] and inequitable workloads at home.[41] One study by researchers at Cornell University found that working mothers are perceived to be less competent than non-mothers and that their recommended starting salaries are lower.[42] And before we go suggesting that mothers are somehow to blame for these patterns, it should be noted that these patterns persist even after taking into account hours worked, work experience, educational background, and partners' incomes. Even more, stereotypes about mothers as less committed to their workplaces fly in the face of recent research by management consulting firm Great Place to Work, which finds that the reverse may be true.[43]

Though it's rare for anyone to come right out and say it, an assumption built into many discussions of work-life balance is that the "life" portion of this equation means children. Work-life balance is a concept that can vary for different people but, at its core, it is about an individual achieving what she or he perceives to be the ideal combination of time and effort spent on lifestyle interests (e.g., health, well-being, family, pleasure, hobbies) and professional pursuits (e.g., career, professional development, work hours, work expectations).

On some level, most people understand that we all have lives outside of work that must be balanced with work. Nevertheless, the perception that childfree people's "life" time is both less valuable and more plentiful than that of their parent colleagues is common in the workplace. Amanda, a media strategist in her mid-thirties, reflected on how she has struggled with the perception that she has more time than the parents with whom she works. As she put it, "If

I wanted to leave my work to take care of something personal, the people that were parents were, like, 'No.' They felt their stuff was more urgent. My dog having to go to the vet was not equal to their child being sick. I was getting more judgment on that."

Amanda explained further. "It was totally okay for the parents to leave at five o'clock sharp, but there was more of an expectation that I could stay late so I could help out with an event because I didn't have kids. . . . I had to protect my personal time in a way that people with kids didn't have to because they have this personal trump card; there's a toddler that needs me or I'm breast feeding. No one questions that stuff, but if I'm like 'I have a date,' that's not as legitimate. My viewpoint on it is that all these choices we make in our personal life are equal. That I have to leave work an hour early on Thursday to get a ski weekend in with my fiancé should be treated equally to 'We're preparing the kids for spring break' or 'I have a parent-teacher conference so I need to leave early.' I feel like parents enjoy a certain degree of flexibility in the workplace that childfree people don't. I believe your personal life is your personal life and your employer should respect whatever decision you're making in your personal life. . . . I've had employers ask me to cancel a vacation or come in when I'm sick or work from home if I was dealing with a family emergency when I don't perceive that parents would be asked the same thing."

Matt, a teacher in his late twenties, has also faced the assumption that he has more time—and that his time is less valuable—than that of his colleagues who have kids. Matt said these assumptions tend to reveal themselves in the course of casual conversations at work, particularly when a deadline is looming. As he put it, "A lot of people will say, and kind of make offhand comments like, 'Oh, so you've got the time to revise this before Friday!'" Matt says his colleagues do not make the same assumptions about the available time of employees who happen to be parents.

As childfree people, when we do take the time to balance our lives with our work, we're sometimes greeted with the raised eyebrows of our colleagues. My own experience using the benefits provided by the Family and Medical Leave Act (FMLA) for a sports injury brought me to this awareness. When a concussion forced me to significantly reduce my work hours for a month, the assumption that I'd quit the sport that caused the injury was common. One parent from work heard my tale and responded with "That much time away from work? I assume this means you're quitting roller derby." While this may have been a well-intentioned query, I couldn't help but wonder how much time she'd taken after having each of her two kids. This and other queries came with the implication that I should have known better than to put myself at risk like that and that the correct choice would be to avoid doing it again.

Obviously, roller derby and babies are not anywhere near the same thing, but I couldn't understand why, after using the same benefit others rightfully use when the need arises, the expectation was that I would quit. I'd made a choice to engage in a completely legal outside-of-work activity that was now impeding my ability to work. Was it a risky activity? Yes, absolutely. But pregnancy and childbirth are not without risk themselves. In the U.S., maternal death rates range from 12.7 to 24 per 100,000 births.[44] Preeclampsia, a pregnancy complication likely to impact mothers' need for FMLA, occurs in 2 to 8 percent of pregnancies.[45] Roller derby, too, comes with risks. One study found that derby injuries are common, though most are minor hits to the knee, foot, or ankle that don't cause a need for extended leaves from work.[46] Risk alone is not a reason to avoid childbirth or roller derby, both of which can enhance the "life" portion of that holy grail we all seek, work-life balance.

Even for parents, equating "life" with "children" to the exclusion of everything else is limiting. Though this may be an observation that doesn't seem to require extensive investigation, studies do confirm that we all have roles that are not related to parenting that sometimes conflict with work.[47] These parts of our lives—which include activities like volunteering, involvement in clubs and organizations, caring for friends or parents, self-care, and hobbies—must be balanced with work. Everyone loses when work conflicts with people's lives. Employees suffer, their friends and families suffer, and employers suffer, too. One study found that workers who struggle with work-life balance are not only more susceptible to psychological strain, depression, and anxiety but also less committed to their organizations.[48] Unhappy workforces don't come cheap. According to Gallup, active disengagement in the workforce costs the U.S. $450 billion to $550 billion each year.[49]

The childfree people I interviewed do understand that it's different when you're a parent. They also understand that their own outside-of-work lives have value, too, and that their time is precious as well. Laura, a librarian in her early forties, was quick to note that she does favor parents having the flexibility needed to be involved in their children's lives. But she needs flexibility sometimes, too. Laura explained, "I don't want to sound like I'm not in favor of this because I am but if someone needs to have time off for going to their children's event at school, or parent-teacher conferences, or whatnot, those seem to be given priority over someone who is childfree wanting to have an afternoon off to do something else. I really do believe that jobs should be much more flexible so that parents can take the time to go to their events, those are very important to children, but I just think that if I'm choosing to take an afternoon off to do something else, that doesn't mean that my choice is less important than their choice."

Ames, a project manager in his mid-thirties, said parents are sometimes treated differently from nonparents in his workplace. As he put it, "In the workplace environment, there are concessions made to people with children that aren't made for people without children. Like, someone will say, 'I have to stay home because my child is sick' or 'I have to leave early because my child is sick.' These are understandable situations, but it's also an easy excuse for people. There's a certain amount of respect that is given to people with children that sometimes is not given to people without children."

Placing a higher value on how one employee chooses to spend her or his time outside of work over another's choice is a slippery slope. And unless employers want to be in the questionable business of judging the relative value of employees' private lives, there has to be a more effective way to handle the reality that all employees do indeed have private lives. In her book *Unfinished Business*, Anne-Marie Slaughter argues that we need to shift the conversation away from balance and toward fitting work with life.[50] Slaughter points out that conversations about work-life balance not only ignore workers in the lowest income brackets, often women, but they also miss the chance to expand the conversation and envision broader changes in how workplaces organize themselves and understand productivity. On-demand contracting, OpenWork environments that give employees voice in shaping their workplace conditions and environment, and other flexible work options can improve productivity and loyalty and they don't require one-size-fits-all notions of how employees live their private lives. Taking a closer look at how we understand work-life balance and what the consequences are of those understandings also reveals that sometimes childfree people benefit from existing notions that equate "life" with children.

Like so many others whom I've interviewed, Brittany, a legal secretary in her early fifties, said one drawback of being childfree is that the lawyers she works with feel freer to co-opt her time, and they do so more often than with her fellow legal secretaries who have kids. At the same time, Brittany acknowledges that the perception that she is more available and more willing to work long hours may have served her well at work in the past. She stated, "As a legal secretary, my bosses really liked that I was childfree because . . . they didn't have to worry that I had to rush home for kids. I guess that made me more available and made it easier when it came to finding a job." Brittany frames her employers' perception of her as more available as a benefit, and it may well have facilitated her job search. Yet hiring or not hiring a person on the basis of parental status, while not an explicitly protected class under federal law, does not seem to be the wisest course of action for employers.[51]

Mandy, an engineer in her mid-thirties, shared a similar experience. "My boss was pretty happy when he found out I was childfree. He knew I wouldn't have to leave work in the middle of the day, that scheduling would be easier, and very easily I can just be gone tomorrow if I have to be, in terms of traveling for work and that sort of thing. His reaction, I would call it glee. He was like, 'Oh really?!' He says, 'Oh geez, that's *great*!' He was definitely pleased."

And Jennifer, an underwriter in her mid-thirties, says her status as childfree is viewed most positively by male managers in particular. "I think that there are definitely advantages of being childfree at work, especially around men, because when I've had a male manager, I've never had to give them the 'Oh, my kid is sick, I can't come in' excuse. Or 'I can't work late because I have a kid.' Or 'I can't do this because I have a kid.' I've always been very up front that I don't have those things holding me back at home, so if I'm needed at work, I will be there."

The preference for childfree workers over parents may even extend beyond management, to colleagues. Christina, a lab tech in her early thirties, said, "I have coworkers who have children at work and I think in some ways they view me as more responsible about work because I don't have kids. You know, they can ask me to do something without worrying that I won't be able to stay late if they need me to."

Indeed, childfree people sometimes benefit, in the short term at least, from the impression their employers and colleagues have that they are more committed to their jobs than parents. Yet it strikes me as a bit of a paradox to assume both that childfree people are more selfish than parents and that they are more willing to put in more time at work. And while the childfree, like parents, have family needs they must balance with the demands of work, 80 percent of respondents in a survey by *Personnel Journal* reported that employees without children are left out of the range of work-family programs being introduced by employers to help employees balance work and home.[52] The childfree aren't happy about it. In the same survey, 69 percent of respondents said corporate America could expect to see some backlash from single and, researchers implied, childless employees as a result. Whether they benefit or ultimately lose out from current arrangements, employees without children should not be excluded from employer programs designed to support, retain, and attract employees. Whatever we call them—work-family, work-life, or flexible—making such arrangements available to parents and non-parents alike is in the best interests of everyone. As a 2018 study of 2,700 workers found, it isn't just mothers who suffer in workplace cultures where work-life balance isn't supported—men and employees without kids also report lower work satisfaction when they fear they will be penalized for attempting to balance their work lives with their lives at home.[53]

LEAVING A LEGACY

Where do childfree people leave the piles of money we're supposed to be accruing as we reap the benefits of all those extra hours at work? To whom do they go after we die? And while we're on this line of questioning, who will even remember us when we're gone? The question of legacy is a tricky one in the context of selfishness. On one hand, I've heard it's selfish *not* to think about the legacy you'll leave behind; what, you don't care about the future?! At the same time, I can't help but wonder, isn't worrying over one's legacy just a little bit narcissistic? As aging scholar Rosalie Kane put it, "Surely, once dead, one would no longer care whether a business passes out of the family, whether an orchard is well-tended, whether a university building exists in one's name, or whether one's children quarrel."[54] But care, people do.

The question of legacy is a popular one in childfree and childless circles. At the NotMom Summit, where breakout sessions fall into one of three categories—Life, Legacy, or Passions—legacy is central. In fact, the overarching theme of the summit is "Redefining Feminine Legacy."[55] Participants learn about and reflect on engaging in philanthropy, telling their stories, planning for old age, and making a difference in the lives of other people's children. Childless and childfree people's concern about how to leave a legacy certainly aligns with our broader cultural values and norms.

Some of the most visible childfree folks today will leave some of the most significant legacies when they're gone. Think, for example, of Oprah Winfrey's significant philanthropic work. Just one aspect is her Leadership Academy for Girls. The academy opened its doors in South Africa in 2007 and has been serving approximately 290 girls from grades 8 to 12 each year since.[56] Also, Ashley Judd's work on the Advisory Council of Demand Abolition, an organization dedicated to eradicating the illegal commercial sex industry.[57] And of course there's Ellen DeGeneres's support for numerous charitable organizations[58] and her touching and hilarious shows featuring kids.[59] And don't forget that the kid-friendly charity Yum-o!, which aims to feed hungry children and educate kids interested in food careers, was founded by childfree celebrity chef Rachael Ray.[60]

For centuries, voluntarily childless nuns have dedicated themselves to civic engagement and social justice. Mother Teresa is one example. Though some, including writer and social critic Christopher

Hitchens, challenge mainstream conceptions of Mother Teresa as someone truly interested in or effective at alleviating poverty, she did receive recognition for her efforts in the form of the 1979 Nobel Peace Prize.[61] Other voluntarily childless religious figures include Sister Simone Campbell and her fellow rogue Nuns on the Bus who have traveled the country since 2012, educating those they visit about immigration reform, protesting cuts to social services budgets, and highlighting problems associated with big money in politics.[62]

Of course, most of us don't have the resources to build full-fledged charities or to take lengthy rides on buses for justice or pay to send hundreds of kids to go to school, but making a positive mark on the world is not limited to the rich and famous or those who dedicate themselves to a particular religious practice.

In 1996, Robert Rubenstein interviewed 109 non-mothers in Philadelphia with an average age of seventy-five about what constitutes legacy for them.[63] Many of these women created what Rubenstein calls a "social legacy" by meaningfully influencing people in their lives through careers such as teaching and nursing and their sense of social responsibility toward their communities. One woman told Rubenstein, "You have to have some way of hitching on to the future . . . and it seems to me that it doesn't have to be biological children."

Rubenstein's subjects also made the observation that leaving a legacy without children required some ingenuity on their part as we're not institutionally or culturally adept at understanding that legacy can mean more than passing something on from parent to child. Rubenstein explained, "They had to overcome something, a hardship, an absence, a loss, or mindless social rules, in order to create a legacy." But the women, like many other childfree people, outwitted the roadblocks placed by our cultural lack of imagination and left their mark in spite of, or perhaps because of, their status as non-parents. One woman, a former teacher, shared that she has former students scattered throughout the U.S. who are now teachers themselves. She told Rubenstein, "I have the next generation who are largely doing teaching, and I think that's very rewarding." Others developed parent-child–like ties with their siblings' children and with younger nonrelatives. In the end, Rubenstein concludes and I concur, if legacies reflect the self at the same time that they foster a nurturance of others, then they require a bit of both narcissism and selflessness.

WHAT'S WRONG WITH BEING SELFISH?

Exploring these questions about finding fulfillment and leaving a legacy has left me wondering, has selfishness been treated unfairly? Has it gotten an unnecessarily bad rap? Fifty-three-year-old childfree Susan, for her part, embraces the selfish label. "I view a 'selfish' person as a person that knows themselves. I view it as a positive. I know myself well enough to know that parenting was not for me." On the whole, the childfree people I interviewed did not identify as selfish. For those who did, it was a qualified version of the term like Susan's.

For Susan, knowing that parenthood was not for her is selfish but another way of looking at her choice is that having a child would be unfair to the child. One theme that came through clearly in my interviews with childfree women and men who described having happy childhoods is that they understood the effort their parents put into providing those happy childhoods. And they knew that they were not prepared to do the same for a child. Perhaps there are wrong or selfish reasons to have children—to have someone to take care of you when you're old, to see what a "mini you" looks like, out of a need for unconditional love—but are there wrong reasons to avoid bringing an unwanted child into the world? Certainly bringing a child who is not wanted into one's life does not benefit the child. If we really do care about kids as a culture, shouldn't we support those who know they don't want to be parents when they make that choice?

In the trailer for Therese Shechter's documentary *My So-Called Selfish Life*, childfree writer Chanel Dubofsky asks, "What's wrong with being selfish?" When I first heard the question, my reaction progressed along the lines of the stages of grief. First came denial: "But, but, *empirically*, we're *not* selfish!" Then anger: "Who is Chanel Dubofsky to tell me I'm selfish!?" (Never mind that she hadn't.) Next up, bargaining: "If I show up to that fund-raising thing tonight, can I be not-selfish? How about if I volunteer at that other thing?" From there, I entered funk and reflection: "Volunteering won't change how people see me. As a childfree person, some people will always think I'm selfish, no matter what I do. Maybe what matters most is how I see myself. Yeah, that's the ticket! But how *do* I see myself? And what does it all *mean* anyway?" Finally, I turned a corner, "What *is* wrong with being selfish? So sometimes I'm selfish. Sometimes I'm not selfish. And maybe, just maybe, we're not talking about selfishness at all."

In the same trailer for the film, poet Molly Peacock asks viewers, "What is selfish about a conscious, considered choice?" What indeed. Walking through the stages of my reaction to Dubofsky's question brought me to the realization that coming to some understanding of what one wishes out of life, embracing the journey on the way there, and then just going for it looks a lot like what psychologist Abraham Maslow called self-actualization.[64] Perhaps that's what the childfree have achieved. Perhaps anyone who has made a conscious decision about parenthood, for or against, has achieved this. The childfree know and have accepted what they want, they're comfortable with some unknowns and the knowledge that their choice is unconventional, and they accept that they are not perfect. But even if that's so, the belief that childfree people are self-ish lives on. And for many of us, knowing that the idea is out there takes its toll.

Research by social psychologists finds that having to contend with the threat of judgment posed by stereotypes lodged against you has serious repercussions. Originally developed as an explanation for racial differences in performance on standardized exams, further studies found that stereotype threat in a variety of contexts can influence job performance and even memory.[65] Other research finds that negative stereotypes about one's family type, such as those about the childfree, can lead to lowered self-esteem.[66] In short, the stress and anxiety of knowing that others think you are less than wears a person down.

As others shared as well, Amanda struggles with how to respond to the singular comments people make, not large enough to make a scene of but not so small that they're insignificant, and together they become much bigger. She went on, "A lot of people in my life make comments to me about being selfish and I don't feel it's appropriate to lash out to each of them and set them straight because in their head they are making a pretty harmless comment, which considered individually, is pretty harmless. But it's the fact that everyone is making them. It's a thousand paper cuts."

Amanda isn't alone. Angela, a professor in her early forties, said she is sometimes treated like "a pariah" for not having kids. And being treated like a pariah is exhausting. As Angela put it, "Some people think I'm broken or selfish or weird or counter—I don't know—traditional. Not having kids has definitely well-established me as 'the other.' I am well aware that many people stereotype me as a childfree person." These microaggressions—defined as subtle everyday events that denigrate individuals because they are members of particular groups—take their toll emotionally, intellectually, and physically.[67] Microaggressions also harm those who employ them, limiting perpetrators' capacity to connect with others and their ability to utilize the beneficial qualities of those around them.[68]

As a fellow childfree person who has struggled with how to defend myself against the selfish label, and how to express my right to work-life balance and to find fulfillment in the ways that work for me, I think that we ultimately do ourselves a disservice by engaging the language of selfishness and selflessness. We are neither more selfless nor more selfish than our colleagues, friends, and relatives who happen to be parents.

Rather than touting ourselves as more committed to our communities and our jobs, or encouraging assumptions that we are or should be so, we would be better served by noticing the flaws in these sweeping generalizations, understanding our commonalities, pushing for better work-life balance policies for all, and letting go of the name-calling. Challenging—and changing—misimpressions of who we are and what we bring to the table means challenging all stereotypes, including those that might benefit some of us on occasion. When we examine how the childfree live and why they've made the choice not to have children, we quickly discover that our lives and motivations are not so different after all from those who choose a path different from our own.

FOUR

LESS OF A WOMAN:
THE MYTH OF
MATERNAL INSTINCT

I have no maternal instinct. I am barren. I ovulate sand.
—COMEDIAN MARGARET CHO

Though the specific talent of ovulating sand may be unique to Margaret Cho, her lack of maternal instinct is not. In fact, the idea that any woman is innately driven toward motherhood is among the most widespread misunderstandings about why people have kids. Culturally, we hold dear the belief that women are uniquely wired to want children. This belief serves to help us identify roles, organize labor within and outside the home, and understand our own—and others'—place. Challenging it means questioning everything we were taught about our place in the world and even our very social structures. It is much more comfortable, and comforting to others, to joke about one's individual lack of maternal instinct than it is to suggest that it doesn't exist.

As psychologist Gilla Shapiro once put it, "The stigmatization of the voluntarily childless is intertwined with the construction of womanhood as motherhood."[1] Though social worker Carolyn Morell found that some women "seem to be impervious to popular beliefs about not-mothering women as incomplete, as inadequate, as having inferior lives," others find themselves dispirited by the unrelenting and omnipresent cultural message that childfree women are not fully women.[2] Remaining childfree is an act in itself of resistance against a pronatalist ideology that posits that women's value comes from their ability to bear and rear children.

MOTHERHOOD AND APPLE PIE

Maternal instinct is a myth. Ellen Peck made this point nearly five decades ago when she observed, "And since one [sex] precedes the other [reproduction], it would seem that the basic human desire operating is sexual rather than reproductive. Reproduction is simply the more or less inevitable result of sexual activity."[3] Peck proposed these ideas in her 1971 childfree manifesto, *The Baby Trap*, but she and a diverse roster of collaborators, including sociologists, psychologists, political scientists, policy makers, and journalists, developed them further in a co-edited 1974 follow-up, *Pronatalism: The Myth of Mom & Apple Pie*.[4] In the book, sociologist Judith Blake asserts that parenthood is a precondition for all aspects of gender roles and that women's sexually differentiated relation to childbearing in particular drives what we think of as natural roles for women.[5] In other words, the predominant belief is that womanhood equals motherhood.

Despite the fact that motherhood and womanhood remain inextricably entwined in most people's minds, scientists have found little evidence to support the notion of a maternal instinct in humans. In her extensive dissertation on the history of scientific views about the maternal instinct, Professor Maria Vicedo-Castello concludes that "there is no scientific evidence to claim that there is a maternal instinct that automatically gives women the desire to have children, makes women more emotional than men, confers upon them a higher capacity for nurturance, and makes them better equipped to rear children than men."[6] Vicedo-Castello interrogates research, theories, and philosophies as far ranging as Charles Darwin's and Herbert Spencer's ideas about evolution and the origin of species to the first-wave feminist movement's challenges to women's roles in parenting, to debates during the shameful eugenics movement to the postwar baby boom, and, more recently, to the second-wave feminist movement's emphasis on reproductive choice. In none of these queries and theories does Vicedo-Castello find evidence to support the idea of a maternal instinct.

Even more, not one of the seven hundred entries in Sage Publishing's three-volume *Encyclopedia of Motherhood*, a hefty tome summarizing knowledge from the scholarly study of motherhood, is dedicated to the concept of maternal instinct.[7] The volume is thorough—in its 1,300-plus pages, it covers topics as wide ranging as the history of motherhood, terrorism and motherhood, discipline of children, and transnationalism. And yet not a single entry is dedicated to the topic of maternal instinct. When maternal instinct does come up in entries, it is generally described as nothing more than a figment of our cultural imaginations. Between Vicedo-Castello's wide-ranging query of work spanning multiple disciplines and hundreds of years and the thousands of pages in the motherhood encyclopedia, it would appear that scholars have as much to say about maternal instinct as an empirical concept as they do about the existence of unicorns and Santa Claus.

Indeed, if maternal instinct were such a compelling force, birth rates would not vary to such a degree with cultural change. The economic downturns of the 1920s and 2000s would have had little impact on how many women became mothers or how many children mothers had—and yet in both periods, fertility rates went down. In addition, the expansion of educational and workforce opportunities for women that we've seen since the feminist movement of the 1960s and '70s should not have impacted fertility patterns. Instead, Gretchen Livingston of the Pew Research Center notes that "childlessness has been consistently rising among younger women since the 1970s."[8]

If the drive to have children were innate, we would also see far less variation in how human mothers do—or do not—raise and nurture their children over time and across cultural contexts. Yet we know that what we think of as a good mother, a natural mother, and of motherhood as a concept varies across time and location.[9] For example, while the notion that biologically related mothers and children are naturally in tune with one another and need each other to thrive is common in the United States and other similar societies, in Haiti's lakou system of group living, children are reared by a wide circle of relatives, friends, and neighbors who share parenting responsibilities for all children in the community.[10] So too in Israeli kibbutzim, where children are raised and educated communally.[11]

As psychologist Steven Pinker put it, people do not "literally strive to replicate their genes. If that's how the mind worked, men would line up outside sperm banks and women would pay to have their eggs harvested and given away to infertile couples."[12] And, as Leta Hollingsworth said in the *American Journal of Sociology* over one hundred years ago, if maternal instinct were universally innate in women, then there would be no reason for "society [to] find it necessary to make laws against contraception, infanticide, abortion, and infant desertion."[13]

What we think of as maternal instinct might better be described as maternal socialization, a product of our culture rather than of our nature.[14] In the U.S., children are taught from a very young age that one of the most important things they can do when they grow up is become parents. Girls in particular learn that they are natural caretakers and that their primary role—and primary aspiration—should be to become mothers. An internet search for "girls' toys" and "boys' toys" quickly reveals that parenthood and homemaking are considered girls' domain. A 2005 study of undergraduates' ratings of toys on a 5-point scale from strongly masculine to strongly feminine supports this claim.[15] Toys associated with nurturance and domestic skill are so clearly "for girls only" that crossing gender boundaries when it comes to toy preferences comes with sanctions for boys. Research shows that while girls are allowed to venture into boys' worlds, boys who engage in "cross-sex behavior" are viewed more negatively than girls who do so.[16] In other words, caretaking and child-rearing are thought to be roles for women, not men.

Indeed, the women I interviewed noticed the ways they were taught to become mothers. Heather, a married nurse in her early thirties, told me, "It's what we've been raised to believe as kids, as girls. I mean you get dolls at a very young age and you feed them bottles and you dress them, and you play Mommy. It's just so ingrained in our culture to want to have the white wedding and get married and then pop out kids. When you disrupt that flow there's something wrong with you." Thirty-eight-year-old Robin observed that her choice not to have kids is "kind of weird, especially if you look at the toys that girls have. You think, how come I wasn't programmed to be a little parent? What went wrong?"

Philosopher Sara Ruddick would likely maintain that nothing went wrong at all. She argues that maternal behavior is learned over time and with practice rather than being innate. According to Ruddick, the behavior we observe in mothers—that appears to be so knowing, so attentive, so natural—is in fact the result of the everyday practice of mothering and the mindfulness that it requires.[17]

Despite the lack of evidence in support of it, research spanning from the early 1970s to within the last few years finds that childfree women are believed to be maladjusted, unfeminine, too involved with work, and less warm than mothers, and so it's unsurprising that many of us struggle to let go of the idea that women are naturally driven to mother. And if all women are naturally driven to become mothers, the logic goes, those who don't wish to parent must surely not be real women. Since the 1970s, scores of academics have challenged this idea.[18] Drawing from psychoanalytic theory, Nancy

Chodorow posited in 1978 that women's inclination toward motherhood came from a deeply internalized desire to reproduce the relationship they shared with their mothers as infants.[19] In the 1980s, Elisabeth Badinter declared maternal instinct to be a myth, citing French mothers' use of wet nurses in the eighteenth century as evidence.[20] Paula Nicolson's 1999 article "The Myth of Maternal Instinct" argued the same, as did my own "There Is No Maternal Instinct" in 2017.[21]

That the notion that women are naturally inclined toward motherhood continues to be challenged suggests that it remains a part of our cultural consciousness. And it isn't just academics considering the question of women's connections to motherhood. In 2017, writer/blogger Destiny Keyes took to the online forum Odyssey to declare, "I don't want kids and that doesn't make me less of a woman."[22] Two years earlier, Mary Elizabeth Williams wrote in *Salon*, "It's high time women weren't judged exclusively in terms of how maternal we are."[23] And yet it continues.

In reality, womanhood and motherhood, as much as they are commonly thought to be synonymous, are quite distinct concepts.[24] That we think of them as intertwined reveals how we think about women who are not mothers and how we do—or do not—value them as people. Sometimes it seems as if those of us who've chosen a path other than motherhood have pulled one over on everyone. And certainly we can't be allowed to get away with that! Calling our womanhood into question is one tool that those who fear changes in gender relations and power structures use to keep us in our place. If we believe the messages we're given when we go to the movies, turn on the TV, or read the paper, it would seem that those of us who are non-mothers are simply walking around masquerading as women. That we're all some unnamed "other" trapped inside women's bodies.

It's hard to understate the positive impact that public figures such as actress Kim Cattrall have had in helping to reduce stigma by being willing to speak out and challenge the idea that women without children are less than. When, in 2015, BBC Radio Four quoted Cattrall as saying, "It's the *less* that is offensive, isn't it? Child-less. It sounds like you're less, because you haven't had a child," her comments went viral. Outlets from around the world picked up the quote. While I had moments of feeling empowered throughout my earlier adulthood by the notion that I wasn't going to have children just because others thought I should, knowing that public figures like Cattrall, Helen Mirren, Ellen DeGeneres, Oprah, Betty White, and others are increasingly willing to proudly respond to questions about their own reproductive choices makes facing the hostile climate shaped by a pronatalist society much more tolerable, and sometimes even entertaining. As comedian Jen Kirkman once— hilariously and unapologetically—put it, "Parenthood can be very rewarding, but let's face it, so are margaritas at the adults-only pool."

It was only after I began my study of the childfree that Lance and I discovered the truth, that in fact women are not biologically programmed to become mothers any more or less than they're programmed to become engineers. While neither role is biologically predestined, both do require a set of learned skills, and both, more often than not, require some nudge—from what may be well-meaning teachers, family, friends, or mentors and from media and culture more generally—toward the role. That nudge is what sociologists call socialization. Of course for women, the likelihood of being socialized to become a mother is far greater than the chances of being socialized toward a career as an engineer. As feminist poet and cultural critic Adrienne Rich explains, "A woman's status as childbearer [is] the test of her womanhood . . . motherhood [is] the enforced identity."[25] Indeed, social scientists and social commentators alike note that women opting out of motherhood is akin to opting out of womanhood altogether or, at the very least, to directly challenging our most deeply held beliefs about female identity and femininity.

YOU'D BETTER WATCH OUT

Though many childfree women know from their own experience that maternal instinct isn't real, the fact that so many around us believe it to be so has very real consequences for our lives. Santa Claus may not be real, yet he manages to have a very real impact on children's behavior. And while wrongly accused convicts may not have committed a crime, the consequences of the belief that they did so are certainly real. Stereotypes of childfree women as not quite real women, even if they are based in myth, shape how others view us and how we think about ourselves and our choice.

Like most women, I grew up assuming I'd become a mother one day. I had certainly trained for it. As a child, I couldn't wait until I was old enough to babysit. I enrolled and completed a babysitter certification course at the age of eleven. As a teenager, I often spent weekend evenings babysitting—not just for the extra cash but because I loved the work. And a highlight of my time in graduate school was the summer I spent caring for my baby nephew after his parents went back to work. I was, it seemed, destined to become a mother. Of course, that never happened. My so-called biological clock had just one button: snooze. And I never felt an urge to do anything but keep it there.

It took a great deal of soul-searching, pages of reading, and hours of research to get to the point of accepting that not feeling the pull toward motherhood didn't mean there was something wrong with me. When I finally came to see maternal instinct as a myth, I understood not only that my lack of it had nothing to do with incompetence or unworthiness on my part but also that countless other women had grown up believing the very same myth. And I came to understand that the social forces keeping us blind to the reality that motherhood is taught rather than innate are so strong that we often perpetuate the myth without even realizing we are doing so.

Many women I've interviewed share experiences similar to my own. They, too, wonder why they never felt compelled to follow the path toward motherhood that so many of their friends have chosen. These women also feel the impact of their choice in the way they're treated when people find out they are childfree. Dawn told me she is acutely aware that she has made a choice that others assume is "unnatural" for women. She explained, "There's a way that people look at women who don't have children. . . . Like something's missing. At least that's how it feels. A lot of people in my family look at women who don't have children with suspicion." Dawn went on to say, "People are more judgmental of women without kids. For women, children are looked at as a status symbol. It's different for men. People don't look down on childless men."

Kim, who posed the question about whether she is less a woman if she doesn't have kids, described how people, married fathers in particular, assume she'll change her mind at some point about not having kids. As with other childfree women I've interviewed, it's as if the men Kim describes cannot imagine that all women don't, or at least some day in the future won't, want to bear children. "I've had married guys, when they find out Jack and I are not having kids, going, 'Yeah, yeah, believe me, we didn't used to want them and suddenly she changed.' Or other comments like that. I find that a very uncomfortable place to go. I can't always tell if it comes from a place of joking or if it's a little bit of jealousy of our lifestyle, but it's uncomfortable. And it's always the woman who is driving the decision to have kids, so the assumption is that if I'm a woman, I'll do that someday too."

Robin and Amber both say they're treated like oddities. Robin, a married IT worker, told me, "I've had a couple of people try and get to the question of asking whether I'm capable of having children. I think people find it kind of strange to find a woman in her mid-forties who has decided not to have them. They're like, 'Why? You're not able?' Nobody's ever actually said that out loud but it's an attitude that I perceive. Like I'm strange."

In Amber's case, as with Kim, it is men in particular who seem unable to place her. Amber, a married communications specialist in her mid-thirties, shared, "It's just an innate thing that you have to have kids or want kids. Men look at me like—not actually like there's something wrong with me, but like what's up with me, why am I like this. It's like they're trying to figure out what happened to me that I don't want kids. Like there's something weird going on with my womanhood. It's like they're thinking, 'What happened to her? Is she just more masculine than most females that she doesn't want kids?' It's strange. I think wanting children is so tied to gender sometimes that for men it's almost like, '*I* wouldn't want kids, but for a woman to not want kids? I don't know.'"

It is common for women who challenge heteronormative gender ideals, such as the notion that women "should" want children, to face confusion and even hostility from people they encounter. In the case of Kim, Robin, and Amber, all three women are conventional in their presentations of self when it comes to what we think of as typical feminine ideals for women, and all three are in heterosexual marriages. These facts have not, however, protected them from having their womanhood called into question by strangers, acquaintances, and even friends and family. All three women say they've come to terms with the fact that some people, men especially, don't know how to place them. Nevertheless, they remain frustrated and sometimes feel isolated by the reactions they've received when people find out they are childfree. And they have noticed that their husbands have a different experience.

Christina, a chemist in her early thirties, also says that people treat her differently than they treat her husband. Though they're both childfree, and they made the decision together, Christina receives "more grief" than her husband as a result of their mutual decision. "My husband hasn't gotten any grief from our families but I do. Like, my mom focuses on me. His family doesn't even ask him but his mother asks me and I'm just like, 'Ah, not right now.' And they focus a lot more on women, like it's the woman's decision but yet they treat it like it's *not* a decision, it's just something that everybody does."

Kelly, another married heterosexual childfree woman, explained, "It can be isolating to be the only woman without kids. I've had some conversations with people about my decision and I think they don't really get where I'm coming from. They don't have the same experiences I do or my experiences aren't the experiences they think women should have. My husband sure doesn't have the same baggage and feelings about it as I do. It probably affects my relationships more than it does his. And with new people, especially women, it's sort of their leading line. Like, 'Do you have kids?' or 'When are you going to have kids?' It makes it hard to have a really good connection or conversation. It's hard not to feel like that decision is influencing your relationships. Is that really so important to everyone that they have to ask you that all the time?"

The stigma childfree women face does not happen in a vacuum and is sometimes exacerbated by a complex set of identities and forms of stigma and prejudice. Sociologist Kimya Dennis describes childfree black women and men as a "minority within a minority" and notes that while having a strong support system is relatively uncommon for all childfree people, "this is especially the case for racial and ethnic minorities."[26] In her study of childfree people of the African diaspora, Dennis found that some childfree black women report feeling alienated and ridiculed based on their decision. Dennis suggests that these feelings may be particularly pronounced among black/African American/African diaspora childfree women whose cultural traditions may emphasize their roles as mothers and the expectation that they will become mothers even more than is the case for other childfree women.

Research by sociologist Nancy Mezey shows that the experience of being childfree does not vary by race alone, but sometimes race, sexuality, and social class work together to shape childfree women's experiences. In her work on how lesbians decide about parenthood, Mezey found that white lesbians wanting to remain childfree were "more selective in their choice of partners" than black lesbians who preferred not to parent.[27] Mezey suggests this may be because childfree white lesbians have a larger pool of potential partners to choose from, particularly if they are from middle-class backgrounds, as these women are most likely to be connected to extensive lesbian communities.

In a twist on the more dominant childfree narrative that we often hear, the women in Mezey's study who found it most difficult to find a community of like others from whom to receive support were those who *wanted* to become mothers, especially working-class lesbians of color. For these women, finding doctors willing to inseminate lesbians and accessing other needed information and services was complicated by their lack of a supportive network that for other lesbians proved essential to making motherhood possible. In later work, Mezey argues that internalized homophobia can also be a barrier to parenthood for LGBT people who wish to become parents.[28] Other researchers have found the same.[29] In short, Mezey's and others' work makes it clear that in some cases parenthood may be the more stigmatized choice.

Amy, a black middle-class lesbian interviewed by Mezey, points out that within the lesbian community, conversations about what choosing to parent means for one's identity as a lesbian are nuanced and complex. As Amy put it to Mezey, "If you were a pioneering lesbian who wanted a child, you were looked down upon in the community as selling out, as becoming part of this, this—you were being heterosexual-like . . . now they're having this major debate in the community itself about, well, are you really a lesbian if you choose to have children and live in a home and to parent those children like straight people?" But whatever differences may exist between lesbian and heterosexual childfree women, Mezey found, like so many studies of heterosexual childfree women before her, that a top reason the women in her study wanted to remain childfree was because they desired personal freedom.

While the pressure to parent (or not) may be experienced differently by heterosexual and lesbian women, the historically recent expansion of how we define marriage and family means that LGBTQ people may be pushed toward parenthood more today than they have been in previous periods. A 2012 *New York Times* article noted that the pressure to parent is seen by some gay and lesbian people as a "welcome sign of their increasing inclusion in the American mainstream."[30] For others, however, this new pressure is less welcome. Kate, a lesbian in her thirties, told me that the increasing pressure on lesbians to become mothers is just "one more thing" she has to contend with. As Kate put it, "Being a vegetarian, being a lesbian, not wanting kids . . . it's just one more aspect in our society where I don't fit in. I'm not *trying* to buck the system, honestly. The system just doesn't fit me very well."

Kate's experience is similar to those described in an emerging literature focused on childfree lesbians, which finds that as constructions of motherhood expand, so too does the reach of the motherhood mandate. In her 2018 master's thesis on childfree lesbian couples in South Africa, Nicole Attridge found that some couples express underlying conflicts in articulating their choice and the reasons for it.[31] While the ten couples Attridge interviewed expressed feeling a lack of desire to become parents, they at the same time struggled with "the perceived ideal of heteronormative parenting in South Africa," finding it difficult to imagine a lesbian motherhood alternative.

In another recent study, psychologist Victoria Clarke and colleagues interviewed five childfree lesbians about their motivations for and experiences of remaining childfree.[32] Clarke and colleagues refer to their interview participants as "essentially or innately childfree" because they did not express any maternal or parental desire. But even without a maternal drive, participants did take pains to express that they like children. They also said that their choice not to have them was motivated by both political and biographical factors. The study authors conclude that the increased visibility of lesbian parenting has resulted in "the unwelcome imposition of heteronormative expectations" such as parenthood on lesbian and other queer women.

These questions may be even more complicated for bisexual women. Though little research to date has focused on this population, a 2007 study from the Urban Institute found that more bisexual women (59.2 percent) report a desire to have children than do their lesbian (41.4 percent) and heterosexual (53.5 percent) counterparts.[33] A more recent study of twenty cisgender college women, five of whom identified as bisexual, found that heterosexual women were more likely than bisexual women to suggest they wanted children "because they wished to replicate elements of their own childhood."[34] While most participants in the study expressed interest in becoming mothers one day, the authors note that bisexual women lack supportive resources and recognition within both lesbian/gay and heterosexual spaces. And the authors of a 2016 study of sexual minority—including lesbian, bisexual, same-gender loving, and queer—women note that these women's marginalized social status and lack of social and legal support for becoming parents may lead to more ambivalence about motherhood than that experienced by heterosexual women.[35] No doubt this challenge shapes bisexual women's experiences when making choices about their fertility, whatever their plans.

Childfree people's experiences vary not just by race, sexuality, and class but by gender as well. Matt, a childfree man in his late twenties who lives with his long-term female partner, describes a much different experience from those of the women I've interviewed. As a childfree man, Matt says his friends who are fathers often express that they're envious that he has managed to "dodge that bullet." Matt suggested that at least among his male friends, being childfree is an envied status rather than one that is reviled, misunderstood, or pitied. He explained, "If it [my being childfree] comes up with men, it's mostly, 'Oh man, I'm so jealous!' That's the kind of thing I get. Not so much judgment. More jealous. I find that women [who are mothers] provide most of the judgment about being childfree toward women who are childfree. Men are much more likely to respond positively or neutrally to childfreedom, at least to mine."

Though we all—women and men alike—may experience pressure to have children, the women I've interviewed describe ways that the pressure on them is unique because it is tied up with their very identities *as women*. The experience can be isolating, leading to feelings of self-doubt (not about the choice not to have kids but about one's place in the world), worry, and fears—and the reality—of disappointing family and friends who believe so strongly that "real" women must feel a maternal instinct.

A WOMAN'S PROBLEM

We know what others think about childfree women's womanhood, but what do childfree women themselves think? For the women I interviewed, gender was a theme woven throughout the reflections they shared. Though I interviewed women and men, partnered and single, gay and straight, questions about the extent to which they are authentically "their gender" arose only among the women with whom I spoke. While parenthood is arguably culturally linked to men's gender identities as well—indeed to their very virility—men did not recount experiences related to their childfree choice that caused them or others to question their manhood. Childfree as a gendered experience, it seems, is a uniquely feminine experience.

When asked about the role that gender plays in his decision and experience of being childfree, Cory, a partnered man in his early thirties, said, "I'd say zero. It's a totally gender-neutral experience." Joel, married and in his late thirties, said he didn't see how gender really could play a role. While Bruce, married and in his mid-thirties, acknowledged that gender might somehow be relevant, he explained, "I haven't framed gender as related to my choice not to have kids as a bigger question for myself." And why should he? For men, the question of whether or not they are parents is not as explicitly linked to the question of whether or not they are "real men."

Steve, a partnered man in his early thirites who reports that his girlfriend is more inclined toward parenthood than he is, was one of the few men I interviewed who expressed that gender probably does play some role in his decision to remain childfree. He admitted, "I'm sure I would feel more pressure to have kids if I was a woman." Likewise, Janet, a partnered woman in her early thirties who works in real estate, observed, "If I were a man, no one would give me a hard time about not having kids."

The men I interviewed responded much differently than Allison, a partnered woman in her mid-thirties, when asked about whether gender plays any role in their childfree decision or experience. Allison's response—an impassioned "HUGE!"—came almost before I'd finished the question. She went on to explain, "I think I am realistic enough to know that no matter what arrangement I have in any relationship, the women are the primary caregivers." Similarly, when Robin imagines what her life might be like if she and her husband had kids, she says, "I'd be the one waking up more often to feed the baby and more involved in the personal care of the child, much more involved. I would have more responsibilities than my partner. I know I would feel that burden more than if I were a man."

Though parents' relative involvement in caregiving for their kids has changed over the years, Allison and Robin aren't wrong that as the women in their relationships, they are more likely to be left with the lion's share of child-rearing work, even today.[36] Nearly thirty years ago, Arlie Hochschild observed that even among couples who consider themselves to be egalitarian, when it comes to caregiving, their arrangements are less shared than they imagine.[37] As one *New York Times* writer put it in the title of his review of Hochschild's book: "She Minds the Child, He Minds the Dog."[38] Findings from the Bureau of Labor Statistics' American Time Use Survey show that even as recently as 2015, 48 percent of married mothers who work full-time and have kids under the age of eighteen at home reported doing housework on an average day while just 17 percent of comparable married fathers did so.[39] In a 2016 study, respondents reported that they believe mothers should be primarily responsible for all aspects of child-rearing except discipline, which just over half of respondents said should be fathers' domain.[40] Given these trends, it is no wonder that marital satisfaction declines after couples have their first kid.[41]

Despite—or perhaps better put, because of—the gains made by women toward greater equality in all domains, women remain the primary laborers at home, particularly when they have children. The growth of pronatalism in the 1980s was no accident, nor was the shift toward intensive mothering.[42] Each came in direct response to the feminist movement of the preceding two decades, with the goal of keeping women "in their place"—at home, with their children. And though fathers' increase in time spent with their kids does correspond with the timing of the feminist movement, their time with their children never caught up to the time put in by mothers. Women continued to spend more time with kids and on household chores, even as they entered the paid labor force.[43] It is no wonder, then, that motherhood became increasingly stressful for women between the 1950s and 1970s.[44]

Because the expectation that women will be the primary caretakers of children remains so prevalent, it also remains women who face the greatest amount of social pressure from others to become parents. This pattern does not go unnoticed among childfree women. As Emily put it, "I think I'm probably a little more evangelical than others [about being childfree] because of my gender and all of the ramifications that go along with that. In a sense it's easier for men. I feel like women have to be more strident in their decision and more solid because of the stuff you get from society and people. I just feel like I've got to be more clear and definitive in what I say when people ask me about my child status."

In her clarity and definitiveness, Emily challenges the assumption that womanhood and motherhood are one and the same. She also makes the association between femininity and reproduction explicit, a connection that philosopher Myra Hird says is normally kept implicit.[45] Calling attention to this implicit connection is one way that childfree women challenge the stigmatization of their choice. Stating it out loud reveals its absurdity.

Janet says she takes some solace in the joy she gets from pushing back against others' pressure on her to have kids with what she views as an equal absurdity: juxtaposing having kids against her carefree childfree life. "I think if they're gonna put their thoughts on me, I'm putting it back on them. When they tell me 'Oh, Janet, you won't have lived until you've had children. It's the most fulfilling thing a woman can do!' then I just name off the ten fulfilling things I did in the past week that they didn't get to do because they have kids. I'll say, 'Oh you know what? When *this* woman was in Jamaica last week, that was a lot of fun. I was pretty fulfilled. And when I head to DC next week to hang out with my friends? I'm gonna be fulfilled. Oh, and I went out last night! Went out, had a really great time. That was fulfilling for me.'"

Though it comes off as glib, there is something real and serious in Janet's response, and it reflects the sentiments of some of the other childfree women I spoke with as well. Flipping on its head the more common notion that women without children are missing out on something (they're child*less*, after all), Janet suggests that in fact it may be parents who are missing out. Just as for Janet and others I interviewed, sociologist Rosemary Gillespie found that childfree women associate motherhood with loss and the sense that something is missing—primarily, free time, energy, and their very identities.[46]

In some ways, Janet's sarcasm is self-protective. This comes through when she describes the pressure she faces to have kids from her mother and grandmother. It's overwhelming, she says, but she is strong in her conviction that she's made the right choice for herself. Janet explains, "I literally got a phone call from my mom at seven o'clock in the morning on a Monday morning, when she knows I do not get up until eight, and it was like, 'Hi, sweetheart, how are you, how was your weekend, I want a kitten and a puppy and a grand-baby. [Increasing her volume, Janet yells,] WHEN ARE YOU GOING TO GIVE ME GRANDBABIES?!' . . . And my grand-mother would be okay if I had a bunch of one-night stands and got knocked up. She wants me to have kids that badly. . . . It's like she doesn't care if I'm married first or happy. . . . So I just live my life. I'm very adamant about it. Ultimately this is who I am. I'm a happily non-married woman without children and I'm hot to trot!"

April's response to her mother, after years of incessant pressuring, is more direct than Janet's. When the harassment gets to be too much, April says she sometimes responds with an "Oh, screw you. Don't try to force me to live the life you want for me." That seems to stop the pleas for grandchildren for at least a while, says April. In Jessica's family, her aunt has been the biggest source of pressure to have children and Jessica eventually lost touch with her aunt and cousins as a result. "We don't really have a connection with them anymore. . . . There was definitely a pressure from her to be a certain way. I just wonder if we had grown up in an environment where it was like here are all the choices, choose what you want to do as opposed to here's the [only] choice . . ."

In the face of unsupportive family members, some childfree redefine family in a way that is not dependent on their fertility. The women and men I interviewed define family in ways that are not bound by biological or socio-legal connections such as marriage. I describe these findings in greater depth in chapter 4. Though notions of family are not always or necessarily linked to womanhood or gender, Jan takes on normative conventions of gender and family quite directly in her reflection on her childfree choice. "On the whole, the institution of marriage as a transfer of property from one family to another, where the whole purpose in life is to create babies, is pretty ugly. My definition of family has nothing to do with that. It's about making a better life for ourselves, together. I guess I feel like the expectation that every woman is gonna have children is some kind of way to control women's bodies. Women have a lack of control over their own reproduction. And I feel like we're going backwards in that. I mean, with regulatory language in the law and reducing access to abortion. It's pretty scary. I think this is kind of a way to control women's sexuality."

Knowing that pronatalism shapes many people's beliefs about

family, legacy, and meaning—often without their even knowing it—can help us understand, and perhaps even forgive, pressure from family members. Yet many women also report being pushed toward motherhood by those whose own familial legacies are not at stake and whose job it should be to support women's reproductive choices: their doctors and other health care providers. In 2016, Holly Brockwell made headlines after going public with her story of undergoing voluntary sterilization at the age of thirty, four years after she began making a series of unsuccessful requests to the United Kingdom's National Health Service (NHS) to receive the procedure. Taking the position that they know better than the adult women who come to them hoping to receive sterilization, the NHS recommends that women receive counseling prior to the procedure, and that they "ideally" do so together with their partner.[47] The NHS also notes that surgeons generally prefer to perform the procedure only after patients have had children and are over the age of thirty.

In a piece written for the UK's *Daily Mail*, Brockwell describes the long battle with health care providers—she was "patronised, ignored, harassed, judged, and demonized"—that ultimately led to her being "allowed" to make the choice that for her was both deeply personal and well informed.[48] Brockwell's doctor even suggested a vasectomy for Holly's boyfriend in place of her receiving a tubal ligation, in spite of the fact that her boyfriend was twenty-four years old when the suggestion came, two years younger than Holly had been when she'd first made her request four years prior. Consider Brockwell's experience in contrast to that of Randy Almont, a participant in historian Elaine Tyler May's research on childlessness, who in the 1960s at just twenty-three received a voluntary vasectomy "for the sole purpose of sexual freedom."[49] Or consider Justin Holt, who in the 2000s received a vasectomy at the age of twenty-seven.[50] Holt says his "doctor grilled him with 'what-if' questions" before agreeing to the procedure. But in Holt's case, the grilling lasted forty minutes before his doctor acquiesced. In Brockwell's case, it lasted four years.

Though research examining the gendered nature of experiences with voluntary sterilization is scant, studies do suggest patterns similar to those found in the more anecdotal cases described above. Psychologists Gareth Terry and Virginia Braun find, based on their interviews with twelve childfree men who underwent voluntary vasectomies in New Zealand, that men's voluntary sterilization is experienced as an act of rebellion rather than as something that is stigmatized, as is often the case for women.[51] Terry and Braun explain that rebelling against what is understood as a masculine act—producing offspring—is in itself a way of asserting one's masculinity. Such a man, according to social psychologists Margaret Wetherell and Nigel Edley, is one "who knows his own mind and who can 'see through' social expectations."[52] For men, their very resistance to the pressure to reproduce is understood as an act of manliness. For women, on the other hand, resisting the pressure to parent calls their womanhood into question.

Research shows that childfree men undergoing voluntary sterilization also describe their vasectomies as heroic, worthy of notice and praise.[53] In framing their efforts in this way, men position reproduction—and the work of avoiding it—as "women's work," work that they may, as a result of their own generosity, engage in but that should not be understood as typically their responsibility. Sociologist Andrea Bertotti links the gendered nature of "fertility work" to that of housework, noting that in both cases racial and socioeconomic factors play a role in shaping the division of labor in heterosexual couples.[54] In Bertotti's study, white and socioeconomically privileged women were more likely than other women to have vasectomized partners. This finding about race is consistent with Kimya Dennis's research and with the claim made by Doreen Akiyo

Yomoah, whose blog *Childfree African* is predicated on the assertion that African and African diaspora people come from cultures that "place great importance on family, and by extension, having children."[55]

In my own interviews, just one of the men I spoke with had received sterilization. Jason, a twenty-nine-year-old actor, had a vasectomy in his mid-twenties when he realized that his fear of getting a woman pregnant was preventing him from "going further with relationships and being willing to go to the next level." He knew he didn't want children and he says that knowing it was a potential created a "fear of intimacy" for him. Jason did not describe any difficulty finding a doctor willing to perform the procedure and he says the only reaction from his male friends has been jealousy that he doesn't need to use condoms. The reaction of Jason's female friends supports the narrative of men who undergo vasectomies as heroic; when he told two of his closest female friends, he says, "it was a moment of excitement," and they were impressed that he'd done it. None of the other men I interviewed mentioned either receiving or requesting sterilization.

Sterilization was a more regular topic in my interviews with women. Julie, who had a tubal ligation at age thirty-six, was "forced to watch a film" in her doctor's office about the permanence of the procedure. It also took several visits to convince him to approve the procedure. When she first asked for it, Julie's doctor said, "'Oh, you really don't want to do that.' I said, 'Yes, I do.' I was very honest with him and told him, 'If I get pregnant, I'm gonna abort it.'" Her doctor then acquiesced, but not before making her watch the film. Angela, a forty-year-old single woman in the military, said she asked four different doctors during her mid- and late thirties to give her a tubal ligation and they all said no. "I literally couldn't believe it," she told me. "When I got to the third doctor I was like, 'You have got to be kidding me!' I asked men, women, doctors of all different ages—in New York, New Jersey, and Japan—I literally tried every-one and everywhere and they all said no."

Mandy, who was in her late twenties when she first asked about tubal ligation at a regular annual exam, reports, "Every time I asked my nurse practitioner about sterilization she'd dismiss it and say, 'Oh, you're too young.' . . . She would talk about 'Is your husband okay with this?' And that doesn't really matter, you know? I would say, 'Yes, you know we've talked about this but really this isn't his decision. This is me and my body but yes you know I have talked to my husband about this. It's not about him.'"

Mandy says she stopped asking for a while but became inter-ested again a few years later when a friend of hers became uninten-tionally pregnant, and subsequently had a tubal ligation. Mandy's friend told her she wished she'd pushed to have the tubal ligation years earlier. This time Mandy avoided her nurse practitioner and went straight to her friend's doctor, finally receiving the surgery she had been requesting for years. At her next appointment with the nurse practitioner, Mandy shared what she'd done: "The very inter-esting thing about it is that when I went back to my nurse practitio-ner and told her what I did, she said, 'Well, good for you for taking control of your body.' . . . It was odd. Sort of like a reactionary thing and not genuine. I didn't really feel comfortable seeing her anymore after that."

Emily, too, faced medical professionals who doubted her ability to make the decision for herself. "I was twenty-six when I had my tubes tied. And I had several physicians come up to me and say, you know, 'Are you sure? Are you sure? Are you *sure*?' And in fact the *day of* the surgery, the doctor went into the waiting room without my knowledge or permission and asked my *parents*, 'Are you sure she's really sure?'" Emily's parents were supportive of her decision and assured the doctor that this was what she wanted but they and she both were shocked that the doctors would inquire in this way behind Emily's back and without her consent.

While doctors' objections to performing sterilization procedures on women are often couched in terms of their permanence, some research shows that other forms of birth control can also be difficult for women to access. In interviews with family physicians, pediatricians, and obstetrician-gynecologists, physician Susan Rubin and colleagues found that primary care providers use a "paternalistic counseling" approach when discussing contraceptive options with adolescents.[56] Though respondents in the study reported that adolescents' primary concern is pregnancy prevention, providers themselves prioritize sexually transmitted infection prevention over pregnancy prevention and therefore don't offer longer-lasting and more reliable intrauterine devices to their patients. Thus, even in the case of nonpermanent solutions to preventing pregnancy, the message seems to be that physicians know their patients' own needs and desires better than the patients themselves.

REAL WOMEN. REALLY.

Childfree women are not the only people driving us to think more deeply about what makes a woman a woman. The idea that gender can be represented by a dichotomous two-and-only-two system has long since been abandoned. As trans celebrities such as Caitlyn Jenner enter the mainstream and the efforts of trans activists such as Nicole Maines succeed in helping us to understand that gender is not always determined at birth nor linked to sex, our cultural understanding of who and how women are is expanding to include the breadth and diversity of ways to be a woman.

"Real" women aren't only those who exude a very limited set of stereotypical expressions of femininity—and plenty of evidence suggests that the childfree are not typical in our expressions of and beliefs about gender. Non-mothers rate much higher than mothers, for example, on measures of independence and autonomy, while mothers rate higher on nurturance and warmth, traits thought to represent "authentic" or "traditional" womanhood.[57] Women who have no desire to become mothers also value personal, social, and financial independence more than those who want kids, and they place higher value on having stimulating intellectual interactions with their partners.[58]

Not all studies reach the conclusion that childfree women reject the ideals of "real" or stereotypical womanhood, however. Childfree women are, like mothers, mostly employed in female-dominant fields such as day care and art history.[59] They are also equally likely to rate themselves highly on traditionally feminine qualities such as friendliness and sensitivity to others. And at least one study suggests that women without kids are in fact quite conventional in their thinking about gender.[60] More recent work also finds few significant differences between mothers and women without children with respect to their attitudes toward women and motherhood.[61]

In spite of both differences and similarities between mothers and non-mothers, I think the question of whether or not childfree women qualify as real women does a disservice to both groups, especially since most of the hand-wringing over childfree women's womanhood comes from fears about women's independence and a desire to keep women in their place. So while I admit that the question of what makes a woman "real" is one I've pondered myself, especially as I tried to reconcile my own lack of "maternal instinct" with what appeared to be happening in my early thirties to my friends and relatives of similar age, I have, like so many of the women I've interviewed, learned that bucking the trend and releasing ourselves from the constrictions of pronatalism can be a source of strength and empowerment. And of course mothers challenge traditional notions about womanhood as well. Single mothers, lesbian mothers, and mothers in the labor force—particularly those who serve as primary breadwinners—would not be such a source of angst for conservatives if this weren't true.

Rather than pondering whether childfree women qualify as "real" women, perhaps the better question is why we are so hell-bent on forcing narrow and constricting rules on what makes a woman. Some women choose to be mothers; others do not. Real women are whoever they wish to be.

FIVE

WE ARE FAMILY:
MAKING A HOME AND BEING A FAMILY

Contrary to popular opinion, *Leave It to Beaver*
was not a documentary.

—STEPHANIE COONTZ

n 1992, historian Stephanie Coontz made the case that families have never really been the way we like to think they were.[1] The "traditional family," it turns out, is "an ahistorical amalgam of structures, values, and behaviors that never coexisted in the same time and place." This amalgam includes some notions from the 1800s, when white, middle-class ideals held that families should place the mother-child relationship at their center. Other parts of our beliefs about what counts as a traditional family come from the 1920s, when we believed that mothers should avoid "overinvesting" in their children lest those relationships interfere with the more-valued intimacy between husbands and wives. These conflicting values culminated in what we think of as the traditional family today, a standard from the 1950s that virtually no human can achieve, one that requires women to be simultaneously everything for their children and for their husbands.

Though we are in some ways still stuck in the nostalgia trap that Stephanie Coontz described in the early nineties, we're a long way from believing that there is a singular way to be a family. And we understand that the *Leave It to Beaver* version does not represent most people's circumstances. In fact, between 1940 and 2012, the share of households made up of married couples with children was cut in half, going from 40 percent of homes in the U.S. to just 20 percent.[2] Even the U.S. Census Bureau, which defines family rather narrowly as "those related to each other by blood, marriage, or adoption," does not limit its definition to groups that include both a mother and a father.[3]

Today it is commonly understood that families don't require two parents, that they might include children from multiple relationships, that they aren't limited to people of the same race or ethnicity, and that they can include partners of the same sex. We also know that many people choose their families. Kath Weston explored this idea over two decades ago in her book on gay and lesbian kinship, *Families We Choose* (though astonishingly, even as late as 2010, Americans were more open to the idea that pets make a family than they were to the notion that same-sex couple households count as such).[4] Yet google the phrase "start a family" and you'll quickly discover that for many people, even today, families don't begin until children enter the picture.[5]

This is not lost on the childfree. Jason, a twenty-nine-year-old single actor, says that even if he had a partner, his friends and relatives won't ever think of him as having a family. As he put it, "A lot of my family and friends are starting to get married and starting to pair off and have kids and they're always like, 'Hey, when's that going to happen for you?' And 'I want grandkids!' And 'When are you going to start a family?!'" What Jason says these well-meaning people in his life don't understand is that he "enjoy[s] kids just fine. I just don't need them to start my family."

For the childfree, families are marked by indicators other than children. Thirty-two-year-old Annette told me she defines family as "anyone who cares for and loves each other." Bill, a thirty-seven-year-old who works in IT, defines family as "your supportive community. It's the people you feel a sense of responsibility to that you don't simply give up on and you don't simply throw away." Emily, also in IT and in her mid-thirties, says that for her, family is "a collection of the individuals that you can rely upon. They have your best interest at heart regardless of any sort of biological ties or not." For Erin, a twenty-seven-year-old administrative assistant who shares a home with her husband and their two dogs, family is "just us two and our pups. We don't need kids to finish out our family. We love the quiet and peacefulness." And fifty-year-old Brittany defines family as "comfort. It is a feeling of belonging."

Jan and Fred, a childfree married couple who have been together for over twenty years, say they think of themselves as a family because they are "a unit that cares for each other and depends on each other." But they also shared a time when it was made very clear to them that not everyone sees them in the same way they view themselves. When reentering the U.S. after a recent trip abroad, they approached the immigration and customs window together to have their passports checked at the same time, as they'd seen families in line ahead of them do. But, says Fred, "when we got to the window, they kicked me out of line. They told me to go get back in line when I walked up to the window with Jan. We're a family. We assumed we'd be able to go through together, like other families do. But they refused us." Not being recognized as the family that they are has practical implications like the one Jan and Fred encountered. It is also stigmatizing to be told that your family isn't a real family.

Childfree families are often cast as not-families because they don't fit the image that is most typically called to mind when we hear the term *family*. Culturally, what counts as "family" is shaped by a narrow understanding of how humans form and nurture bonds with one another. Our understandings come from a pronatalist—and heteronormative—ideology that posits that women should bear and care for children (or should at least *want* to do so) and that men should aspire to procreate and rear children with women.

These cultural norms—centered on heteronormative binaries of gender (man/woman), sexuality (heterosexual/homosexual), and family (biological/chosen)—prescribe not only that adults must couple with and marry individuals of the other sex but that they must then go on to rear children together.[6] Because such norms exist, the choice to remain childfree is sometimes interpreted as a rejection of these binaries. Even women who adhere to the binaries of gender and sexuality, with feminine self-presentations and marriages to men, are suspect unless they go on to have children. Thus, while some childfree people engage in what has traditionally been considered the first step toward creating a "normal" family (marriage) that they opt out of the next step (child-rearing) means that, to some at least, their unions don't count as families.[7]

Precise definitions of family are difficult to pin down, but most family scholars agree that families meet the following needs for their members: They offer emotional and sexual companionship, facilitate reproduction, facilitate economic provision, and provide a home.[8] The experiences of the childfree adults I interviewed, along with evidence from additional social scientific research, show that the families nonparents create indeed fulfill all four of these functions.

INTIMACY AND ADVENTURES

For many of us, family is a place of refuge from the harsh realities of the world outside. It's where we recharge so we can get back out into the world and participate as contributing members of society. The companionship families provide—be it emotional, sexual, or some combination of the two—makes this possible. And most adults, whether they have children or not, form relationships that help them fulfill their emotional and sexual needs. But studies over the past four decades show that nonparents are stereotyped as incapable of fulfilling this function of families. Compared to parents, we're believed to be emotionally unstable and cold[9] despite the fact that marital satisfaction, sex frequency, and affection are higher for couples without kids.[10] Even more, desire to maintain emotional closeness and an active and satisfying sex life with one's partner fall among the top reasons some adults choose not to have children.[11]

In her interviews with twenty-five voluntarily childless women, sociologist Rosemary Gillespie found, "Often, the intimate, couple relationship with a partner was an integral part of what participants sought to preserve in remaining childfree."[12] This certainly reflects Janet's experience. Janet, who lives with her partner, told me, "One of my favorite things [about my childfree life] is my healthy sex life. One thing I've seen with people who have kids is how horrible their sex life is. I don't want to lose that." Fred and Jan also said intimacy is important to them. That they can be intimate without having to worry about pregnancy is a relief for Jan, who believes the pressure to have children "is simply a way to control women's sexuality."

Robin and Joel, a childfree married couple who'd been together for eighteen years when I interviewed them, cited their connection with each other as essential for their well-being, as individuals and as a couple. In reflecting on why they don't want children, Robin said, "I love our life together. I don't want to give it up to a different way of being. And I feel sad for children whose parents have kids only to fulfill a need to have someone love them." Joel followed up by saying, "Do parents feel the need to have something that's going to make their life better? I mean, if they're looking for something that's going to add something to their life other than their partner, I don't know. I think *we're* enough."

Sociologist Anthony Giddens describes the sort of intimacy that Robin and Joel enjoy as a "pure relationship," wherein each person involved stays in it based on choice and companionship.[13] Couples who have kids may, of course, enjoy "pure relationships" with each other as well. Such connections aren't limited to the childfree. But some parent couples may be held together more by "ties that bind," such as child-rearing. This is not to say that one reason for staying together is better or worse than another—it's all a very personal choice—but for childfree couples, it is usually their connection with each other that drives them to stay together. There's no "staying in it for the kids" in a childfree partnership.

Jack says he's enjoying staying in his marriage precisely because he and his wife, Kim, don't have kids. If they were parents, "everything would be different!" Jack said, laughing. "So much different. I guess we could go on for a while but our marriage is very independent. We're very fluid, and with a child, you need to have built-in routines and times and stuff like that. We're very flexible with everything that we do." As Jack explains, his partnership depends on each member of the couple enjoying their connection to each other but also appreciating their individuality. Jack also talked about the importance for him of having time to travel, both with his partner and on his own. He said the travel alone allows them to be individuals, which is important to them both, and the travel together helps them stay connected with each other.

Like Jack, Mandy says her relationship with her partner is enhanced by their ability to travel together. She and her husband, Tim, love exploring new places together and revisiting favorites. They both say travel, particularly the kind of lengthy and adventurous travel they enjoy, allows them to take the time to nurture their relationship in ways that wouldn't be possible if they had kids. "Last year, we went on vacation for seventeen days," explains Mandy. "That's a long time to be hauling kids around. It would never have been possible with kids because of the nature of it."

Tim and Mandy went on to reminisce about that trip along with others they have taken together, saying the trips were essential for their connection as a couple. They also talked about their shared love of skiing. "We like going on ski vacations and we like having ski passes and skiing every weekend," says Mandy. "It's one of the reasons that we really like not having kids." Mandy explained that skiing together provides a sense of adventure, it's "a little bit dangerous and fun." Tim concurred, noting that their freedom to spend time together, both planned and spontaneous, is crucial for them.

Mandy and Tim's experience resonates for Lance and me. We love to travel and it's an important part of our relationship. Over the past decade, we've developed the habit of spending a month every spring on Roatan, an island in the Caribbean off the coast of Honduras. We took our first trip there in 2007, for two weeks. It was the first time I could remember taking off my watch and letting go of my obsession with knowing what time it was for longer than a day. I left my watch on the dresser that first day so that I'd have the freedom to play in the sand and water. I've never put it back on again since. It may seem like a small change, but for a person with anxious tendencies, it's been a lifesaver and a life changer for me personally and for us as a couple.

Roatan helped teach me to appreciate the moment I was in at the moment I was in it. That lesson translated into a deeper connection with Lance; suddenly, I could pay attention to a conversation with him without being distracted by looking at the time! Returning every year, we look forward to the opportunity to check in with each other, be present, and pay attention that our time there provides. Could we do those things at home? Of course. But the travel has facilitated our ability to nurture our relationship. I'm not sure we would have had that opportunity had we chosen to become parents. Or perhaps better put, understanding the pressures that pronatalism puts on women to be all-in all the time for their kids, I doubt I would have been capable of balancing motherhood with the sort of connection with my partner that I desire. Certainly, some parents are able to do this, but I feel confident I would not be among them. Anne, a forty-four-year-old married professor, put it in a way that resonated for me: "I worry that if I had a child I'd become a terrible partner because I'd be so focused on being a good parent."

For Lance and me, our trips to Roatan also give Lance the chance to enjoy his lifelong love of coral reefs and tropical fish, and to share that passion with me. Since our annual treks began, Lance has become an avid diver. My irrational fear of sharks, combined with my love of lounging in the sand with a drink in hand, led me to take my time, several years in fact, before mustering the courage— and energy to get out of my lounge chair—to go for my diving certification. I finally did it in part because I wanted to share in and learn about something that Lance loves so much. On our first dive together after my certification, Lance was beaming with pride that I'd done it, which tickled me. And I was delighted to have finally taken the plunge after putting it off for so many years. The icing on the cake was the discovery that I loved diving, too. Sharing Lance's love of the ocean was exhilarating. It gave us—long-married, middle-aged folks who have experienced the repetition provided by nearly three decades together—the chance to share in something brand-new.

The childfree have been blasted for citing travel as a benefit of not having kids—recall Tucker Carlson's quip about the real meaning in life for the childfree residing in vacations and spin class. Even some childfree people raise this criticism themselves. In an interview for the podcast *Pregnant Pause*, childless-by-choice writer Meghan Daum said, "We need to reframe how we talk about this choice. . . . The childfree tend to go into this reductionist sort of rhetoric . . . we tend to sometimes answer the question 'why don't you have kids' with some kind of jokey answer like 'oh, I'd rather take expensive vacations' or 'I'd rather sleep in late' and frankly that's not the reason that anyone chooses not to have kids. It's a really personal, complicated decision."[14]

In one sense, I agree with Meghan Daum. The choice not to

have kids is personal and it is complicated. Where I think Daum gets it wrong is in her easy dismissal of what for some childfree people are real and legitimate reasons for their choice. I did not interview anyone for whom expensive vacations or sleeping in late were the singular or primary reason for their choice not to have kids, but plenty of my interviewees identified these as important parts of their list of reasons.

As Mandy and Tim, Robin and Joel, and Jack and Kim explained to me, their desire to nurture their marriage by sharing in new experiences and spending concentrated time together through travel was at the top of the list of reasons they'd opted not to add kids to their family. Other research, too, shows that spontaneity and freedom are core reasons many people make the childfree choice. In her review of twenty-nine studies examining why people choose not to have children, Sharon Houseknecht found that freedom from childcare responsibility, greater opportunity for self-fulfillment, and spontaneous mobility were among the top reasons provided by the childfree.[15] So too was the value of sustaining a satisfactory marital relationship, and research shows that creating opportunities for spontaneity and engaging in exciting or novel activities together enhances couple relationships.[16]

I do understand how unusual my and Lance's own circumstances are, as were those of other couples I interviewed. Not all childfree couples are off gallivanting on annual treks to tropical islands. Nor do they have the opportunity or means to purchase season ski passes and head to a mountain every weekend. Some couples I interviewed talked about ways that they enjoy nurturing their connection with one another at home. Bruce and Emily, both thirty-five and married to each other, told me they enjoy having "pretty much complete autonomy over how we want to spend our time. We spend the evening reading or we decide on a whim to go out for dinner. We love being completely free to determine what we do together in the moment."

Anne said she enjoys exercising with her husband, saying they both like being physically active and that it helps them de-stress and connect. For Beth, in her late thirties and married, spontaneity keeps her feeling close with her husband. "If we don't feel like going straight home after work," she said, "we can decide on the fly to go to a movie or go out for dinner."

For those who do want to travel together and are able to do so, these experiences provide much more than shallow, meaningless party time. They are not a joke. Mandy and Tim, for their part, told me their travels help them understand each other, know one another's quirks, and enjoy each other's company. That's true for Lance and me, too. The intensive and distraction-free time together that travel provides is a gift that enhances some childfree couples' connections with one another.

Childfree people's claims that travel has a positive impact on their unions are supported by research on the subject. Relationship quality increases when couples engage in leisure activities together rather than apart.[17] One survey from the U.S. Travel Association found that traveling together has long-term benefits for couples, leading to higher levels of relationship satisfaction.[18] Findings from the survey show that couples who travel together are also more likely to report that they share similar goals and desires with their partner, that they agree on how to spend money, and that they are best friends. The U.S. Travel Association survey also found that travel helps couples build and maintain their relationships and that it ignites romance and deepens intimacy.

Activities needn't consist of exotic trips or ski weekends for couples to realize the positive impact of engaging in them together. Finding the time to plan home improvements as a team, or trying out any other number of pursuits that a couple defines as novel, exciting, or arousing, promotes relationship quality.[19] And of course these activities are not limited to childfree couples. Parents may, however, have fewer opportunities to carve out the alone time required for sharing new and exciting experiences with one another. As Kim observed, "I see the differences with my friends in a similar income bracket and they don't have the money to go traveling. It's really travel where we spend our extra money. It's such an important part of 'us.' A lot of our friends with kids haven't traveled in years. That would be a really hard adjustment for us."

Another difference between couples who are parents and those who are not is in who drives decisions about how leisure time will be spent. A 1993 study found that although new parents and couples without children spend similar amounts of time on leisure activities, they don't reach decisions about what they'll spend their time doing in the same way.[20] Perhaps driven by the need to divide family responsibilities in order to conquer them, the study found that for parent couples, the leisure activities they pursue together are often those enjoyed by the wife but that the husband dislikes. In contrast, the childfree couples I interviewed report that a favorite aspect of leisure time spent together involves not just sharing their own favorite activities but also learning from and about their partner's preferences.

PARTY OF ONE

While family scholars generally think of the companionship that families provide as coming from partners or children, single childfree adults also create households and form connections with people they love.[21] If family is about satisfying emotional and sexual needs, providing economically for oneself and others, and contributing to the rearing and well-being of others, certainly the social units formed by single people can also be thought of as families. A single childfree friend of mine lives alone but travels regularly on her own and has friends—and romantic partners—all over the world who make up her family. I thought of her when I read the claim of scholars Jill Reynolds and Margaret Wetherell that solo living offers a path toward "a politics of self-acceptance, self-transformation, and self-actualization."[22]

Angela, who lives on a military base and has had relationships with men but has opted to avoid any long-term partnership, says she is surrounded by people even though she is single. Though some people on the base don't understand, Angela says, "I have really important people in my life that I've kind of gathered throughout the years. We take care of each other." Twenty-year-old Carlotta lives alone but thinks of family as made up of her large network of friends and their parents and siblings. "I have a lot of people who make up my family," she says. Thirty-year-old James, who has lived with two different girlfriends in the past but was single and living alone at the time of his interview, says his family includes the members of bands he's been involved in over the years, some of which have toured together.

Jason, the twenty-nine-year-old actor, is single and lives with two friends from college who make up part of his family, he says. Jason's arrangement—making a home and a family with close friends—isn't unusual. Having herself studied how singles create family, psychologist Bella DePaulo says that in fact friendship—not marriage, romantic relationships, or relationships between parents and their kids—is "the key relationship of the twenty-first century."[23] Jason also recently became aware of the childfree community and he says he now considers that community part of his family as well. He described his interest in reaching out to other childfree singles who might feel alone. "There's a whole subculture of us," he said. "If people feel alone or like 'Is there something wrong with me?' I just want them to know there's a bunch of us out there, so don't worry."

In each of these cases—whether single by choice or circumstance, whether they enjoy uncommitted relationships or the freedom to move from one relationship to the next without the complication of living together, whether they are close with their families of origin or not, whether they have pets that they care for or children in their lives—the childfree singles I met do not consider themselves as lacking family. This is not to say that all childfree singles consider themselves as having created a family. In their interviews with childfree single women in Australia, psychologists Elizabeth Addie and Charlotte Brownlow found that some women do feel that a partnership is required in order to consider their own households or social configurations a family.[24] Other childfree singles feel differently. As my own interview participant Barb—thirty-three and single by choice—put it, "I would like to be thought of as having a family. My life is just one of a range of options that some people choose and some people don't, but I don't see how it's anything special or to remark about."

NURTURING OTHERS

Reproduction, according to social scientists, is another important function families fulfill for societies.[25] And believe it or not, families without kids can and do engage in this role. This claim may seem strange but sociologists recognize two forms of reproduction, one biological and the other social. Childfree people clearly don't reproduce biologically. But social reproduction is just as important as that which is biological, and perhaps even more so. The concept refers to all of the roles, actions, and responsibilities required for helping our fellow humans become participating and contributing members of society.[26] Parents engage in social reproduction, of course, but they aren't the only adults in children's lives who aid in preparing them for adulthood.

Children learn from numerous sources how to interact with their peers and with the adults in their lives. They learn the rules of the playground not just from their friends but also from their teachers. Some learn the importance of respecting their elders in church settings. Others learn about the values of honesty, kindness, and generosity from books. They watch and learn from the adults they see on TV. They hear from the police officer who visits their classroom that they should "stop, look, and listen" before crossing the street. All of these norms and rules are taught by a variety of people in a child's life. In some cases, those people are parents. In others, they are not. The police officer visiting a child's classroom to teach about pedestrian safety, for example, does not have to be a parent in order to be qualified to teach those lessons. Yet by teaching children these rules, that officer has participated in social reproduction.

I explore childfree people's involvement in social reproduction in more depth in chapter 6, where I describe the roles that childfree people play in children's lives. Some childfree people serve as mentors and friends to children. Others have formal and in some cases legal responsibility for children as godparents or legal advocates—such as a guardian ad litem role—for children. Many work with children in their capacities as teachers, social workers, medical professionals, and other roles. Some enjoy caring for nieces, nephews, and their kids' friends from time to time. Others help out with young siblings. Some attend these children's birthday parties, sports games, performances, and other events. All of these activities involve social reproduction.

Beyond social reproduction for children, another area where childfree people share something in common with parents is in the nurturing roles they play for other dependents in their households. Nurturing others is one way of attaining the emotional intimacy humans require for their own fulfillment and well-being. Some childfree people may care for aging family members. One childfree woman I know invited her mother to live with her after her father died. And those who are in couples care for their partners, of course, but an additional aspect of nurturing that many childfree people engage in—be they coupled with another human or not—is the care they provide for pets. This care, like that required when supporting human companions, helps people meet their need for sustaining loving connections with others, and scholars are increasingly recognizing "interspecies families" as legitimate family forms.[27]

While most of the childfree people I interviewed were quick to make clear that they understand the differences between pets and children, some did say they think of their pets as their children. As she nodded toward her two dogs on the floor, Mandy told me, "Family to me is me and Tim and our little kids." And while I interviewed twenty-seven-year-old Erin, one of her dogs began barking too loudly for us to continue. Erin's response? "Sorry about that. There goes my kid, barking again."

James, age thirty, who describes his dog as his child, had recently quit his job at the time of his interview so that he could attend to caring for frail and elderly Rasta. When the vet told James that Rasta had only a few weeks remaining, there was no question that he would dedicate himself to Rasta until the end. James had saved for this contingency and had the financial security to take the time he needed. Acknowledging that many people would not (or could not) make the same choice, James reflected, "He's been with me since he was a month old and now he's almost fourteen. I could never just throw him away." For James, not throwing Rasta away meant taking time away from paid employment to provide round-the-clock care for him during his final days, just as he says he would for a child or any other family member.

Even those who do not refer to pets as their children did relay a deep appreciation for the bond they share with their animal companions. Whatever terms they use to describe their pets, many childfree people do report that nonhuman companions play an important role in their families, as do many parents. Nicole, a thirty-five-year-old woman in medical billing who lives with her partner, shared that, for her, "pets have always been members of the family." Annie, a partnered thirty-seven-year-old child therapist who lives alone, said of her horse, "I wouldn't describe her as my child but she is definitely babied and really is a member of my family."

While the bonds childfree people develop with their pets are different from those that parents develop with their children, it is possible that those who are being nurtured—respectively, pets and kids—do experience connections with those who care for them in ways that are similar to each other. Research shows that companion animals, like humans, are capable of feeling both love for and jealousy related to their caretakers.[28] And a 2013 study found support for parallels between attachment theory in humans and attachment of dogs with humans.[29] Dogs and humans both are more likely, for example, to initiate physical contact with those with whom they are familiar, a pattern the study authors describe as in line with "the structure observed in child-parent attachment." These sorts of connections with dogs are not limited to dog owners who happen to be nonparents. In fact, sociologist Jessica Greenebaum found that many childfree people and empty nesters alike describe themselves as parents to "fur babies."[30]

Though the term "fur babies" is not one that resonates for me personally, caring for a pet for the first time in my life did help me understand how the desire for companionship and nurturing can be met by bringing nonhuman members into the family. Shortly after Lance and I got married, I felt compelled to add to our household, wanting something to snuggle and care for but knowing that that something would not be a human baby. So we added to our family by welcoming our cat, Edvard Munch (Munch for short), into our lives. Munch was named for the artist behind *The Scream*, a painting I'd spent much of my time admiring at the National Gallery in Oslo during a study-abroad stint in Norway a couple of years before our wedding.

In retrospect, we probably doomed poor Munch from the start. His namesake was, after all, known to have suffered severe anxiety and feelings of persecution.[31] Our own Munch was a bit of a terror himself, bullying guests into submission, playing coy and then lashing out, even screaming—quite literally—at anyone who didn't sit right with him, which, it turned out, was pretty much everyone. Once, Munch trapped an overnight guest in the bathroom for several hours in the middle of the night by stretching out in front of the bathroom door after she went in. When she emerged, Munch hissed and swatted at her as she tried to step over him to exit. After several unsuccessful attempts to cross the threshold, she opted to stay stationed in the bathroom until Munch decided to move on of his own accord.

Munch's emotional problems took a toll on us, individually and as a couple. Though we loved to entertain, it was stressful having people over. Munch's behavior was embarrassing. We felt bad for the stress that visitors placed on him and the stress he placed on our guests. One cat sitter, after having experienced his wrath while we were away, went so far as to suggest that we might have abused our poor cranky four-legged furry friend. I was humiliated and angered by the accusation. We loved Munch and had never harmed him. We had our theories about the reasons for his bad behavior but we were mostly stumped. We did the best we could to care for Munch and took solace in the moments when it was just the three of us at home. It was then that Munch would relax enough to become a cozy, cuddly purr machine.

Munch's behavioral problems were a source of stress, but even more straining was the conflict over his care. I had made a lot of promises to get Lance to agree to bring Munch into our home. Lance liked cats but he was allergic. The biggest promise I made—and very quickly broke—was to bathe the cat weekly, using a shampoo that helped control allergens. A few weeks into our fifteen years with dear old Munch, I got lazy. He hated the baths and they were torture on us both. Weekly baths turned into monthly baths, which turned into annual baths and, eventually, no baths.

In a turn of the ultimate karmic justice, we also learned that not only was I allergic to cats as well but that I was far more allergic than Lance. Though this fact no doubt gave Lance some moments of justified glee, we both paid a price as a result. My severe allergy meant that my immune system was badly compromised and I walked around with constant sniffles, susceptible to every germ that crossed my path. In those years I'd say that Munch, whom we both loved and were committed to keeping (we'd brought him into our home as a member of the family; we weren't about to kick him out simply because he presented challenges for us), became our most argued-about topic. We were both stressed by his behavior "in public" and, pretty quickly, my sneezes turned into something that could easily trigger annoyance in Lance. With each sniffle, he was reminded of that big promise about baths that I'd abandoned as quickly as I'd made it.

Some studies do find that pets can be a source of stress in households, as was the case for Lance and me.[32] But the more familiar narrative, substantiated by some research but not to the extent that media coverage might have us believe, is that pets have a positive impact on families and relationships.[33] One study found that far from causing strain in relationships, "pet owners were just as close to key people in their lives as to their animals, indicating no evidence that relationships with pets came at the expense of relationships with other people."[34] Given the mixed evidence to date, the non-profit National Center for Health Research concludes that although there are benefits to having companion animals, "we do not yet know under what circumstances those benefits are most likely."[35]

Munch died in 2010, fifteen years after our adventure with him began. This creature whom we loved dearly certainly brought us a great deal of joy, but he also brought his share of grief. He was a mixed blessing, much in the way some parents describe their children. Just as we experienced the glee of a new pet when we brought Munch home only to discover there would be challenges as well, parents also report an increase in happiness upon the arrival of their first child, followed by a steep decline in happiness once they discover that their new bundle of joy also comes with new levels of social isolation, lack of sleep, and strain on the couple relationship.[36]

While I would never argue that cat-rearing and kid-rearing are the same, our experience with Munch does help me understand the impact that bringing another being into one's life and family can have. And though there are important—and significant—differences between raising pets and children, there are similarities, too. In his 2009 review of scholarly literature on the subject, demographer Stuart Basten found evidence that the human "need to nurture" can indeed be met by pets.[37] And sociologists Nicole Owens and Liz Grauerholz found in 2018 that although parents of young children were unlikely to refer to their pets as their children, nonparents and parents of older children construct their relationships with pets in similar ways, both emphasizing the similarities between raising pets and children.[38] Even those who resist defining their pets as children occasionally slip into referring to them that way. In a study of individuals involved in the "serious leisure" of dog sports, for example, sociologists found that "the parent/child terminology is so pervasive that even respondents who insist that dogs are not ersatz children may use it."[39]

Whether our pets are our children or not, our approach to rearing them may not differ so much from how we rear kids. A 2016 study argues that the range of parenting styles observed among "dog moms" resembles the range of styles employed by the parents of humans. The study's authors found that "dog parenting" most typically resembles an authoritative style, with dog parents exhibiting a balance of warmth and discipline toward their pets.[40] Other work finds similarities between dog owners and parents in terms of investment in time, energy, emotions, and physical contact.[41] In a 2016 audio documentary on NotMoms, self-described childfree "dog mom" Laurie Qualey talks about her and her husband's inability to travel because of their caretaking responsibilities for their six rescue dogs and one rescue cat.[42] As Qualey put it, "Probably I'm just as tied down by my dogs as anyone would be by their child."

In some ways, Qualey's circumstances may be more similar to those of parents with kids at home than to "fur parents" of cats and other lower-maintenance pets. While my own experience with Munch makes clear that cats are not entirely stress-free or self-sufficient, cats generally reside closer to the low-maintenance end of the spectrum of care than dogs. One thing Lance and I loved about having a cat was that we could leave him for a few days without having to arrange sitters or kenneling him. Though we've always described ourselves as dog people, we've never had a dog as part of our family. They require more time for training and discipline than we're interested in investing right now, they have needy bathroom habits, and they don't pack easily into luggage.

Though my reasons for not having kids look remarkably similar to my reasons for not having a dog, no one has ever told me I'll regret my choice not to get a dog (though some have told me I would regret it if I got one). No one has told me that I'm doomed to be lonely since I don't have a dog (though some have told me that I'd see my friends less, and therefore could feel lonely, if I did have a dog). And no one has told me that I'm selfish for choosing not to bring a dog into our lives (though some have told me it would be selfish to get one given our schedules). Why can I make this choice about my family without judgment but the choice not to have a child rankles so many? For some, children make a family. For others, it's pets. And for others still, neither children nor pets are the key to family. In each case, it is about finding balance between emotional connection with others and commitment of time, energy, money, and love that's right for an individual. One person's family configuration may not work for another. And that's okay.

While for many, pets are a way to bring families together, they, like children, can create complications when couples split. Tanya, who had recently ended her marriage when I interviewed her, said that figuring out how she and her ex-husband would share time with their cats was the most difficult part of the divorce. She explained that they "both view our cats as our children. My ex-husband refers to them as 'the boys.' And for me, my cats really are a big part of my life." Tanya described how her ex-husband "still has contact with me because of the cats," noting that their post-divorce arrangement around the cats obliged her to maintain a relationship with her ex-husband much in the way children serve as a compulsory link between divorced parents. She explained,

Honestly, our whole divorce went very smoothly except for the cats. The only thing that we ever argued about as we went through the process was the cats. I got to keep the cats but he wanted to still have the keys to the house and come visit them when I'm not here. I had interesting conversations with people about, you know, should we be doing this. There are many people who firmly believe "no way, he shouldn't have access to your cats, they're not children so he shouldn't" and then there's a couple of people who have gone through divorce situations, guys especially, who've said to me, "I wasn't able to see my children the way I wanted to and he certainly should be able to see the cats because he treats them as his children."

In the end, Tanya and her ex came up with an arrangement that worked for them, where he would visit only at times that she told him she would not be at home, but she did note that they may not have contact at all anymore if it weren't for their "shared custody" of the cats.

As Tanya's story demonstrates, childfree families face many of the same challenges that families with children do. They care for one another and they share in the responsibility of caring for dependent others. When relationships shift because of a split, all families face challenges in navigating the new terms of their connection to one another. All families serve to meet the nurturing and companionship needs of their members whether they include children or not. And for many couples, parent and nonparent alike, their emotional connections to their pets resemble parents' connections to their children.[43] While the couple relationship may be most central in coupled childfree families, other beings such as pets play a role in facilitating their emotional well-being and providing companionship and, as with children, adding occasional tensions and challenges.

The care that childfree families provide each other and their animal companions isn't limited to emotional companionship and nurturing. Childfree families also provide financially for their members, another of the key functions social scientists say families fulfill in society. As James's story about quitting his job to care for his dying dog attests, for childfree people with pet companions, providing for pets isn't limited to the emotional care they provide; it's also financial. Research by the U.S. Bureau of Labor Statistics indicates that married couples with no children living at home spend more than any other household configuration on care for their pets.[44]

And of course the economic support that childfree families provide isn't limited to pets and partners. Childfree people also provide economically for extended family members. While families without children may not provide for kids in the traditional sense, some do contribute to the financial well-being of nieces, nephews, and others in their lives. As actress Kim Cattrall explained to BBC in a 2015 interview, "I didn't change nappies, which is okay with me. But I did help my niece get through medical school."[45] Annette, who says her family tree includes the children in her life, also supports some of them financially. "I think about the kids in my life all the time. I care for them, emotionally, of course, but also financially. Anything I can do to help them and their parents, I'm glad to do it." I consider additional examples of the economic support that childfree adults provide to the children in their lives in chapter 6.

SMASHING THE PATRIARCHY AT HOME

An additional function of families recognized by social scientists is providing a home to their members, and certainly this function is one that all families aim to meet regardless of whether they have children or not. In making a home for and with their members, families must negotiate who will manage the household, what tasks will be completed to retain a functioning home, and how this work will be accomplished. The management of day-to-day life within households is an important aspect of family operations that helps family members function and contribute to life outside the home. Further, the activities that are necessary to providing a home—such as preparing meals, cleaning, and yard work—occur within child-free households, as they do within all households. This function, however, is met differently by different kinds of families.

In many families, the tasks related to the day-to-day management of life in the home are divided by gender. Numerous studies show that among heterosexual couples with children, women are far more likely to carry the load when it comes to the unpaid labor required to run their homes and that this inequitable division of labor at home translates to negative health and economic consequences for women.[46] Economist Jacques Charmes found that women and girls are typically responsible for more than three-quarters of unpaid family work.[47] And as the United Nations noted in its 2016 Human Development Report, by taking up a disproportionate amount of unpaid work in the home, women forgo "opportunities for other activities, including education, visits to health centers and work outside the home."[48]

The available evidence suggests that children play a role in shaping the disproportionate division of labor at home. For example, gender-role stereotypes increase after couples become parents.[49] Among newly married heterosexual couples without kids, a 2015 study found that these couples tended to share paid and unpaid labor equally but that "their patterns become increasingly differentiated by gender" after they become parents.[50] Similarly, a study seven years earlier concluded that parenthood "is a critical moment in the development in an unequal gap in time spent on routine household labor."[51]

In childfree households, the division may be more equitable. In 1986, Victor Callan found that when compared to women who desired having children, women wanting no children had less traditional expectations of their male partners.[52] Callan also found that childfree women valued personal, social, and financial independence and stimulating intellectual interactions with their partner more than did women who want children. Numerous other studies also find that the childfree hold less traditional gender beliefs than parents.[53] For example, family studies scholars Kristine Baber and Albert Dreyer found that although childfree and parent couples are equally likely to espouse beliefs about the importance of spousal role equality, the childfree are more likely than parents to actually enact these beliefs when they divide up labor within their homes.[54]

These patterns may result in a division of household labor less constrained by traditional gender norms for childfree families.

Without the pressure of having to negotiate dinnertime, bathing routines, or soccer schedules, nonparents are freer to try out new ways of running their households. And in families without children, pressures to stay at home to take care of the household are lessened. Childfree women in particular are aware of the cultural pressures on women to do the work involved in being the primary parent.

In our own household, Lance and I work hard to share the load and, as with many of the childfree couples I interviewed and consistent with other research on childfree couples, we are also very independent and value that independence.[55] We sometimes complete chores such as cooking, laundry, and bill paying together; other times we each take responsibility for our own meals or laundry and one of us may take care of bill paying on our own if we find we have the time and inclination. And, I'll admit, there are times when neither of us takes responsibility for the work that needs doing in our home and something goes undone. In these moments we're grateful to be the only household members affected by our lapse. For us, our childfree home means we can be flexible in how we manage the house though we recognize that not having a set or regular pattern may require more intensive communication to avoid misunderstandings.

Families that don't include kids also appear to challenge traditional arrangements when it comes to deciding who will provide economically for the household. Historically, decisions about who will be the economic provider for a family have been gendered, with men securing the title of breadwinner far more often than women.[56] But in heterosexual households without kids, women are much more likely to work outside the home, and their incomes are higher than those of working mothers.[57] This is not to say that this is right—see chapter 3 for more on this pattern and perceptions of time and parenthood in the workplace—but the study does show that couples without kids fulfill the function of providing economically for their households and do so in less traditionally gendered ways. In addition, research by the Population Division of the U.S. Census found that women in families without children are more likely to work in professional and managerial positions when compared to women in families that include children.[58] As one pair of researchers put it, "The proportion of women in management without children is quite striking."[59]

These patterns are especially striking in the context of a 2010 study of nonparent men, which found these men have lower average incomes than working fathers, and more recent work showing that working men receive an income boost when they become fathers.[60] Given the structural pattern of employers penalizing mothers and rewarding fathers, it is clear that forces larger than the choices made within individual families push mothers toward more traditional household arrangements while freeing women without kids from many of the same constraints. We operate within a society that pushes women toward motherhood and mothers away from work and this has consequences for how couples with kids manage their day-to-day lives at home.

However childfree families provide homes for their members and manage those households, it is clear that they do indeed fulfill the function of providing a home. Making a home is something all families do. And homes require a series of operational tasks to run smoothly—someone has to make (or order!) dinner, someone needs to clean the bathroom, someone needs to mow the lawn, and someone needs to pay the rent. Who that someone is in each of these cases has historically been divided along the lines of gender. But childfree families show that their homes can be managed just fine—and family members can be nurtured within them and revitalized to face the world outside—using less traditional arrangements.

YOU CAN PICK YOUR FRIENDS . . . AND YOUR FAMILY

Family is a community of people who love one another and support one another no matter what. It's a place of nonjudgment, where everyone helps one another out and there's open communication.

—JESSICA

Family is the idea of people bonding together and taking care of each other and becoming a unit.

—KIM

Family is a group of people who share a living environment and know each other very well and who are linked to one another by the obligations they've made and have toward each other. They are united despite any kind of differences; it's a togetherness. Two people can be a family.

—SARAH

For the childfree women and men I've interviewed, family is about belonging, social support, responsibility, and love. Sure, family can and does include blood relations such as siblings and parents. It also includes partners with whom we may have legal ties. But, on the whole, the definitions of family offered by childfree people emphasize the needs that families meet and the functions they fulfill rather than the specific people their families do or do not include. As Sarah told me, family is those who are "united despite any kind of differences; it's a togetherness."

Perhaps childfree people's definitions of family emphasize meanings rather than members because of their own experiences of exclusion. Many of those with whom I spoke shared stories about not being invited to events at friends' and relatives' houses because it was assumed, without asking, that they wouldn't want to participate if kids were present. Others described how "family friendly" events in the community exclude their adults-only families. Annette shared her frustration. "Our town has lots of great activities and most of them are called some variation of 'Family Fun Day.' So does that exclude me? It usually does because it's geared for children, not for *my* family." Annette raises a question we might all consider: Do family fun days and family-friendly environments really mean fun and friendly for all families or only for those that include children?

Of course I'm not suggesting that there is anything wrong with events that cater to families with children. But call them what they are: kid-friendly events, not family-friendly events. Continued use of the term *family friendly* in this limited context only reifies the idea that families without children are not really families. And just as it's okay to reserve special days, events, and spaces for kid-centric activities, so too is it just fine for some spaces, places, and events to be limited to an adults-only crowd.

Bars have traditionally been thought of as adults-only spaces, though in recent years they've become increasingly kid-friendly. In 2018, the *New York Post* wrote that "baby birthday parties have infested Brooklyn's bar scene."[61] The article features a couple who threw their one-year-old's birthday party at a Brooklyn beer hall—and not at an otherwise empty time of day but on a busy Saturday afternoon. Parents interviewed for the story said they appreciate having the option of picking up guests' bar tabs and that hosting children's parties at breweries and beer halls is typically less expensive than renting children's play spaces.

While I can see the appeal, these establishments are likely alienating a significant core of their market—both parents and nonparents—who enjoy time away from kids. Rather than hosting children's parties at peak bar times, perhaps these establishments could open up their spaces for children's events at other times—say, weekday afternoons or weekend mornings. Children's spaces have had success with this model. The children's science museum in my own hometown occasionally hosts events in the evening, after the museum's official hours, for the twenty-one-plus crowd. Having bar times or other community events labeled kid-centric, and museum times and other events and spaces labeled adults-only, makes it clear to whom events are designed to appeal. And it reserves the term *family friendly* for use in reference to all types and configurations of family.

Americans of course aren't the only ones whose perceptions of family are generally limited to household units that include children. In Ireland, couples without children are defined by the census as "pre-family."[62] In some ways, this makes sense; having children is an important milestone and children are an essential part of family for many. But as increasing numbers of women and men around the world opt out of parenthood, our practices and policies must consider that not all families do, nor must they, include children. Whether they have children are not, we all form bonds to create family in many of the same ways. As they do so, childfree people demonstrate that while kids are the right choice for some, having children is *not* a prerequisite to forming families that fulfill the emotional and sexual needs of their members, provide for one another, and contribute to the important task of helping to rear the next generation. Childfree families challenge ways of "doing" family that disadvantage women, overlook gay and lesbian unions, ignore the variety of ways we give and receive love, and, to borrow from Stephanie Coontz, would be better left as amalgams in our imaginations alone.

SIX

IT TAKES A VILLAGE:
CHILDFREE PEOPLE AND THE CHILDREN IN THEIR LIVES

Children exist in the world as well as in the family.
From the moment they are born, they depend on a host of
other "grown ups"—grandparents, neighbors, teachers,
ministers, employers, political leaders, and untold others who
touch their lives directly and indirectly.

—HILLARY RODHAM CLINTON[1]

n her classic treatise *Black Feminist Thought*, sociologist Patricia Hill Collins describes the role of "othermothers" who aid in rearing children who are not biologically their own.[2] Othermothers may be related to the children whose lives they're involved in but they may also be the partners, neighbors, friends, or coworkers of children's biological parents. They serve as advocates and provide guidance for children, may help with daily care, or fill in as needed by providing meals or watching over children occasionally. This practice, says Collins, has its roots in African and African American traditions. It emerged in part out of necessity—in America, black mothers have relied on othermothers in part because the extreme demands on them as laborers, first as slaves and later as high-hour, low-wage workers, forced them to be away from their children—and in part out of a belief in the value of community.

Othermothers also engage in social activism, advocating for the well-being and future of their communities. At the core of the practice of othermothering is the belief that all members of a community share in the responsibility for improving the next generation's life chances. This belief is not limited to the communities or periods that Collins describes. Analysis of an American survey of households conducted in 1910 found that childless couples in that period were much more likely than parents to take in nieces and nephews who needed a home.[3] More recently, Megan Reid and Andrew Golub found that black men often serve as "social fathers" to their partners' children.[4] And, as described in chapter 4, communal child-rearing practices can also be found in Haiti and Israel. Many of the childfree women and men I interviewed share these values.

While this chapter explores the roles that childfree people play in children's lives, let me make clear that what follows is not an apology for the childfree. It is also not an excuse or a justification for the choice they've made. It is neither an ode to the joys of children nor a diatribe on the terrors of having children. Instead, it is a realistic account of childfree people's various relationships with and perspectives on kids. No, we don't all hate kids but neither should we have to justify our choice not to have them with lengthy proclamations about how much we adore them.

Childfree people are often put in the position of being expected to apologize for their choice. Some fear that a new acquaintance will hear they've chosen not to have kids and immediately write them off because of it, assuming that if they don't want to rear children of their own, they must be uninterested in anyone having anything to do with kids. The assumption that childfree people hate any human who doesn't legally qualify as an adult is wrong. Fear of this assumption leads some of us, and I've certainly been guilty of this myself, to overexplain or apologize for their choice by pronouncing how much they adore children. I call this sort of apology the "I love kids BUT" tactic.

The "I love kids BUT" approach is especially common among childfree celebrities who use it to deflect criticism for their choice. For comedian Ellen DeGeneres, this is the go-to response when people ask her about having kids. During a 2012 appearance on the *Tonight Show*, host Jay Leno inquired of DeGeneres, "I heard you and Portia are having a baby. Is this true?" After clarifying that it wasn't true, DeGeneres went on to explain, "They're precious to look at and I love them; we have nieces and I love them very much. [But I] don't want 'em." A year earlier, in her book *Seriously . . . I'm Kidding,* DeGeneres noted that people were "constantly asking" her and wife, Portia de Rossi, if they planned to have kids. In response, DeGeneres wrote, "We thought about it. We love to be around children after they've been fed and bathed. But we ultimately decided that we don't want children of our own. There is far too much glass in our house."

In some ways, offering descriptions of how much we actually, really, truly love kids reinforces the notion that most—*other*—childfree people don't like them. It's sort of a "we doth protest too much" kind of thing. Insisting that we adore kids also normalizes the idea that we should have to apologize for opting out of parenting them. It normalizes the idea that we should have to apologize for making the choice that's right for us. But neither parents nor the childfree should have to apologize for making a thoughtful choice about what their families will look like. And what is especially odd about the stereotype that childfree people hate kids is that, when you look at the research, you discover that parents and the childfree don't really feel all that differently from each other about kids.

PARENTS: THEY'RE JUST LIKE US!

If you're looking for them, rants that pit parents and the childfree against each other are easy to find. Amy Glass's 2014 piece, "I Look Down on Young Women with Husbands and Kids and I'm Not Sorry," resulted in over ten thousand comments online.[5] In it, Glass observes that having kids and getting married "are the most common thing, ever, in the history of the world" and that equating these milestones with "real work" and accomplishments holds women back. Christian blogger and father of twelve Chris Jeub quickly responded with his own rant, "We Look Down on Child Free Ideology and We're Not Sorry."[6] Jeub's piece was as unforgiving and unapologetic as Glass's, and well designed to drive traffic to his blog. Jeub calls up the usual stereotypes, positing that the childfree are selfish "anti-people" people. Neither Glass nor Jeub really pause to try to understand the other's perspective. Though much of what they write can be understood as clickbait, there's an underlying assumption in most such pieces that tells us parents and childfree people are radically different from one another. But the research says otherwise.

In a 2015 study, Melissa Graham and several health research colleagues examined how women's attitudes toward children predict their likelihood of becoming mothers.[7] Contrary to popular belief, it turns out that attitudes toward children are a poor predictor of future parenthood and childlessness. Beliefs about the extent to which caring for kids is a burden did not distinguish those who became mothers from those who did not. Mothers and non-mothers were also similar in their perspective on the impact of children on a woman's career. As with previous research, this work busts the myth that women who work outside the home must be "anti-child" and that those who are mothers must be "anti-work."[8] In reality, all women, whether they are mothers or not, understand that parenthood comes with costs and benefits. Even belief in the notion that children are one of life's greatest joys did not predict whether a woman will ultimately become a mother.

Years before Melissa Graham conducted her research, psychologist Victor Callan also found that parents and the childfree are mostly similar in their perceptions of children, particularly as related to the costs—financial and otherwise—of having them.[9] Parents and the childfree identified the costs of "general restrictions, inconveniences" at similar rates. Both groups also identified "financial cost" as a disadvantage of having children. Along with these similarities in perspective, Callan also found a few differences between parents and nonparents.

Mothers and non-mothers in Callan's study both identified pros and cons to having kids, but which of each they emphasized varied. For example, mothers were less likely than non-mothers to be concerned about the impact of a child on their career. Instead, mothers emphasized the drawback of the physical demands of rearing children. Parents and the childfree also differed in the sort of benefits they saw to having kids. Childfree people were more likely than parents to mention the benefits of having the company of children in old age, the opportunity to teach children, and the pleasure of watching children grow and develop. Parents, on the other hand, more often mentioned love, companionship, and self-fulfillment as primary benefits of having kids.

Callan also found some interesting gender differences, suggesting that gender may in some ways be more relevant than parental status in understanding how perceptions of children vary. All men in the study, whether parents or not, were more likely than women in either category to focus on the financial strain associated with having kids. Later research supports this finding; in 1991, Karen Seccombe found that men were more apt than women to consider the impact that children might have on their ability to make major purchases, and my own 2016 study supports this finding as well.[10] Women in Callan's study, on the other hand, were more concerned than men with the impact of children on a couple's ability to focus on their marital relationship. In most other ways, though, parents and the childfree, whether men or women, reported similar feelings about kids and parenthood.

One notable difference between Callan's study and that of Graham and colleagues tells us something about how our consciousness of the impact that children have on parents' lives has changed. In 1982, Callan found that mothers were less likely than non-mothers to believe that children negatively impact a woman's career. And mothers' optimism about children's lack of impact on their careers was reflected in their rates of labor force participation. In 1948, just 17 percent of married mothers were in the labor force; by 1985, that figure had grown to 61 percent.[11] But by the 1990s, these rates began to decline and since 2000, they have remained relatively stable. Three decades after Callan found that mothers were less likely to believe that children could negatively impact their careers, mothers in Graham's study were as likely as non-mothers to believe that kids hurt women's careers.

Putting these figures into context, we might think of mothers' beliefs about the impact of kids on their careers in the early 1980s as a result of the collective feminist consciousness that had emerged thanks to the second-wave feminist movement of the preceding decade. Women were inspired to believe they could "have it all" and their increasing participation in the labor force reflected that belief. But a generation later, we discovered that the claim, as enticing as it was, was more fiction than reality. Workplace policies, legal protections, and cultural norms around how we rear children and divide labor at home hadn't caught up to the reality that most households now had two earners. As a result, married mothers found that while their roles outside the house may have expanded, there was little corresponding shrinkage in their responsibilities at home.[12]

Indeed, economist Anna Matysiak and colleagues found in 2016 that the decline in parents' subjective well-being after having children is moderated by the level of work-family conflict women face after becoming mothers.[13] For these mothers, it seems, "having it all" includes having high amounts of stress. As Anne-Marie Slaughter, Princeton professor and former director of policy planning for the U.S. State Department, put it in "Why Women Still Can't Have

It All," her pivotal 2012 article in *The Atlantic*: "I still strongly believe that women can 'have it all.' . . . But not today, not with the way America's economy and society are currently structured."

Of course, it isn't just beliefs about the impact they might have on one's career that shape our feelings about kids. And just because parents and the childfree share similar attitudes toward children does not mean that all childfree people's attitudes are the same. Lance and I, though we are very much on the same page about a great many things, can attest from our own experience that not all childfree people feel the same way about children.

I grew up assuming I'd have kids one day. I had, after all, prepared myself brilliantly for the role of mother. From babysitting to working in my church nursery to employment as a nanny, all signs pointed toward eventual parenthood for me. And I enjoyed those roles. I felt I was contributing, doing something important. My attitude today hasn't changed on that front. I do believe that the work I did in helping nurture kids was important. I am fully on board with the notion that it takes a village to raise a child. What I have come to discover as an adult, however, is that I would be perfectly comfortable if my village was mostly childfree. This doesn't mean I don't care about kids or about the future; it just means I prefer to make a positive difference toward our collective well-being in ways that don't require an abundance of interaction with children.

Lance is a bigger fan of kids than I am. And they adore him. While kids and I seem to share a mutual feeling of "meh" toward each other, they glom on to Lance when he's around. Babies coo at him, toddlers toddle to him, and older kids can't seem to get enough of his sarcastic side. I think it's that he considers what stage of life they're at and treats them in an age-appropriate way, while I simply don't have the interest or the patience to do the same. In Lance's own words, from a post on our blog:

Frankly I don't care if you're 1, 2, 5, 12, 16, 25, 50, or 89 years old, I'm going to base whether I like you or not on what kind of person you are and whether or not we click. I'm also going to build in some allowance for where you are in your life. For example, all 1-year-olds—and many 89-year-olds—cannot control their bladders. If you are at one of these life stages I will not hold wetting yourself against you.

My and Lance's perspectives on kids are not that different from what I heard in my interviews with childfree adults. Some do not seek out interactions with children (and the same can be said of some parents). Many prefer the company of adults (and the same can be said of some parents). But outright hating children, or anyone, simply because of their age? That's age discrimination. And though clickbait headlines like one from a 2015 piece in *Salon*—"I hate your kids. And I'm not sorry."—would have us believe otherwise, most childfree people do not avoid parenthood because they don't like children.[14]

In a review of twenty-nine studies of why childfree people choose not to have children, Sharon Houseknecht found that of the nine reasons people give for not wanting kids, a "general dislike of children" does not even rank in the top five.[15] Freedom from childcare responsibilities, greater opportunity for self-fulfillment and spontaneous mobility, more satisfactory marital relationships, career considerations and monetary advantages, and concerns about population growth all ranked higher than dislike of children. And following closely behind dislike of children were early socialization experiences and doubts about parenting abilities; concern about physical aspects of childbirth and recovery; and concern for children, given problematic global conditions.

Some might point to the presence of "general dislike of children" as a category at all as evidence that the childfree don't like kids. But it is important to note that the reasons listed represent a summary of reasons found across twenty-nine different studies and are not taken verbatim from the childfree research participants themselves. I myself might have checked this reason if presented with it on a survey since it matches my feelings about my preference for the company of adults more closely than any other of the reasons listed. At the same time, I'd argue that selecting this option on a survey does not signal *hatred* of younger cohorts. Rather than a dislike of children as people, it seems likely that what this response indicates is a dislike of some of the accoutrements of children—temper tantrums, dirty diapers, noise, stickiness, and a general disregard for personal space. Most adults—childfree or not, child fan or not—understand the social norm that prescribes we should treat our fellow humans with respect and are perfectly capable of doing so, whatever the age of the fellow human in question.

What is clear from these studies is that there are a host of reasons childfree people choose to remain so and most of these reasons have more to do with the kind of life they want for themselves than with the age of the people with whom they prefer to spend their time. For those who are not involved in kids' lives, the question of their feelings about kids is much more nuanced than a simple love/hate dichotomy portrays. Even more, my interviews show that a good portion of childfree people maintain meaningful and fulfilling connections with kids.

CONNECTING WITH KIDS

Childfree people enjoy a range of connections with children. Some are aunts and uncles, others serve as mentors, teachers, and friends of the kids in their lives. They are present in children's lives in all kinds of ways.[16] From my own interviews, several themes emerge when examining the role that the childfree play in children's lives.

First, many childfree people have connections with children through their careers as teachers, counselors, social workers, and other positions that require them to be involved in kids' lives. These roles are important both for the childfree people who fill them and for the children who benefit from them.

In addition, some childfree describe relationships with children that are special precisely because they don't have children of their own. This theme is present in earlier research as well. In their analysis of the roles that aunts play in the lives of nieces and nephews, for example, Patty Sotirin and Laura Ellingson found that these nonparental roles offer "progressive potential" to challenge and change outmoded understandings of care and kinship.[17] As Sotirin and Ellingson note, aunts are distinct from mothers and by ignoring the roles that they play in children's lives, we miss the opportunity to fully understand not just how care and kinship work but also the variations and complexities of "feminine agency."

Some of the childfree people I interviewed report mixed feelings about kids. For most, it isn't that they don't like kids. Instead, their feelings about children are based on factors more complex than age, factors such as how they connect to individual children. But even this doesn't mean that they don't play any role in the lives of children. Below, I explore the role of the childfree—from those who love children to those with mixed feelings—in the lives of children.

PROFESSIONAL CONNECTIONS

One of the most common ways that childfree people interact with children is through their careers. In fact, over a quarter of participants in my study intentionally sought out career paths that would require them to interact with and be involved in children's lives. Elaine Tyler May found a similar pattern in her research on the childfree.[18] As May put it, "Some nonparents took seriously their role as nurturers of children in a wider world, as did many of the childless in earlier eras. They had a sense of responsibility for the children in their lives, and they represent the continuation of a long tradition of childless adults serving the needs of the community's children."[19] Among the childfree in my study, some are teachers, others are therapists, and still others work as social workers, camp directors, pediatricians, or police officers. A number have even worked as nannies, just as I did. Others are just beginning their careers but are planning for their working lives to be centered on children and child advocacy.

Susan, a fifty-three-year-old camp director, babysat from the time she was twelve years old. She always assumed she'd have kids one day, but during college, she worked in a department store where "watching parents with children just disgusted me. To see the way that they treated their children. They'd yank them by the arm, pull them around, yell at them, make them sit down. It just, to me it just wasn't right." That experience led Susan to think more deeply about how she could make a positive difference in children's lives. "I had a lot of experience at being with children at various stages. And I enjoyed it, I loved it, but I said to myself, 'There are way too many kids out there that don't have someone to look after them and don't have someone to be an advocate for them.' And I felt that I could be that person."

So, much in the way of the othermothers Patricia Hill Collins describes, Susan decided that her mission was to become an advocate for kids, focused on securing a better future for other people's children without having the potential distraction of being pulled away from that goal by having her own. "I started working at camps and realized that that was my passion. I could help so many other children who weren't getting the attention that they should be getting or being complimented, you know, given some confidence for what they did and how they felt. That was a big, eye-opening experience for me. All through my twenties and on I'd known that having children was not for me but that making a difference in children's lives was something I could do. There are so many children who are already in this world who need our love and attention. This is more important than bringing our own children into it."

Indeed, making a positive difference in children's lives has become Susan's life's work. Though this path makes sense to her, she knows that it is confusing to some. She explained, "All of my work background has involved children, be it camps or education. I suppose for some people it's strange since I've chosen not to have children myself but really everything in my experience is about working with kids. It's a quandary for some people but there are so many out there who need help."

Like Susan, Jessica, who has worked as an organizer at various nonprofit agencies over the course of her career, told me, "I love kids, and most of my work has been with kids. I want to make a difference in kids' lives. . . . I've always felt like I am able to relate to them in a certain way and I feel like I have the ability to be really patient and I want to make sure that the children have access to other adults [who are not their parents]." Jessica says the kids she works with don't seem to be confused by her choice not to have children of her own, but some parents seem put off by it.

The quandary and confusion that Susan and Jessica describe— that some people can't figure out why they are dedicated to helping kids despite not having any of their own—is one that other childfree people face as well. Kelly, a pediatrician in her early forties, said that despite her years of education and success on the job, colleagues question her expertise because she doesn't have kids. As Kelly put it, "I think some people doubt my ability to do my job as well because I don't have kids. I've seen that. And, you know, I actually had a manager say to me in a performance appraisal, she started out very positive, talking about how I'm very family-centered and I work well with kids. She said I have reasonable expectations for the families that I work with as far as what they can get done, like exercise programs or so forth for their kids. And then she said, 'Even though you don't have kids, you still really understand what these parents are up against.' *'Even though you don't have kids!'* She said that to me! And I thought, 'Really? I didn't know that came into whether I'm good at my job.' I trained for this job. I'm good at it. My manager knows that but she can't seem to reconcile it with the fact that I don't have kids."

Erin, who describes her career as "always having worked in some capacity for agencies having to do with youth and care for youth," said that things always get "very awkward" at work when someone asks her if she has kids. "People at work seem to think that if you don't have kids, you can't possibly understand kids. My professional experience and education are all focused around children so I feel like I have some authority to contribute at work. There's always an awkward moment there for me professionally. And I always feel a judgment being made when I say, 'No, I don't have kids.'"

Other people I interviewed said that they, too, chose work with kids because they enjoy them but that they also value their non-kid time outside of work. Char, a full-time college student, explained that it is because she is not planning to have children of her own that she thinks she'll be able to dedicate herself as a teacher. As Char put it, "I'm an education major. One of my professors said that she's always really admired people that are able to have young children and teach at the same time because you literally spend twenty-four hours a day with kids. And I was, like, god I can't imagine that. I *can* imagine spending seven hours a day with young children; that's fun. But I definitely couldn't imagine spending twenty-four hours a day with them." Char hasn't yet embarked on her career but she believes that not having children will facilitate—rather than impede—her ability to succeed in a career centered on children.

Kim and Jack's experience, as a married couple who are both teachers, supports Char's prediction. They say they love their jobs but that they value their kid-free time when they're not at work. As Jack put it, they get their "kid fix" from their jobs. He said, "We're constantly around kids and we're sort of raising those children. . . . I think we both see our relationships with kids in the classroom as being really important. There are a lot of kids in my life, in both of our lives, and so I don't feel like I'm missing out on anything [by not having kids of my own]." Tanya, who also works as a teacher, put it this way: "I am a teacher. I've been a teacher for seven years. I love being a teacher. My degree is in education. But I'm not a kid person in the sense that I want to be a mom. I enjoy children in educational settings. I worked as a nanny when I was in college. That experience helped me realize that I'm good with kids, that parenthood isn't a decision to be taken lightly, and that it isn't for me."

A UNIQUE CONNECTION

One of the clearest themes to emerge from my interviews was that childfree adults are in a unique position to have special and important relationships with children because they are childfree. Forty-year-old Angela, who travels around the world for work, said her brother James described her connection to James's son Grayson in the following way: "It's cool. There's this mythology around you. We get postcards and discs from you as you travel all around the world and we see you Skype in all kinds of places. You're this cool mythological creature for Grayson. He loves it."

This finding from my own interviews is consistent with that in other studies as well. In a survey of a thousand non-mothers, marketing firm DeVries Global found that children—including nieces, nephews, and the children of friends—play an active role in the lives of 80 percent of women who don't have children of their own.[20] Men, too, serve in similar capacities. Robert Milardo found in his interviews with twenty-one uncles and thirty-one nephews that uncles act as mentors, friends, and sometimes surrogate parents to their nephews, demonstrating a deep concern for the next generation and their roles as caregivers.[21] And a study of aunts found that they serve important roles as teachers, role models, confidantes, "savvy peers," and second mothers in their nieces' and nephews' lives.[22] Research on "othermothers" also shows that these roles aren't limited to aunts and uncles or to other adults who happen to be related to the children in their lives.[23]

As Kim said when she described her relationship with the three-year-old daughter of one of her close friends, "I get to be her playmate." This is a much different role than the child's parents play. Kim's husband, Jack, added that this girl "refers to Kim as 'Kim' but she calls me 'Kim's daddy,' I think because she sees Kim as her peer."

Jack also has a special connection with the kids in their lives. He explained, "We're good with little kids. We try to invite the kids [of our friends] over and we all have this sort of joke that our house is called Summer Camp. Most of our friends have kids and as the couple without kids, sometimes we have more of an ability to play with their kids than other couples. When we come to their houses, since we don't have any of our own kids to watch, we can actually really do that role with *their* kids, like almost an aunt and uncle thing and just get in there and hang out. It's really funny sometimes because the kids can see us as a bigger, older friend. We have a lot of really good relationships with a bunch of kids because we have the time to do that. I mean we can really focus on them. There's a lot of attention we can give them."

Jan, who has been married to her husband, Fred, for over ten years, also talked about her friendships with children. In particular,

Jan and Fred are good friends with their neighbors, and Jan has a close relationship with their eleven-year-old daughter, Emma. "Emma is my little buddy," says Jan. "I think she was two when they moved here. While she was growing up, I spent a lot of time with her in the yard and in our gardens. So I would say that we've been friends now for the past nine years."

Allison, a grant writer, talked about how much she enjoys getting to know her friends' kids. She shared, "I have two really good friends who are pregnant right now and I thoroughly look forward to getting to know their babies." And Allison and her husband believe they are in a unique position to offer their nine-year-old niece a broader view of the world than she might receive without their involvement. Allison explained, "We really, really, really enjoy spending time with our niece. Last Christmas we suggested to have her come stay with us for a few days, and for long weekends especially in the summers. She's always so sad when we leave her house to go home and we thought it would be nice for the parents, but mostly really a nice change of environment for our niece. I just feel like I get some of her issues on a different level than her mom and grandma do. I think it would be good for her to maybe have a connection with someone else who sees her in a different way than the people who interact with her on a regular basis."

Allison's point about "getting" her niece's issues in a way that others may not is reflected in the reports of other children who have close relationships with their aunts. Laura Ellingson and Patricia Sotirin found in their analysis of seventy nieces' and nephews' written accounts of communication with their aunts that nieces and nephews value their aunts' nonjudgmental advice, open-mindedness, and willingness to discuss topics they preferred not to broach with their parents.[24] As Ellingson and Sotirin put it, "The aunt's third-party perspective enabled them to become ideal confidantes. The aunt knew both the niece/nephew and the parent, and hence was in a good position to understand the nature of the problem, the personalities involved, and what steps would best address the problem."[25]

Aside from their unique friendships with children, the women and men I interviewed also described how not having kids themselves makes them more available to take on not just informal roles as friends and buddies but also more formal caretaking responsibilities for the kids in their lives, sometimes through legal guardianship or as godparents. Annette, a professor, said she is able to be the godmother "to several children" because she doesn't have kids of her own, though she added, "That's plenty!" when asked if she had plans to say yes to any future godmother requests.

While they were still married, Tanya and her ex-husband, Chuck, took in Chuck's nephew to live with them for several months. He had been struggling at school and had just been kicked out of college. Tanya explained, "Chuck comes from a family where there's a lot of mental illness and the parents of his nephew have not, cannot, achieve much in life. So when Chuck's nephew was struggling in college, he got kicked out and we took him in. He lived with us for five or six months because we wanted, in a weird way, to help care for an older child. We wanted to provide someone who had so much potential with the opportunity to see a different way of living. It really was a wonderful experience for us and I guess it was the closest we ever got, aside from parenting cats, to parenting a child, a teenager. I think it really did make a difference for Mike, the nephew. It was a fun thing. We took him to different places. We took him to wonderful restaurants, to concerts, to New York City and gallery openings. We took him to Pennsylvania, we introduced him to our friends who are all academics, and I mean it was just a world so far from what he had grown up with."

Kim and Jack have also taken on a more formal role with some of the children in their lives. One couple with whom they are very close asked them to serve as guardians to their two children should anything happen to them. It came up during a conversation about family, and their friends shared that their siblings weren't particularly interested in their kids. They couldn't imagine asking them to serve as guardians and they said they would love for Kim and Jack to do it. "It wasn't something we took lightly," Jack said. Kim explained, "I think it feels more like a family with these friends now because we have this important connection. I think it's going to feel even more like that when we sign the papers. Like, 'Wow, now I'm legally responsible to those kids if anything should happen.' And I think it helps strengthen our friendship. It makes it different, a little more like a family unit. I wouldn't be surprised if the kids see us differently because I remember knowing who was going to take care of me if my parents died and they did feel like my second set of parents because of that understanding. I just remember that security as a child. I knew they were going to take care of me."

Susan, the camp director who says she felt destined to make a difference in children's lives, also enjoys the weekends she spends with her nieces and nephews, who visit her when their parents need a break. She says she's extremely close to the children and she has the financial security to help their parents with expenses. Susan also loves giving to the kids. As she put it, "When they visit me, I take excellent care of them, I lavish them, we have fun, and they have everything they want."

Susan isn't alone. Common practices of "aunting" include encouraging nieces and nephews and providing them with gifts and other treats. Nieces and nephews report that these special meals, trips, and other activities that parents don't typically provide are especially appreciated and remembered.[26]

One study, by "Savvy Auntie" Melanie Notkin and Weber Shandwick, found that it's common for aunts to spend money on the children in their lives and assist kids' parents financially.[27] In 2012, aunts spent an estimated $387 on each child in their lives.

Three-quarters of them spent more than $500 per child. And aunts who are not mothers are more likely to engage in these practices than are those who have children of their own. Data from the Generational Transmissions in Finland survey show that women without children invest more in their siblings' kids than do women with children of their own.[28] Other research shows that aunts without children have more contact with their nieces and nephews than do aunts who are mothers.[29] It is clear that while childfree women may not be giving birth, they do give to the children in their lives in significant ways, both emotionally and financially.

KIDS ARE PEOPLE, TOO

While many childfree people opt to engage in significant—and often cash- and time-intensive—ways in children's lives, some prefer to limit their circle to mostly adults. These folks told me they view children as independent, autonomous beings, some of whom they like and enjoy being around and others with whom they do not personally connect. More often than not, the reasons childfree people cited for not feeling connected to some kids had more to do with the kids in question as individuals rather than kids as a group. But even those who did express a preference to stay away from children described a discomfort with them, not a feeling of hatred toward them. Others noted that they simply don't naturally connect with kids.

In a reflection reminiscent of Lance's position on kids, thirty-two-year-old Annette said she enjoys having kids over to her place and interacting with them at their level. "I get library books and I've got a handful of movies that the kids like and things like that. I've got sippy cups at my house and others of those basic things that I have accumulated over several years. I want everyone who comes over to be comfortable at my house. You know, a lot of people assume that, 'Oh, you just don't like kids. That's why you don't have kids.' And that's not true at all. Although they are sticky." Annette, like other childfree people I interviewed, accepts kids at the level they're at. She also recognizes her own boundaries. Whereas Lance—and, apparently, Kim Cattrall—draws the line at diapers, Annette draws it at sticky.

For some childfree people, discomfort with kids is less about kids per se and more about how cultural norms around and expectations of children have changed since they were kids themselves. As Bill put it, "When I was a kid my parents would take me to the parties they'd go to and I was expected to be responsible and quiet. They enjoyed their adult activities and I was expected to be able to interact with the adults. I think as a kid you need to learn how to function socially rather than just being shuttled away from it all the time. Today kids aren't taught how to interact with adults." Bill, like others, is happy to interact with kids. He also says kids should be provided more opportunities to interact with adults responsibly and respectfully, with the expectation that they learn how to do so.

Childfree people understand that providing these opportunities to kids isn't easy. Barb described one such opportunity she observed. "I was at a picnic last weekend and there were a lot of people there. I was sitting at a table with a mom and a dad and their daughter and her cousin and they were interacting with these little girls all day long. It was interesting because I really appreciated the way they dealt with the girls. It was really age-appropriate and they were joking around with them and yet they were also all interacting with the adults. I was very impressed watching them, like this is really like watching good parenting in action. But at the end of the afternoon I was so exhausted. I was like, 'Thank god that is not me!'"

In addition to learning how to interact with adults, others noted that kids should be allowed to be on their own as well. Steve shared,

"The whole notion that kids have to be hand-held and helmeted and padded and overprotected, it's just so different from when I grew up. You know, my mom said, get out of the house. In the summer especially, get out of the house and find something to do. I don't want to see you until dinner. Kids don't get to be kids anymore." While an increased awareness of child safety and worry over abduction may be the cause of the shift Steve identifies, it is also likely linked to the cultural shift toward more intensive parenting. And, as described in chapter 3, helicopter parenting can go to extremes that are not necessarily safety based and not always in the best interests of children or their development.

For others, not wanting to be around children is no different from not wanting to be around people more generally. Bob, a professor, initially told me he doesn't feel particularly comfortable around kids. He then went on to explain that it's less about kids and more that he just isn't a "people person." He says he is working on it, though. As Bob put it, "I want to make a conscious effort to be more comfortable around children. You know, I want to spend more time with them, maybe get to know them. Maybe as I understand what it's like to be them, I'll be comfortable with them." And he confesses, "When I go over to people's houses who have kids, I prefer playing with the kids. I enjoy it. In fact, it's often easier to hang out with some people's kids than with the parents." Once, Bob volunteered to watch a colleague's children for an evening so his colleague could enjoy a night out with her husband. In recounting the experience, Bob shared, "I absolutely loved it. But I also loved it when ten o'clock came around and their parents came and picked them up."

Robin and Joel, a married couple who are self-described "computer geeks," say they each need plenty of alone time. Joel explains, "We like people but we like them in small doses, and only when we want to be around them." Robin went on to say, "Even with each other, there'll be plenty of hours where he's in the living room surfing channels and I'm in the other room on the computer. It's not that we're not thinking of or into each other. It's just that we're doing our own stuff for some periods of time. And we like that." For Robin and Joel, and other childfree people, introducing any additional human into their household—child or adult—would disrupt the pattern of everyday life that they've come to value.

The question of whether to welcome another person into one's life is huge, whatever age that person happens to be. And there will always be people with whom we simply don't connect—including, for some, certain children. As Kim put it, "Not all kids are equally charming to be around. It's not that I don't like kids, I just don't want to necessarily be around some of them all the time." Replace "kids" with "people" in Kim's statement and I've no doubt we could all agree. That there are childfree people who treat kids *as people* should not be confused with the notion that they hate them.

Some parents also take this approach toward children. Several of my own friends who happen to be parents have confessed that while they think their own kids are cool, they are far less enamored of other people's children. One friend—who happens to be a dedicated and excellent parent—once confessed that she's not really a kid person. That some parents are also not especially interested in children is likely the root of the "But it's different when they're your own!" that so many of us childfree hear when we share that we're not having kids.

The "kids are people, too" tenet can also be seen in what's been dubbed the free-range parenting movement. In 2008, writer Lenore Skenazy set off a firestorm when she wrote in *The New York Sun* that, after weeks of begging from her son, she'd allowed the nine-year-old to find his own way home—in New York City, via bus and subway—armed with just a subway map, a MetroCard, a twenty-dollar bill, and a few quarters in case he needed to call her.[30]

According to Skenazy, "Half the people I've told this episode to now want to turn me in for child abuse." But Skenazy stuck to her guns, arguing that when children think they can't do anything on their own, they soon find that they can't, and two years later published a manifesto of sorts, outlining her philosophy of rearing "free-range kids."[31]

Skenazy was never arrested but writer Kim Brooks describes a somewhat different fate in her 2018 *New York Times* opinion piece on motherhood in what she dubs "the age of fear."[32] Brooks learned there was a warrant out for her arrest—and she was eventually charged with contributing to the delinquency of a minor—after leaving her four-year-old son in the car, windows cracked and doors child-locked, for five minutes on a "cool March day." In the end, Brooks was able to avoid having the charges pursued in exchange for one hundred hours of community service. As Brooks notes, she was lucky—she didn't lose her job, and her family and friends stood by her. And the experience brought her to an awareness of a "slow-brewing backlash to the idea that we should let our lives be ruled by the twin fears of danger and of disapprobation."

Much in the way we criticize women for whatever choice they make about children or how many children they have (or don't have), Brooks observes that when it comes to exposing kids to even the smallest bit of independence and the risk that goes along with it, "we're contemptuous of 'lazy' poor mothers. We're contemptuous of 'distracted' working mothers. We're contemptuous of 'selfish' rich mothers. We're contemptuous of mothers who have no choice but to work, but also of mothers who don't need to work and still fail to fulfill an impossible ideal of selfless motherhood." Brooks's experience and those of the fellow "bad moms"—moms who had also faced criticism after leaving their children to play on their own or wait in the car without company—whom she interviewed after her ordeal suggests that treating children like people by allowing them some modicum of independence and freedom comes with the risk of stigma and, for some, even arrest.

There's some evidence to suggest that the pendulum may be swinging away from intensive parenting and back toward a more "kids are people, too" model of parenting. The fact that Kim Brooks and the other moms she spoke with were compelled to speak out in her op-ed suggests as much. And in 2018, Utah became the first state to legalize "free-range parenting."[33] The law reframes child-neglect to allow for children "of sufficient age and maturity" to do things like play outdoors or stay at home alone. Kids are also free to walk, run, or bike to school without supervision and remain unattended in a safe and ventilated vehicle. I sincerely doubt that the legislators who passed the bill into law hate kids, but they certainly seem to recognize kids' autonomy and their humanity, as do many of the childfree people I interviewed.

A COMMUNITY EXERCISE

We hear proclamations all the time that it takes a village to raise a child and we know from childfree people's own accounts that they are an important part of that village. It may well be in the best interests of children—and of all villagers—that not everyone wants to have children of their own, even those who might make excellent parents. These nonparent figures are essential for children, they provide needed support for parents, and the childfree value these relationships as well. Indeed, research conducted for Big Brothers Big Sisters of America shows that having caring adults who are not their parents involved in their lives improves kids' confidence, grades, and social skills.[34]

Jessica Valenti, feminist writer and author of the edgy critique of the pressures of modern-day parenthood *Why Have Kids?*, argues that "we need to start thinking about raising our children as a community exercise."[35] I couldn't agree more. The childfree have an important role to play in that exercise. And it isn't that all childfree people *must* do so—but it is important for us to recognize that many of them *choose* to play a role in children's lives. This too often gets overlooked when we busy ourselves worrying about the fact that *some* childfree people don't like kids. The notion that this is true for all, or even most, childfree people simply isn't supported by the available evidence.

Childfree people's relationships with kids are meaningful not just for children and parents but also for the childfree themselves. In his interviews with 104 aunts, uncles, nieces, and nephews, social scientist Robert Milardo found that aunts and uncles don't just mentor their nieces and nephews; these children mentor the adults in their lives as well, offering advice in dealing with family members and other support.[36] Just as children benefit from the involvement of parents and nonparents alike, Milardo's research shows that adults, parent or not, get something from having children in their lives as well.

We know from the reports of childfree people themselves that the decision not to have kids has very little to do with kids. The childfree choice is made with an eye toward the life one hopes to carve out for themselves, not out of fear of the life they hope to avoid. Though some pundits, preachers, and politicians would like us to think it's all always about the children, the childfree choice is one case where it truly is not.

SEVEN

HAPPINESS AND AGING IN A WORLD NOT DESIGNED FOR THE AGED

In the end, this marriage comes to old age in solitude, with the bitterness of loneliness.

—POPE FRANCIS

Twenty-some years ago, on a balmy zero-degree day in Minnesota, Lance and I opted to enjoy the legal right to file joint tax returns forever and ever—at least until one of us dies or we can no longer stand each other, whichever happens to come first. Having conquered love and then marriage in the requisite order, we assumed that babies would eventually follow. I imagined they'd be adorable, smart, and witty, just like Lance. We assumed we'd have babies because that's simply *what people did* after they got married. But we veered off that path and decided to keep ours a family of two. One of the reasons Lance and I don't have kids is that we enjoy having the time and energy to nurture our connection with one another. Does this mean it's all sunshine and roses all the time over here at Chez Blackstone? Of course not. But most of the time it's pretty darn good.

Lots of childfree couples opt out of parenthood in order to retain and nurture a relationship with their partner.[1] And though it feels like stating the obvious to say that all adults—whether they are parents or not—form lasting, loving, and nurturing relationships with others, studies over the past four decades show that nonparents are perceived to be incapable of doing so. We're believed to be less emotionally stable than parents, less warm, and more selfish, cold, and materialistic.[2] These stereotypes lead people to assume that the childfree are doomed to a fate of dying bitter and alone. As sociologists Pearl Dykstra and Gunhild Hagestad note, "There has been a strong tendency to view the lives of childless older adults through a lens of deficiency, seeing them as lacking life course structuring, 'normal' development, family life, and mechanisms of social integration."[3]

As with the selfish myth, we have Pope Francis to thank for helping to propagate this tall tale. In 2014, he said of childfree marriages, "It's better not to have children! It's better! You can go explore the world, go on holiday, you can have a villa in the countryside, you can be care-free. . . . It might be better—more comfortable—to have a dog, two cats, and the love goes to the two cats and the dog. Is this true or is this not? Have you seen it? Then, in the end this marriage comes to old age in solitude, with the bitterness of loneliness."[4] The Pope's remarks might seem over the top, but the childfree people I've interviewed report incredible stories about the predictions friends, family, and even strangers make about what's in store for them as they age.

When Lance interviewed her for our blog, comedian Jen Kirkman told him, "The craziest thing people have said to me is 'You're going to die alone if you don't have kids.' What's crazier about that comment is it isn't said in a beautiful setting as two female friends walk on the beach and share their most intimate thoughts. STRANGERS SAY THIS TO ME at weddings, cocktail parties, waiting rooms, anywhere they can get their two cents out—they say it."[5]

I think there are a few things going on when people assume that the childfree will die alone, and bitter. First, they're assuming that their own children will be around to care for them in their old age. They're also falling for stereotypes about the childfree as emotionally unstable, coldhearted, and not good at relationships. And they are playing into fears that many people have—parent and non-parent alike—about end-of-life regret. Memes about people lying on their deathbeds expressing regret over not spending more time with their families (read: children) are no accident. They perpetuate pronatalism and they support the notion that though it may be all fun and games for childfree people now—while they have their health—they will one day regret their choice. Of course, research shows that none of these assumptions is true.

REGRET

The possibility of later regret is a concern that lots of childfree people face when they share their intentions with others. Indeed, as social worker Carolyn Morell notes in her published doctoral dissertation, "Threat of regret is one way that pronatalism is promoted."[6] Yet Morell found little evidence of ongoing or serious feelings of regret among the thirty-four middle- and older-aged "intentionally childless" women she interviewed. Instead, the women described "ongoing comfort and reinforcement of their childlessness over time." And in their study of well-being later in life, Karsten Hank and Michael Wagner found no difference between elderly parents and nonparents in how they fare economically, psychologically, and socially.[7]

Rather than fretting about the possibility of regrets themselves, it is outside others who tend to express fear of regret on behalf of the childfree. This fits with Morell's assertion about threat of regret as a tool for reinforcing pronatalist ideals. I once had an Uber driver insist—unsolicited, of course—that I would "live to regret [my] choice" when he learned that I've chosen not to have kids. And yet regret isn't a fear that comes up often for childfree people themselves. Considering that parental status is not a circumstance that can easily be changed after a certain age, some fear of regret would be understandable. Of course, when people express this fear on be-half of the childfree, they are often overlooking an important dis-tinction between childfree and childless. It is reasonable to think that a person who always wanted children, but didn't for any num-ber of reasons, could regret not having had them.

Comments like that of my Uber driver have the potential to be quite harmful. For the childfree, having to defend their own valid choice in the face of unsolicited predictions of regret is frustrating and exhausting. But imagine if I hadn't chosen my particular cir-cumstance of a kid-free life. My driver didn't know my circum-stances. Sure, I told him my husband and I had chosen to forgo kids, but what if I'd framed it that way as a self-protective measure, to avoid having to think about the pain of unwanted infertility? And why is the reason for my circumstance any of his business? Parents, too, are sometimes confronted with unsolicited observations about their need for another child, or a child of a different sex from the one they happen to have. Their choice to stop at however many chil-dren they have ("Your kid could resent you for not giving them a sibling!") or to opt out of trying for a boy or a girl ("But don't you want to walk a daughter down the aisle? Play catch with a son?") is just that—their choice. The point is that respecting the childfree and the choice that they've made is in a way respecting all adults, parents included.

When it comes to regret, the available evidence suggests that feeling regret over never having married is more likely than regret over not having children.[8] But this is not a cautionary tale about the dangers of remaining single. Plenty of recent research shows that singles are doing just fine.[9] As psychologist (and happily single woman) Bella DePaulo put it in her 2017 TEDx Talk, positive sto-ries of single life are rarely heard but that's not because they don't exist.[10] In fact, DePaulo shows that while people's happiness levels increase slightly on average after getting married, over time, levels of happiness among married people are similar to those of singles. Single people also have more friends, do more to contribute to the life of their towns and cities, and do more than married people to stay in touch with their siblings and tend to their parents.

As for regret about the choice not to be a parent, the (admittedly limited) research out there suggests the childfree—those who have explicitly chosen not to have kids—are unlikely to regret their choice. Even women at midlife who are facing the end of their reproductive years, the point when some worry regret will begin to kick in, report that they do not experience feelings of regret over their choice not to have kids.[11] As a woman who has herself reached that mid-stage of life, I can say that my own experience has been one of ambivalence but not one of regret. Though I know with certainty that my choice to remain childfree was the right one for me, I've always had a curiosity about what pregnancy and childbirth might be like. I toyed with the idea of surrogacy, though not ever very seriously at all. I wanted to understand an experience that so many women share, but I knew when I made the decision to undergo sterilization, and was again reminded with the first signs of perimenopause, that I'd allowed my window of opportunity to pass.

From other studies of regret, we know that older people who've chosen not to have kids are much more likely than those who are childless by circumstance to report advantages of nonparenthood.[12] Another study of well-being among a sample of seventy-two middle-aged and older women found that women who chose nonparenthood are less likely than non-mothers who wanted kids to have child-related regrets.[13] Surprisingly, this research also found that one-third of women who once identified as involuntarily childless eventually came to think of themselves as "childless by choice" as they came to accept and enjoy their childfree lifestyle.

When I asked my study participants if they saw any drawbacks to being childfree, most said none. Those who did mention drawbacks most often discussed the possibility of regret or loneliness in their old age. But usually those concerns were countered with a positive spin or strategies for combatting them. As Becky told me, "Just this past Thanksgiving we had a friends' dinner with wine and delicious food. It was one of the best evenings ever! I look forward to having that down the road instead of thinking 'oh, I'm gonna be lonely when I'm sixty years old.'" Though *CNN Money* in 2015 called it a new trend and credited millennials with its development,[14] Friendsgiving isn't really a new phenomenon. Gay and lesbian people have been gathering on the holidays with their families of choice since well before millennials thought to do so.[15] Lance and I have been gathering with friends "from away" (Maine's term for transplants like us) during the holidays for all of our fifteen years in the state. The specific locales and the guest lists vary from year to year but the constants are great food, fun company, and much too much wine.

Janet recounted a similar experience. "I guess if there was any drawback it would be that if I don't have a kid, then who am I going to spend Christmas with? But then my brain says I have lots of friends who don't have kids and something tells me they'll be looking to spend Christmas with someone. That sounds fabulous to me! Maybe we can go to Colorado or the Bahamas. That sounds way better than staring at presents under the tree. I just spent Thanksgiving with some friends in Seattle. It was just a bunch of people and me and my boyfriend; fifteen people without kids just sitting around a big makeshift table in the living room. We drank wine and had a blast!"

Fabulous evenings drinking wine with friends is not a terrible way to celebrate the holidays, if you ask me. Apparently, such gatherings appeal to many of my childfree compatriots as well. Indeed, people without kids are more likely to drink alcohol than their parent counterparts.[16] We're also more likely to smoke, though perhaps these patterns are counterbalanced by the finding from another study that women without children are more likely to engage in physical activity than are mothers.[17]

Though these behaviors may translate into an up to twenty-two-month shorter lease on life,[18] the childfree people I've interviewed say they're happy to trade those months in exchange for living the life of their choosing during the time that they do have.[19] If the reports of my interviewees and our social media followers are any indication, these risky behaviors result not just in possible lower life expectancy but also good times and fun memories with cherished friends and family. I'm not asserting that childfree people do nothing but party, but the evidence does suggest that these are not sad and lonely people drinking alone at home. They are likable and well-liked people enjoying the benefits of their strong social networks and having a grand old time doing so.

WHO WILL CARE FOR YOU?

One of the most common questions childfree people field during discussions about regret is "Who will care for you when you're old?" Kim, for her part, is not worried about later regret or an absence of companionship that children might otherwise provide. She says that even if she had kids, she wouldn't want or expect them to care for her in her old age. "It takes so much to take care of aging parents that I wouldn't like that for my kids, to have to give up so much of their life to take care of me. I feel like I've had a really full life and I would want my kids to have the fullness of life that I had and not, when they're forty, have to give up their own lives for me."

Kim's "full life," and that of many other childfree people, includes a strong network of friends and relatives. And while relying on networks of friends for care in old age might strike some as a new phenomenon, LGBT individuals and communities have long relied on each other in old age, creating intentional families of choice and selecting "voluntary kin" who adopt caretaking activities for elders.[20] In 2014, Catherine Croghan and colleagues observed that the typical "hierarchy of seeking assistance" in old age—starting with a spouse, then child, then other relatives, and finally friends and neighbors—does not apply to the LGBT community.[21] For LGBT individuals without a partner, friends and neighbors were the most frequently identified sources of care. This finding highlights both potentially untapped sources of support that heterosexual nonparents might consider as they age and the need for inclusive caregiving policies. As the study authors note, "Many federal and state laws and policies are reserved for caregivers caring for someone to whom they are legally related."

These arrangements don't benefit just the recipients of care. One of the most common explanations that caregivers of chronically ill older lesbian, gay, and bisexual adults gave sociologists Anna Muraco and Karen Fredriksen-Goldsen for why they provide care is that it makes them feel good about themselves and, as one caregiver put it, "that's what friends do."[22] But caregivers and recipients of care also made clear that caregiving was just one aspect of their friendship and, though it deepened their connection, they engage in other activities together as well. Participants in the study made clear that they are not just friends; they're family. Muraco and Fredriksen-Goldsen note that because of the social context of the particular time when the LGB elders in their study came of age, their connections to blood relatives are often tenuous.

Though their composition may be smaller,[23] some research suggests the networks on which older nonparents rely offer similar levels of social support as the networks of parents.[24] In fact, marital status is a better predictor than parental status of where support will come from in old age.[25] And although many childfree people are married, even those who age without a partner are not necessarily worse off.

Sociologist Eric Klinenberg notes that aging alone is not only increasingly common but that single seniors are happier than ever and that most are not truly alone.[26] In fact, Benjamin Cornwell and colleagues found that single seniors have as many friends as their married counterparts, and that they're more likely to socialize with friends and neighbors.[27] Nonparents' support networks also appear to be more diverse than those of parents. Older adults without children are closer to "collateral kin," such as siblings, nieces/nephews, and cousins, than are parents and they attach greater importance to their friendships.[28] Though some researchers note that early investment in nurturing social networks and, for those who are able, good financial planning will help ensure positive outcomes in later life whatever one's parental status.

When I interviewed thirty-eight-year-old self-described "computer geek" Robin, she mentioned some worry about not having the companionship of children in her old age, though she put a comical spin on it. "I think I might regret it when I'm eighty-nine years old and don't have grandchildren and the woman in the room across the hall from me in the nursing home does and brags about 'em. But I can always shut my door and go back to the internet." And though Robin's imagined neighbor may brag about her grandchildren, there's no certainty that they or their parents will show up to visit. While two-thirds of grandparents have at least one grandchild within easy visiting distance, 39 percent report having a grandchild more than five hundred miles away.[29] As psychologist Victor Callan notes, the idea that children or grandchildren will care for their elders when they grow old may be a traditional value but it is also part of the "folklore of parenthood."[30]

NOT A CARE(TAKER) IN THE WORLD

The folklore of parenthood tells parents that if they invest time, energy, money, and love into their children, they can avoid a life of loneliness in their old age. But if the plethora of media pieces about loneliness among the elderly are any indication, it would seem we have an epidemic on our hands, and not one that is limited to the childfree. One *Washington Post* story described the plight of Han Zicheng, an eighty-five-year-old grandfather in China who in 2017 put himself up for adoption.[31] "Lonely man in his 80s," began Zicheng's pitch. "My hope is that a kindhearted person or family will adopt me," he wrote, "nourish me through old age and bury my body when I'm dead." While loneliness in old age is a concern many express on behalf of the childfree, having children is not a guarantee of protection against it. It was not for Han Zicheng, nor was China's elderly rights law, which requires children to visit their elderly parents.[32]

One study by a team of researchers at the University of California, San Francisco, found that 43 percent of older adults felt lonely.[33] And loneliness isn't limited to those who live alone; only 18 percent of older adults in the UCSF study lived on their own. Some call it a public health crisis; others say it poses a greater public health threat than obesity.[34] Indeed, research shows that among older adults, loneliness is a predictor of functional decline and death.[35] A 2017 review of scholarly articles on the topic showed that all but 2 of the 128 studies examined found a detrimental effect of loneliness on health.[36] Another review of scientific studies concludes that the "joint contribution of family members, health care providers, and volunteers is necessary to break the vicious circle of loneliness."[37] In other words, just as it takes a village to raise a child, it takes a village to shepherd people through their golden years as well. For some, that village may include adult children but it shouldn't rely on one's offspring exclusively.

Despite idealized notions of generations caring for one another from womb to grave, things rarely work out this way for most people, particularly in the United States, where more than eleven million elderly Americans live alone and, say experts, "many millions more will do so" in the coming decades.[38] The childfree people I've interviewed are quick to point out that children don't always turn out or behave in exactly the way a parent might wish, though research suggests that parents may have more reasonable expectations than the childfree of what help children are likely to provide to them in old age. In a study comparing parents and childfree people's attitudes toward children, Victor Callan found that just 6 percent of mothers and 0 percent of fathers cite companionship in old age as an advantage of having kids. Twelve percent of childfree women and 14 percent of childfree men, on the other hand, believe this is one advantage of having kids.[39] Of course, most childfree people—and most parents—understand that there are no guarantees. As Barb, a committed animal rights activist whose political leanings reside far to the left, put it, "Hell, my kid could turn out to be a Republican!"

Though some adult children do tend to their parents as they age, most don't provide care for their elderly parents to the extent we might think they do. Twenty-five-year-old Ashley told me, "My mom has three kids and I'm the only one that helps take care of her. She has two other children who don't do anything. It would take one of them five minutes to get to her home and the other one a minute to get there. She had surgery two weeks ago and neither of my siblings has visited her." In 2015, the Pew Research Center found that 58 percent of Americans with parents over sixty-five help them with errands and other chores.[40] Fourteen percent help their parents with more intensive kinds of care like getting dressed and bathing. Most adults who care for elderly relatives provide help on a weekly basis at most; daily care is provided by just 20 percent of familial caregivers.[41]

Not only do fewer adult children care for their parents than we might think, research also shows that estrangement between parents and their adult children is more common than folklore about families might have us believe. In her systematic review of fifty-one studies on estrangement, psychologist Lucy Blake says, "This literature confirms that contrary to dominant expectations and assumptions about the involuntary, everlasting nature of family relationships, some parents and children have a distant and/or inactive relationship."[42] Exactly how many parents and children this is true for is unclear, but a 2014 survey of British adults found that one in five families in the UK is touched by estrangement.[43]

Though fewer adult children help or retain connections with their parents than our cultural ideals would have us believe, an increasing number of adults find themselves being supported by their parents. Twenty-eight percent of adult children say they've helped their aging parents financially while 61 percent of parents report helping with the finances of their adult children.[44] Though not common, the most shocking story of a parent caring for an adult child that I've ever heard came in 2017 when *Travel & Leisure* profiled a ninety-eight-year-old mother who had moved to a nursing home to care for her eighty-year-old son.[45]

Parents are also taking on increasingly more debt to fund their adult children's education, particularly at the very moment when they should be building their own nest egg.[46] Data from the Federal Reserve's Survey of Consumer Finances show that fewer than 1 percent of "substantial" financial gifts that households report receiving come from children.[47] More often, financial gifts come from older relatives including parents, grandparents, aunts, and uncles. And, as noted in chapter 2, nearly one-third of adult children aged eighteen to thirty-four are living with their parents today, a rate that exceeds all those recorded since 1880.

It is possible millennials will eventually return the favor and provide for their parents one day. While I am not personally suggesting that they must, doing so would align with our values as a culture. Despite the fact that more parents provide for their adult children than the other way around, the public *believes* the reverse should be the case. Seventy-five percent of the public says that adult children should provide financial support to their parents while only 52 percent believe that parents have a financial responsibility to their adult children.[48] Time will tell, as millennials age alongside their parents, whether their behaviors will eventually reflect the values that most members of the public espouse by taking on care for those who raised them. Or perhaps our cultural beliefs about who is responsible to care for whom will change.

Of course, if current trends are any indication, it is unlikely parents will want to move in with their children later in life. As sociologist Eric Klinenberg notes, "Elderly singletons often report that one reason they prefer living alone to living with family is that their children do not merely host them, they put them to work—with child care, help with the cooking, even cleaning."[49] It's not surprising that parents who spent a significant share of their earlier life taking care of their children might resist doing so in late life. Most people envision an old age that involves something other than continued care for others, and the childfree are no exception. Many are thinking about and planning for their old age.

PLANNING FOR OLD AGE

Some of the childfree people I interviewed said they were more concerned about the practical implications of not having someone looking out for them than with the possibility of regret or the companionship children might provide. When I asked if he saw any drawbacks to not having kids, thirty-five-year-old Bruce told me, "I think about what happens when we die. I mean, who does that sort of cleanup after people without kids are dead? I think we'll just have to be a lot more responsible. We're going to have to figure out how to clean up after ourselves when we die." Jan has similar questions. "I wonder if anyone is going to notice when we die. I guess eventually they will, when we don't show up to board meetings or something. But that could be a real mess if we're sitting here dead in the house for a long time!"

Childfree people know that they need to plan for their old age. Annette, the thirty-two-year-old professor, jokes with her students, "While I don't have a child to take care of me, I am also going to have more money to pay someone to do it. One day, you and your kids are going to need jobs and one of you is going to wind up taking care of me! I'm going to pay you to do it, and I will be able to afford to pay you to do it because I haven't put all that money into child-raising." Researchers suggest that indeed paying for care in old age will become more common given women's increased rates of labor-force participation and the growing practice of paying for childcare, which has normalized paying for services once thought of as best left to the private sphere.[50] Data from Norway show that elders there have long preferred to use homemaker services over relying on family to take care of them, even those who have children living nearby, when they need long-term assistance.[51] That Annette is planning for care in her old age is reflective of her childfree status. One study comparing mothers and non-mothers in nursing homes found that the women without children had taken charge of their planning, making choices about care and housing without prompting from others.[52] Mothers, on the other hand, were more passive, waiting for others to make decisions for them about how and where they would age.

On the whole, the childfree people I interviewed did not have deep, lingering concerns about their old age, mostly because they'd thought about it and were confident they'd be prepared. But not everyone was as nonchalant as Annette. Thirty-five-year-old Bob admits, "Honestly it scares the hell out of me to think that I will be old and have no one below me, who I am responsible for in a very real sense and who will feel responsible for me. I know that's a very selfish response but I think maybe people have kids so that they have someone to support them when they cannot support themselves. I understand that fear." Bob may be tapping into the reality that older men without children don't always fare as well as women. Some evidence suggests that non-fathers who are divorced, widowed, or never married are more likely to experience loneliness in old age than non-mothers in comparable circumstances.[53] For Bob, any fear he's felt has not been enough to change his mind about not wanting to be a father. It was, however, enough to motivate him to place the maximum legally allowable into his retirement savings.

Cory talked about retirement savings, too. "This guy I work with has three kids. He's chosen to have three kids. And one day we were talking about retirement and he mentioned he'll have five hundred thousand dollars saved by the time he retires. And I was thinking 'I will have one and a half to two million dollars more than you and it's got nothing to do with our salaries.'" Reflective of Cory's observation, research shows that a person's net worth is not determined by earnings alone; having children negatively affects wealth accumulation.[54] Of course, it is also true that parents need considerably less wealth in retirement than nonparents in the same income bracket since they are accustomed to an overall lower standard of living. This may be a non-concern, however, since there is evidence of an inverse relationship between children and wealth.[55] The childfree may require more wealth than parents to retain their standard of living in retirement but are also more likely to accumulate it.

On our blog, Erika shared, "I'm investing the money I would have spent on kids to pay for a qualified caretaker in my later years. A much more reliable solution. I also invest in friendships—those people you actually choose to spend time with—as I have time to because I'm not looking after offspring for decades. My childfree friends, and even parents who are not visited by their children, will be our own support clan into the future." I can relate to investing in friendships as a strategy for late-life companionship. I played roller derby for a few years in my early forties and, as a result, cultivated friendships with a number of women much younger than me, some less than half my age. I've joked with them that I befriended them so that they'd be around to visit and take care of me when I'm old. I'm only half kidding.

Gloria, another reader of our blog, told us, "I find that women in the 55+ crowd (of my ilk)—both parents or not—are talking A LOT about plans for creating/reviving communities of friends to relocate in one area, even compound living quarters and modular housing. Senior 'warehousing' will be a thing of the past. Technology will allow a host of alternative situations. The Boomers will age and think about caregiving differently—especially after they've seen what their elderly parents have faced or are facing now. . . . There are going to be so many changes ahead in the way we age and live. It's daunting and also exciting." In my interview with Tanya, she also talked about wanting a more creative plan for aging than what she's seen others do. "I've talked with one of my girlfriends, she also doesn't have children, and we say maybe we'll live together."

Gloria and Tanya are onto something. Golden Girls–style living arrangements are increasingly common and baby boomers are driving the search for innovative solutions to aging in community.[56] In 2014, retired lawyer Bonnie Moore founded Golden Girls Network, a national roommate matching network for "single mature women and men" who wish to form shared living senior communities.[57] Three years later, the Cohousing Association of the United States founded a new initiative, Aging in Cohousing, focused exclusively on supporting the development of age-friendly cohousing communities throughout the U.S.[58] Multigenerational cohousing is another model that people without an established connection to younger generations are embracing. In this model, apartments or other multi-unit buildings mix older residents in with younger people. The older folks are therefore able to develop connections with younger people who may be able to assist them in times of need and both generations have the chance to enjoy the companionship provided by living communally. Writer Michele Coele, who herself has experienced cohousing, also notes that older residents might provide "housing equity" to the younger generation in exchange for services or assistance.[59]

Some intergenerational services focus on housing but intergenerational programs of all kinds benefit young and old alike. Programs include services like preschools located in nursing homes and artists-in-residence programs in which younger artists receive housing in retirement communities in exchange for sharing their talents with residents. In San Francisco, Little Brothers–Friends of the Elderly organizes a cadre of volunteers who provide advocacy and companionship for elders sixty-five and older.[60] The organization, which started in France, has several chapters throughout the United States.

Such programs are popular; according to a 2018 report released by Generations United and the Eisner Foundation, 85 percent of Americans say that if they needed care services in their old age, they would prefer a setting with opportunities for intergenerational contact over one with only a single age group.[61] In the report, researchers from Ohio State University describe findings from their survey of 105 intergenerational programs across the United States. They conclude that intergenerational programs reduce ageism and loneliness while they increase older people's level of engagement and younger people's empathy.

AARP and others estimate that interest in communal living will continue to grow as the number of elders without children increases[62] and as more aging adults discover the benefits—such as companionship, lowered expenses, and the security of knowing others are looking out for you—of shared housing. At the eleventh conference of the International Communal Studies Association in 2013, anthropologist Margaret Critchlow Rodman noted that senior cohousing "creates socially, financially, and environmentally sustainable communities."[63] More elderly adults will also be without children in the future. As one article on realtor.com put it, "To those who are joining the geriatric group-living parade, it's a bit like college living, 50 or 60 years later—minus the keg stands."[64]

BETTER OFF OR MORE BITTER?

Any woman who says she's happy to be childless is a liar or a fool.
—KATE SPICER, *DAILY MAIL*

Keg stands or not, college living doesn't strike me as a particularly miserable experience, but in our pronatalist culture, the belief that people without children *must* be unhappy—even if we're unable to admit it to ourselves—is hard to shake. Never mind that the authors of a 2001 study of the well-being of older adults without children found "no statistical evidence for the hypothesis that childlessness increases loneliness and depression."[65] In fact, the reverse appears to be true. After kids, parents tend to grow apart from each other and marital quality declines significantly.[66] Another study found that middle-aged and older adults without children "had the lowest predicted levels of depression across all marital groups."[67] While it may be true for some that children are blessings that give life meaning, on the whole, the available evidence suggests it is the childfree who come out ahead when it comes to emotional well-being.

A number of studies addressing the "who's happier?" question have made headlines over the past couple of decades. In 2004, Robin Simon and Leda Nath found that parents who live with minor children report feeling significantly more fear, anxiety, worry, and anger than adults who don't live with young children. Parents also report significantly less frequent feelings of calm and contentment.[68] That same year, Nobel laureate Daniel Kahneman and colleagues published findings showing that working mothers derive about as much joy from caring for children as they do from reading their e-mail, doing housework, and napping.[69] Child-rearing activities fell well below other activities like eating, watching TV, and socializing. Just before the Kahneman study came out, analysis of a large number of prior studies found that marital satisfaction among nonparents is much higher than that of parents.[70] Other studies show that parents experience depression more often than nonparents, get less sleep, and are generally less happy than nonparents.[71]

Though it is safe to say that research generally supports the claim that nonparents are more satisfied with life than parents, findings across studies aren't totally consistent. A 2008 review of sociological research on the subject was mixed, showing that parents derive more meaning out of life than nonparents but that they also experience less emotional well-being.[72] In a working paper for the Max Planck Institute for Demographic Research, Mikko Myrskylä and Rachel Margolis, whose data come from Britain and Germany, found that parental happiness actually increases with the first two children but that it declines when couples add a third child.[73]

Adding further uncertainty to the question of "who's happier?," a study published in 2013 found that parents report relatively higher levels of happiness than nonparents. In contrast to Kahneman's findings, authors of the 2013 study argued that parents actually do derive greater joy from caring for their children than from most other day-to-day activities.[74] This study was criticized, however, by another group of researchers who attempted—but failed—to replicate its findings. According to the authors, the study showing that parents are happier made "premature" claims and its findings were not well supported by the analysis.[75] Rather than children driving happiness in the 2013 study, a reanalysis of the data suggests that, in fact, marital status and parental age are what explain the positive relationship between the presence of children and well-being.

One lesson from these studies is that we need to be very clear about exactly *who, what,* and *when* scientists are talking about when they collect data, conduct analysis, and present findings. For example, happiness levels vary a great deal over the course of parenthood, dipping quite low right after a child's birth and during the teen years but going higher at other stages of life. And of course cultural context matters, too. Though most research finds little effect of childlessness on well-being in old age, for example, a 2014 study in China found that widowed parents over the age of sixty fared better than widowed individuals without kids.[76] The authors explain this finding as a function of the fact that "Chinese persons tend to rely on their families for emotional and practical assistance" and that the Chinese "emphasize having filial children."

A reasonable question to raise, then, about findings on parents' relative unhappiness is which parents are being considered. Certainly, cultural context matters. And single parents arguably endure more stressors than partnered parents. Also, new parents may experience relatively higher levels of stress as they face the steep learning curve that more experienced parents have already summited. As Amanda observed during my interview with her, "Obviously there are factors that I'm not privy to, but when I see what some new parents are going through I'm like 'Oh, my god, you did this on purpose?! You seem miserable!'" Among those who are partnered, relationship satisfaction no doubt influences parental satisfaction. Yet in spite of these differences, Ranae J. Evenson and Robin Simon say, based on data from a national survey of families and households in the U.S., "there is no type of parent who reports less depression than nonparents."[77]

As noted, national context shapes the relationship between

parenthood and happiness.[78] Comparing data from eighty-six countries, Rachel Margolis and Mikko Myrskylä found that parents are happier than nonparents in post-Soviet states where an "increasingly important role of adult children in providing care for their elderly parents" has emerged.[79] In 2016, a team of sociologists led by Jennifer Glass found in a comparison of twenty-two nations that differences between the happiness of parents and nonparents are greatest in the United States, where nonparents report higher happiness levels than parents. The researchers explain this finding as the result of the lack of strong parental support policies in the United States.[80] Sara McLanahan and Julia Adams predicted as much nearly thirty years earlier when they wrote, "Differences [in happiness] between parents and nonparents stem from economic and time constraints. . . . We expect these trends to continue in the near future, reducing the desire for children. . . . Parental strain might be alleviated by some form of state-supported childcare or child allowance."[81]

Even more, Glass and colleagues found that parental support policies seem to increase the happiness of nonparents as well as parents. Apparently, happiness spreads! This isn't especially surprising but it is a finding that policy makers in the U.S. would do well to understand. As the researchers explain, offering employees paid vacation and sick days makes all employees happy. Sure, parents may have occasion to use these policies more than nonparents (say, if a child is sick) but any additional relief such policies provide for parents does not appear to take away from the happiness of nonparents. Another reason for the (somewhat) inconsistent findings across studies could be that most studies comparing the happiness of nonparents to that of parents don't distinguish childlessness-by-circumstance from childlessness-by-choice. There are plenty of reasons to think that happiness levels might differ between those who choose not to have kids, and are therefore living the life of their choosing, and those who want kids but can't or don't have them for some reason.

In addition to the belief that children are life's greatest joy, we're also told that even if it's tough while they're growing up, parents will reap the rewards once their kids reach adulthood. Even some of the childfree people I interviewed adhere to this belief. But while it is true that parents' happiness fluctuates over the years and the greatest investment of time and money comes before kids reach adulthood, there's no guarantee that the most intensive parenting years will be capped by an emotional high once children leave the nest.

One study using data from the 1970s found "little evidence that important psychological rewards are derived from the later stages of parenthood."[82] In fact, once parents become empty nesters, their happiness increases to about the same level of nonparents' happiness.[83] Bob tapped into this reality when he told me, "Basically when people have children, their quality of life gets minimized and stays put for just about eighteen years. Maybe your quality of life eventually returns but eighteen years is a long time to go without being happy."

As for stereotypes about the childfree being less good at relationships, it's actually the case that the desire to maintain and nurture emotional closeness and an active and satisfying sex life are among the top reasons some adults choose not to have children.[84] Childfree couples are clearly onto something; in one study comparing nonparent couples to new parent couples over a period of twenty-one months, parents experienced more change, all in a negative direction, in their individual sense of self and marital satisfaction than did nonparents.[85] Bill says he noticed changes in his closest friend's marriage after his friend became a father. "He can't go out anymore after work. Now he has to ask for permission from his wife and he makes comments like 'yeah, she's *letting* me go out tonight.' Where's the joy in that? For either of them!" Indeed, one of the themes I explored further in chapter 4 is that childfree families may offer greater emotional rewards to their adult members than families with children.

Studies over the last five decades show fairly consistently that marital satisfaction among nonparents is higher than that of parents. For example, sociologist Karen Renne found in 1970 that parents were less satisfied with their marriages than nonparents.[86] In the 1980s, Jay Belsky and colleagues found that although new parents may experience a "honeymoon period" in the month immediately following the birth of their first child, "overall marital engagement declined significantly" after the new baby's first month.[87] The following decade, Marsha Somers found that childfree couples displayed higher levels of cohesion and satisfaction than parent couples.[88] In the 2000s, Jean Twenge and colleagues' meta-review of studies on the effects of parenthood on marital satisfaction concluded that marital satisfaction declines after children due to the restriction of freedom and role conflicts caused by the new family structure.[89] And more recently, psychologists Alexandra Chong and Kristin Mickelson show that new mothers who perceive that the division of household labor and childcare is inequitable are especially likely to report a decline in marital satisfaction after having kids.[90] A multitude of additional studies over the past fifty years also find that marriages suffer when children are brought into the family.[91]

Starting from the well-established finding that nonparents report higher marital satisfaction than parents, sociologist Michelle Zagura explored what mechanisms drive this pattern in her 2012 master's thesis. She found that time spent together was the strongest factor driving differences between parents' and nonparents' satisfaction with their marriages.[92] In the same year, Thomas Hansen's review of scholarly research on the topic revealed that while the widely held assumption is that "children enhance well-being by fostering greater marital happiness," the empirical evidence does not align with folk theories on the matter.[93] Instead, Hansen found that raising children comes with marital costs "that are either direct (by reducing sex, affection, and time spent together) or indirect (via psychological distress)."

Hansen's findings align with an observation Janet made in my interview with her. "I find it really intriguing that my friends who are parents tell me how fulfilling it is," said Janet, "but they're the same people who you get the phone call from about how miserable they are and how tired they are and what an asshole their husband is and how they haven't had a break and how they haven't had a day to themselves." In line with Janet's reflection, economist Luis Angeles's study of British households concludes that satisfaction with one's spouse is negatively affected by having children.[94]

It's not all bad news for parents. In fact, research suggests that marital status is a better predictor of life satisfaction than parental history.[95] One study of older women in nursing homes found no difference between mothers and non-mothers in their reports of overall life satisfaction.[96] Others, too, report that parents and nonparents may be more alike than they are different when it comes to well-being in old age. In a 2011 survey of 496 of "the oldest old," Josefin Vikstrom and colleagues found no differences in the psychological well-being between childless eighty-five-year-olds and those who were parents.[97] Even more, the authors discovered that parents and nonparents "were equally likely to end up in institutional care, to have friends close by and to be in contact with neighbours."

Some researchers argue that the jury is still out on the "who's happier?" question. Others, though there are significantly fewer in this camp and the studies they cite have been criticized, say that it is actually parents who are happier. Whatever the case, perhaps more important than the question of who's happier is the question of what will make an individual happiest.

Not everyone is cut out for parenthood. There's no shame in that. Despite the pervasiveness of cultural messages suggesting otherwise, parenthood is not the key to a fulfilling life for everyone. Even parents need something more than parenthood to be fulfilled. And for some of us, parenthood isn't a part of the equation for fulfillment at all. As Janet explained, "I'm really fulfilled with my career and my life and I don't need kids to make that happen. Not because something horrible has happened to me, or that I grew up in a family where horrible things happened. It's the complete opposite of that and I'm happy, happy, happy! Why would I want to change that?" Indeed, when I asked Tim what he wanted people to know about being childfree, he shared, "You can have a happy and full life even if you choose not to have kids. It's all about freedom of choice!"

EIGHT

A NEW CHAPTER

You know what it's like, picking up the paper and reading about you accepting the award as Non-Parent of the year? . . . It's like picking up the paper and reading that one of your dearest friends has become a Nazi.

—FRIEND OF DAN WAKEFIELD, 1974'S NATIONAL ORGANIZATION FOR NON-PARENTS' NON-FATHER OF THE YEAR[1]

Marcia Drut-Davis was thirty-one the year she made her television debut, in 1974.[2] An elementary school teacher, Marcia and her husband at the time, Warren, broke the news to Warren's parents that they did not intend to have children—ever—during a televised conversation with them that aired on *60 Minutes*. They hadn't planned to share their news in this way. In fact, the opportunity to do so came suddenly and Marcia and Warren had only minutes to decide if this was how they would "come out" as nonparents by choice (the vernacular at the time) to his parents. Not only that, they had to decide in the presence of the *60 Minutes* producer who had invited them (and very much wanted them to say yes) along with Ellen Peck, author of *The Baby Trap*—a woman Marcia deeply admired, and whose book changed her life.

Peck had invited the *60 Minutes* crew to film a segment of the very first convention of the National Organization for Non-Parents in New York. As the convention drew to a close, producers hoped to shoot some more intimate footage of childfree couples and the struggles they faced. Peck introduced Marcia to a producer, just as she and Warren were preparing to leave for home. The producer urged her to call her mother-in-law in that moment so that they and the film crew could head to her in-laws' home, where they would tape Marcia and Warren breaking the news that they would never become grandparents. Marcia says the producer got to her when she said she wanted to "explore the beauty of honesty" that would "make this puzzle whole for our viewers." Marcia thought, *What's the worst that could happen?*" So she said yes.

When the show aired, the footage had been, in Marcia's words, "edited to death, mutilated," from a taped hours-long, intimate conversation to "three minutes of pure propaganda." Cutting out Marcia and Warren's acknowledgment of the positive aspects of parenting and the heartbreaking reality of living a life they knew so many found objectionable, even offensive, the show kept only Marcia's words, removing Warren's contributions entirely. The description Drut-Davis offers in her memoir reminds me of the period that the show aired, at the height of the feminist movement, when paranoia about women speaking for their husbands and taking charge of family decisions reigned supreme. The *60 Minutes* presentation of Marcia and Warren's heartfelt and difficult talk with his parents played perfectly into those fears.

Marcia says she and her husband were depicted as "very sad, selfish, not sure of what they were doing, sort of immature" as were the other childfree couples represented by the show.[3] The choice to air the episode on Mother's Day was most certainly intentional on the part of *60 Minutes* producers. And Mike Wallace's sign-off from the show that evening, "Pardon our perversion for airing this on Mother's Day," was no doubt intended to raise the hackles of viewers. It worked.

Marcia was no longer called for the regular substitute teaching jobs that had always kept her busy and that she and Warren relied on for making ends meet. The threats and letters soon followed. Neighbors, saying they had seen her on *60 Minutes*, told Marcia they felt sorry for her husband because, as one particularly virulent letter described, she was "a Godless baby-hating bitch" who "should not call [her]self a woman because it's unnatural for any woman not to have kids." Some warned that she should watch herself carefully and be careful about her dog as well, who was obviously taking the place of a baby. Why would Marcia even have a dog? they asked. And wouldn't it be better to give death to the dog than allow it to stay in Marcia's home?

In many ways, times have changed since Marcia's 1974 television debut. In 2013, at age seventy, Marcia published her memoir, *Confessions of a Childfree Woman: A Life Spent Swimming against the Mainstream*. Today, she says she has no regrets about her choice not to have children and she supports thousands of childfree people through her two Facebook pages, one a public forum for anyone curious about the choice and another a private space limited to those who identify as childfree. And she is part of an ever-growing system of support for people who've made the choice not to have children, and for those who are unsure but want to learn from and about not just the experiences of those who opted into parenthood but also those who opted out.

In 2014, Marcia was recognized for her groundbreaking involvement in the childfree movement with a Lifetime Childfree Contribution Award from a group of writers and bloggers who had reinstated NON's Non-Parents Day as the renamed International Childfree Day.[4] Three years later, Marcia was invited to serve as a keynote speaker at the second NotMom Summit in 2017. Today she runs a blog, as well as her Facebook groups, and has organized several group cruises for childfree people. But while Marcia's story highlights that resources for the childfree have expanded since she first went public with her choice, and that more people are talking about their choice, we still have so much further to go. As Marcia herself told Lance and me in 2013, "I wish I could tell you there's acceptance . . . acceptance is not here. Families and friends still reject childfree people. Some tell me their parents have taken them off their wills, as they are not going to have grandchildren to carry on the family's DNA! . . . So, it's up to us. We must keep on keeping on. We must speak our choice with pride and dignity."[5]

In some ways, it seems that the more things change, the more they stay the same. But they needn't do so. In this final chapter, I consider both how far we've come and how much further we have to go to reach the point where either choice about parenthood, yea or nay, is accepted and where all people understand choosing one path over another does not mean choosing a life that is "less than." My aim is not to suggest that the childfree should receive special treatment for their choice, but simply that they deserve to be treated fairly and with respect. All families benefit when all families have the same opportunities to thrive.

COMING OUT AS CHILDFREE

Ten years Marcia's junior, Gloria de Leon, a self-described "mature Latina of Mexican American descent," grew up in the fifties and sixties and assumed she'd become a mother one day.[6] As she wrote in her childfree story on our blog, she understood that's what was expected of her. She watched as her four older sisters married right after high school and became mothers even before they'd reached the legal drinking age. Despite expectations that she, too, would marry young and begin having children right away, Gloria knew this wasn't the path she wanted to follow. Instead, she would become the first in her family to graduate from college and the first to choose a role other than mother around which to center her goals and identity. Eventually, Gloria became the co-founder and executive vice president of the National Hispanic Institute, a nonprofit leadership organization for Latino youth.

Though her story is one of success, at each step Gloria was breaking new ground, building a path that would remain for future generations in her family but had not been laid for her. Having worked with many first-generation college students, I appreciate the courage required to make that choice. And while today's first-generation students typically find support on their campuses specific to their circumstances, formal programs for first-generation students were not common in Gloria's time. In addition to being the first in her family to navigate college, few women—whether college was new to their families or not—attended college in the eras preceding that of Gloria and her peers. Gloria's family, and the culture more generally, assumed that college wasn't necessary for women. Instead, the transition to adulthood was marked by the roles of wife and mother.

As Gloria notes, "My generation would be the first sizable group of women to attend college." And attend college, Gloria's generation did, going from about a third of women in the 1960s to nearly half by the mid-'70s. Coming of age in this period meant being part of the first generation of women to have legal access to abortion and to be able to take a pill that could prevent pregnancy. These changes, along with the expansion of other legal rights and protections for women at home and in the workplace and a slowly emerging new definition of womanhood, would forever shift the way we thought about parenthood. No longer a likely inevitability for any fertile person engaged in heterosexual sex, we began to think of parenthood as something we choose rather than something that happens to us. This shift occurred slowly, though, and not everyone welcomed the change.

While Gloria and Marcia's experiences occurred a decade apart, both women came of age in a time when few women chose a path other than motherhood and those who did lacked the resources— such as information about and access to birth control, the possibility of connections with other childfree people through meet-ups and social media, and media coverage of potential childfree role models—that many of us without kids enjoy today. Since Gloria and Marcia's experiences, people feel increasingly freer to "come out" as childfree, sharing their intentions with partners and parents and even celebrating their choice with announcements and parties. In her description of this trend in the *New York Post*, writer Anna Davies asks, "Is anything comparable to the miracle of life?"[7] She continues with "Ciara Pressler says yes. The 37-year-old business strategist and entrepreneur [has introduced] her latest business venture with a Saturday afternoon shower—complete with an Amazon .com registry link on the invitation." But these announcements are not without critics, and the Davies piece itself was ultimately a harsh indictment of this trend. As Davies says, "Last year, a photo shoot depicting a couple cradling their puppy as if it were a child went viral—proving that navel-gazing knows no bounds." She goes on, "In our special-snowflake society, a nonevent like not having a baby has increasingly become a moment worthy of 'likes,' accolades and even presents. Look at me—I'm not having a baby/getting married/ having a housewarming party!"

Davies mentions our blog's "birth" announcement in her article, too. She leaves out, of course, that it was meant to be tongue-in-cheek, lighthearted, positive, and fun. And though that's exactly how she pitched her story when she called me to ask for an interview—saying she was writing about the variety of fun ways people celebrate such milestones—in retrospect the bait and switch should not have come as a surprise. I'm reminded each time I write an op-ed about the childfree choice or do an interview with the media that the idea that some people might opt out of parenthood is still hard for others to accept. One piece I wrote came with this comment from a reader, not so different from the reaction to Marcia Drut-Davis over four decades ago: "LOL. I feel sorry for this woman's husband." Another reader, a nonparent herself, wrote, "Sounds like you're jealous that people with kids get more attention than you.

I don't have kids but I don't go bragging about it or whining that we don't get the same respect. Blah, blah, blah. I guess it really is all about you and your selfishness."

Though Davies's portrayal in the *New York Post* is ultimately unflattering, it does mark a shift from a half century ago when Gloria de Leon and Marcia Drut-Davis were making their own choices about parenthood and the lives they would lead. Today, though we still face pushback, we have a name for our choice—childfree—and with the click of a mouse, we can easily find others whose circumstances and choices we share. We are less alone than perhaps ever before. And the occasions we celebrate have expanded to include our lives and choices. As I told Davies myself when she called to interview me for her story, we're used to celebrating significant milestones in our culture—we have parties to celebrate engagements and weddings, parties to celebrate graduations from school, parties to celebrate the purchase of a new home. But the milestones we most typically acknowledge epitomize a very narrow life path—bridal shower, bachelor party, the birth of a baby, baby's baptism, baby's first communion, baby's first birthday, baby's preschool graduation—that doesn't represent everyone's experience. What "I'm not having a baby" celebrations do is expand the repertoire so that life choices that feel significant to those who don't follow the love/marriage/baby carriage trajectory have the same chance to be seen, to celebrate their own choices, and to feel heard.

HEALTH AND MEDICINE

Not only do people feel more free to claim their childfree status with pride, women and men now enjoy greater access to medical solutions for controlling their fertility than at any prior point in history. Most people are familiar with treatments focused on women's fertility—hormone-based pills, patches, rings, and shots and surgical options including tubal ligation and abortion—but men, too, have more options than ever before.

Though historically used by eugenicists and others to control the fertility of vulnerable populations against their will, vasectomy eventually came to be seen—and used by men *with* their consent—as a highly effective and safe method of birth control.[8] In fact, vasectomy is both safer and more effective than tubal ligation.[9] Though rare, female sterilization comes with risk of infection, bleeding, and anesthesia-related complications, with tubal ligation resulting in 1 to 2 deaths per 100,000 procedures.[10] Yet vasectomies, as reported in *Reviews in Obstetrics & Gynecology*, come with "no major complications."

Vasectomies are also cost-effective. The Male Health Center notes the average cost of a vasectomy is $750–$850 while tubal ligations average around $2,500 each.[11] For reasons of lower risk and cost combined with higher effectiveness, the Brookings Institution recommends vasectomy over tubal ligation.[12] Why, then, considering its higher effectiveness, better safety record, and lower cost, are vasectomy rates half those of tubal ligation rates in the United States and one-fifth the rate of tubal ligations worldwide?[13]

Around the world, researchers find that social norms against vasectomy serve as a barrier to its adoption. These norms, report researchers in the journal *Global Health*, come from men's—and women's—misperceptions that vasectomy causes men to become physically weaker and that it is equivalent to castration.[14] And though cultural lore suggests that men's sexual performance might be at risk, the Mayo Clinic lists this along with four additional fears—damage to sexual organs, risk of cancer, risk of heart disease, and severe pain—as "unfounded concerns" regarding vasectomy.[15]

Though some men manage to frame their vasectomies as heroic acts of rebellion, as described in chapter 4, for many the procedure represents loss—loss of masculinity, loss of control, loss of power.

For these men, the experience is more likely to call up questions about their gender than to affirm it. As one team of medical researchers note in their study of men's experiences of vasectomy, "There is an intensity of gender role self-evaluation around this time" and early studies of vasectomy found that men adopt "more stereotypically masculine" behaviors following vasectomy as a way to compensate for "a diminished sense of masculinity."[16]

More recent research also finds that men connect vasectomy with a decline in masculinity. As one man recounted—jokingly but tellingly—to psychologists Gareth Terry and Virginia Braun in their study of men's experiences with vasectomy, "I'm not a real man and I've got a certificate to prove it."[17] In an autoethnographic account of his vasectomy experience, sociologist Ryan Cragun recounts a "troubling question" he found himself asking—one that other men have confronted as well—following the procedure: "Am I less of a 'man' now that I'm sterile?"[18] Individual men's angst over what their vasectomies reveal about their masculinity feed into and are fed by both broader cultural beliefs about what makes a man and global misperceptions of the risks and effects of vasectomy.

Not only do studies find that we don't understand the risks of vasectomy, there also seems to be a lack understanding—or perhaps lack of care—that sterilization for men is a far less invasive procedure than it is for women. The combination of an idealized masculinity that cannot be achieved without productive sperm and worldwide confusion over what vasectomy actually entails has brought us to the current moment, when vasectomy remains far less common in most nations when compared to tubal ligation. As documentary filmmaker and World Vasectomy Day co-founder Jonathan Stack put it, "Even though modern techniques [of vasectomy] require neither needle nor scalpel, and for the vast majority of men it takes only a few days to recover, it's still a tough sell."[19]

Stack, in partnership with urologist Doug Stein, is working to allay men's reticence to pursue vasectomy. As co-founders of World Vasectomy Day (WVD), Stack and Stein and their work help men and their families become more informed about family planning choices.[20] World Vasectomy Day is a year-round communications project, marked each year in November by a "vasectomy-thon" that includes live streaming of men getting vasectomies around the world and Q&A sessions with vasectomy providers. In 2017, on WVD's fifth anniversary, more than twelve hundred vasectomies were performed in more than fifty countries around the world.[21] Though these numbers are impressive, the founders of WVD say the family planning community could do more to engage men. As their mission statement notes, "We believe men worldwide are ready to make the choice to do right by themselves, their families and our future by becoming engaged in conversations about family planning."[22]

Whether men are ready to take on a more active role in family planning or not, our health-care system is not structured to fully engage them. In the United States, rates are driven in part by health-care policies, shaped by legislators who cling desperately to an outdated belief system that tells them men's masculinity is driven by their virility—and their fertility. Health reformers passed up the opportunity to change this when they left coverage for vasectomy out of the Affordable Care Act but included female sterilization. Indeed, in areas where access to vasectomy is free—including the United Kingdom and Canada—vasectomy rates are more than double those for female sterilization.[23]

Vasectomy isn't the only way for men to control their fertility, though expanding men's options requires continuing medical research. Today, medical researchers are pursuing less permanent solutions for men. Though still in development, hormonal birth control for the male population could be available one day. Testing of an injectable version was halted in 2016, with numerous media outlets attributing the halt to the 20 of 320 men in the trial who reported that the contraceptive's side effects—including depression, muscle pain, mood swings, acne, and changes to the libido, all shared by hormonal birth control for females—were intolerable.[24]

A review of the study reveals that, yes, twenty men did discontinue their participation after experiencing effects such as changes in mood, acne, panic at first injection of the hormone, palpitations, hypertension, and/or erectile dysfunction and that the study was halted after an independent safety board concluded that "the risks to the study participants outweighed the potential benefits to the study participants."[25]

Considering the story of female hormonal contraception trials, whose history is marked by "a lack of consent, a lack of full disclosure, a lack of true informed choice, and a lack of clinically relevant research regarding risk," the 2016 decision from the male trial is striking in its difference.[26] While no one is suggesting that men be subject to the same mistreatment that women endured, an opinion piece by Anna Rhodes in *The Independent* concluded, "I don't blame the men who dropped out of the trial for doing so. I blame the medical establishment for treating women like cattle who can deal with the risk of cancer and blood clots to avoid the world being populated by unwanted babies, yet aren't willing to let men suffer even a slight headache to the same end."[27]

The effects at least some men in the trial reported were more severe than a slight headache (nobody enjoys erectile dysfunction), but Rhodes does have a point. As evidence, one need only glance at the now infamous photo of the all-male panel of House Freedom Caucus members who in 2017 lobbied President Trump to drop the ACA requirement that insurance companies offer maternity care in all health plans. The image represents not just policy makers' historical lack of care to involve women in decisions that concern them most directly, but also a lack of inclusion of medical research funders and institutions.

In 2018, the Endocrine Society announced the study of a new birth control pill for men—for which eighty-three men took the pill for one month—that showed "hormone responses consistent with effective contraception."[28] The report notes that longer-term studies are under way and that "these promising results are unprecedented in the development of a prototype male pill." Also unprecedented, though perhaps one day possible, would be men's equal participation in family planning. Women and men must share the right—and responsibility—to control their own fertility. Until women and men are considered equal partners in planning their fertility, solutions for men will continue to be misunderstood, underutilized, and understudied. For now, the United Nations notes that contraceptive methods requiring men's "direct participation—male sterilization (vasectomy), the male condom and withdrawal" account for just 21 percent of contraceptive practice worldwide.[29]

Because most contraceptive methods rely on women's involvement, and because it is women who most directly experience the consequences of failed contraception, we must also work to improve women's access to sterilization, abortion, and nonpermanent forms of birth control. While vasectomy is a great option for partnered people and single men, tubal ligation is the better option for single women who never wish to become pregnant. Nothing better ensures the right of everyone to choose whether (or when and how) they will become a parent than access to the health care that allows women and men to control their own fertility.

Those fortunate enough to have decent health insurance are better off than many, but the fate of our fertility shouldn't be left to luck. The Affordable Care Act in the United States brought us closer to the sort of access that our neighbors to the north in Canada and throughout much of western Europe enjoy but it didn't go far enough. As long as employers are allowed to opt out of providing basic health coverage to their female employees, as long as the Hyde

Amendment—which effectively limits women's legal right to abortion to only those who can afford it—is in place, and as long as state courts are allowed to further limit access to medically safe, legal procedures like abortion, we will continue to see people become parents who wish they'd had another option.

Access to care is just part of the key, though. We must also embrace more inclusive education. Comprehensive sex education for children and teens is essential for reducing unwanted pregnancy; scientific evidence supports this conclusion and further shows that sex education programs do not entice adolescents into sexual activity.[30] Though teen pregnancy rates have plummeted in recent years, state-specific rates vary widely. States with the highest rates of teen pregnancy, teen birth, and sexually transmitted infection are those that either lack sexuality education or that require abstinence be stressed in what programming is offered.[31] A 2008 study of 1,719 teenagers found that those who receive comprehensive sex education were 60 percent less likely to report pregnancy (either becoming pregnant or impregnating someone) than teens who received no sex education, and 50 percent less likely to report pregnancy than those who had received abstinence-only education.[32]

MONEY AND WORK

Our education system needs change but so do the processes of employment, saving, and tax paying that adults face when they leave school. We need a tax policy that doesn't penalize poor working nonparents. In the United States, the Earned Income Tax Credit was designed to lift people out of poverty by ensuring that they don't begin to owe income tax until their earnings exceed the poverty level. It works this way for families with children. Those without kids at home, however—including singles and couples—receive little or no EITC and begin owing income taxes while still below the poverty line. An example developed by the Center on Budget and Policy Priorities in 2016 showed that a single, twenty-five-year-old childless worker employed year-round for thirty-five hours per week at the federal minimum wage would fall below the poverty line but still end the year owing nearly $1,000 in federal taxes.[33] Driving poor working nonparents further into poverty is in no one's best interests.

Inheritance tax laws in some states also disadvantage nonparents. While estate taxes are covered by a deceased person's estate, inheritance taxes are the responsibility of individual beneficiaries. As of 2016, six states collect inheritance taxes: Iowa, Kentucky, Maryland, Nebraska, New Jersey, and Pennsylvania.[34] Of course there are exceptions to the law—spouses are exempt in all six states, children are exempt in all but two (Nebraska and Pennsylvania), and charitable organizations are often exempt. But for nonparents, there is no relative or loved one to whom they can leave their estate (unless they happen to be married to someone who is still living when they die) without also leaving the person receiving their inheritance with a hefty tax bill.

One childfree couple I know plans to leave the bulk of their estate to a sister, sixteen years their junior, who works in geriatrics and who they expect will be their primary caretaker as they age. But if they die in the home and city they love and have known their entire adult lives, in Iowa, the sister will end up handing over $10,000 to $15,000 to the state for every $100,000 in their estate. Though the sister's anticipated role resembles that more typical of a child, she is not exempt from the inheritance tax as a child would be. The beneficiaries of nonparents should not be treated differently from the beneficiaries of parents. Even more, parents who have strained relationships with their children might prefer to leave an inheritance to other loved ones, but the inheritance tax laws in these states privilege only a narrow conception of love and family.

Another issue related to money is how and where the childfree spend theirs. Not enough companies pay attention to this question. While some are beginning to recognize nonparents as a market worth courting, they need to do more. The 2014 Land's End ad featuring a presumably childfree woman is a start. In the ad, the woman is laughing with two young children, perhaps around five years old, with the copy reading "Being their aunt means when we're #together there are no rules."[35] But even this ad places its protagonist in the position of mother figure, having fun with her young niece and nephew and clearly excelling at her role as auntie. Representing women in a more diverse array of roles, some of which might involve children but all of which needn't, would better reflect the reality of all women's lives, mother or not.

Even moms have had enough of stereotypical mom tropes, according to a 2016 study of nearly eight thousand mothers from eight different markets around the globe.[36] The study, by ad agency Saatchi & Saatchi, found that moms feel that marketers have "outdated and inaccurate" views about them and that they want to be represented as the interesting, fun, inspiring, knowledgeable people that they are. Childfree women want this, too. As described in the opening pages of this book, "Savvy Auntie" Melanie Notkin and "NotMom" Karen Malone Wright are working to change the current reality that, in advertising, women are primarily limited to the role of mother.[37] Others should join them in this mission.

Finally, as discussed more deeply in chapter 3, we need to improve work-life balance policies. We all need time away from work. Rather than viewing our collective interests as competing, parents and nonparents should work together to push for better balance. We will all be better off when we come to see our interests as shared. And employers will have happier, healthier, and more productive workforces when they accept that providing time away serves their interests as well. Absence makes the heart grow fonder, after all.

AGING

We need to be much more creative about how we age, developing systems that promote healthy aging for all. And prevention strategies for combating loneliness among the elderly should focus on approaches that don't rely on nuclear family connections alone. The Golden Girls–style arrangements and intergenerational programs described in chapter 7 are great examples. So too are the programs for combating loneliness—such as Little Brothers–Friends of the Elderly—also discussed in chapter 7. An AARP review of intervention studies offers a number of strategies for combating loneliness in seniors, including telehealth interventions for those who are homebound, elder mentor programs, intergenerational living communities, and citywide initiatives that teach neighbors to help neighbors and expand transportation and civic engagement opportunities.[38]

There is widespread support for such initiatives. A study by researchers from Ohio State University found that 79 percent of Americans believe that the government should invest in programs that bring older adults together with youth. Even more, 82 percent report that they would support their tax dollars going toward building intergenerational facilities in their communities.[39] Loneliness in old age is a real problem but it is solvable. We should build from this support and the momentum of programs already established by our foreparents (and fore-nonparents) to grow these and other models of healthy aging and caring for our elders.

SPACES AND PLACES

Today the childfree are more able than ever before to talk openly about their choice. But there are still spaces and places where they are not welcome or where the extent to which they are welcome is unclear. In chapter 5, I raised questions about the meaning of the term *family-friendly* and consider how it is often used to exclude adults without children. I also pointed out that having events, spaces, and places that are geared toward children is perfectly acceptable but that these should be described as kid-friendly rather than family-friendly. And I note, too, that it is okay for some spaces to be limited to adults. Others should be open to all configurations of family.

In recent years, some restaurants—airlines, too—have decided to go entirely childfree, a choice met with mixed reviews but, in one case at least, also leading to a 50 percent increase in sales.[40] While we won't always agree about where or how to draw the line between kid-friendly and adults-only, we should be able to acknowledge that all adults, whether parents or not, need and value time alone with their peers. Nurturing friendships and other connections in ways and in places that are centered on adults' needs and interests is just as important as providing kid-friendly spaces to children. We should be careful not to further divide parents and nonparents, but we must also move past misplaced accusations that wanting no-kids-allowed spaces equates to wanting a no-kids-allowed world.

IT'S COMPLICATED

We should accept that for many of us, no choice will feel like the perfect fit at all times, even when we know we've made the right one for ourselves. I know parents who sometimes wish they had the freedom Lance and I do to decide on the spur of the moment that we feel like grabbing a beer after work at our neighborhood bar. And I've spoken with childfree people who truly enjoy activities with children that are typically limited to parents and their kids—school concerts, dance recitals, sports events, and the like. It's okay to have some ambivalence about whatever path we've chosen. If parents and the childfree are encouraged to be open about the fact that their choice comes with pros and cons, those still deciding which path is right for them will be better able to make the best decision for themselves.

One positive trend is that parents are beginning to open up about the difficulties of parenting. Say what you will about the proliferation of mommy blogs, but one consequence of their omnipresence has been a more public and open discussion about the joys *and* frustrations of parenthood. Dooce.com's Heather Armstrong— former stay-at-home mom, or as she put it, "Shit Ass Ho Motherfucker" and current "FTSWM—a Full-Time Single Working Mom, or, Fuck That Shit Where's Marijuana"—was among the first. Armstrong launched her blog in the 1990s, documenting motherhood as it really was for her, often with the wit of a professional comic.

Others followed Armstrong's lead. Of particular note, and internet fame, is Jill Smokler of Scary Mommy, "a massive vibrant community of millions of parents, brought together by a common theme: Parenting doesn't have to be perfect." As these and other mommy bloggers show, there should be no shame in honestly discussing the very real and very hard (and often very funny) work it takes to parent well. Doing so not only benefits parents who can feel less alone knowing that others, too, sometimes struggle with the role, but it may also serve to reduce the stigma for those who choose to opt out of parenthood. Recognizing that a single role is not the be-all, end-all for anyone serves everyone, including those who may be undecided but want to make an informed decision.

Mommy bloggers weren't the first to open up about the difficulties of motherhood. In her 1973 book, *Mother's Day Is Over*, National Organization for Non-Parents co-founder and mother of two Shirley Rogers Radl described the ways that motherhood not only disrupted marriage but was also sometimes a source of "resentment, hostility and rage."[41] Openly calling attention to the difficulties of motherhood is one thing. In more recent years, the public conversation has opened up to include honest conversation about the reality that motherhood is hard and also to acknowledge that some women regret their choice to become parents.

Though motherhood is popularly framed "as a mythical nexus that lies outside and beyond human realms of regret," sociologist Orna Donath found that motherhood regret is very real for the twenty-three Israeli biological mothers, aged twenty-six to seventy-three, she interviewed between 2008 and 2011.[42] Though her sample is small, the public reaction to Donath's work suggests that she is onto something. Since the 2015 publication of her book and subsequent articles, Donath's work has been covered in numerous media outlets, from the BBC to ABC, *The Guardian* to Yahoo, and numerous others.[43]

It isn't just maternal regret that's getting attention. A 2018 BBC News piece notes, "It's not just women who sometimes regret parenthood."[44] The article features forty-five-year-old Martin, a father who shared, "If I could turn back time, if I knew then what I know now, children would never have been on the agenda." Martin, like some of the women Donath interviewed, reports feeling constrained by his kids, even now that they are adults, and wishes he'd made the choice to remain childfree.

The increase in both popular and scholarly attention to the reality that some parents regret their choice should, I hope, bring attention to the importance of not pressuring people to have children before they are ready and not pressuring people at all when they know they never want to become parents. It also reveals the importance of supporting parents in their roles. One conclusion by Orna Donath, for example, is that regret is shaped by external factors such as how much support mothers receive from their spouses and the extent to which mothers give up careers in order to raise children. People concerned about declining fertility rates among some portions of our population would do well to understand how offering better supports for parents might change the dynamics of regret.

The childfree should also be given the space to be open about the complexities of their choice. We've been accused at times of being defensive, and this defensiveness can be off-putting. In chapter 1, I outline some of the reasons we may come off as defensive (hostility directed toward us and our choice, lack of interest on the part of some parents in interacting with nonparents, faulty assumptions about why we've made our choice, etc.). Approaching a childfree person, whose choice you may not understand, with respect and nonhostile curiosity could help. And for the childfree, responding to curiosity about our choice openly and patiently could aid in promoting the respect and understanding we desire and deserve. And of course maintaining an awareness that we've all been reared in a pronatalist environment, based on a whole host of assumptions not always grounded in fact, should help as well.

FROM BABY SHOWERS TO BALLS VOYAGE

We have an announcement to make! We are thrilled to say we will NOT be adding any more tiny humans to our family! My husband is taking one for the team and to celebrate this momentous occasion I felt the need to throw him a little "Balls Voyage" party for his upcoming procedure.

—KIMBERLY HEMPERLY

In late 2017, mother of two Kimberly Hemperly, taking inspiration from the cast of *The Real Housewives of Orange County*, threw her husband a "Balls Voyage" party to celebrate his pending vasectomy. Her husband donned a T-shirt with the line TIME TO RETIRE THE SWIM TEAM, and their two kids wore shirts identifying them each as a SWIM TEAM SURVIVOR. Hemperly's post about the party went viral, generating over 45,000 shares on Facebook.[45] While Hemperly isn't childfree, the party signifies an important moment in our culture, one where we are finally free to discuss openly what humans have done in private for centuries: control our own fertility.

Since the U.S. Census Bureau began tracking the numbers, the percentage of people who choose not to have kids has nearly doubled and we've come a long way toward accepting reproductive choice. Today, while some people host baby showers, others throw vasectomy parties. While gift registries for some mark the birth of a new baby, for others they mark the birth of a new business.

When Lance and I started our blog, the same year Marcia Drut-Davis published her memoir, we set out to contribute to that effort and we wrote a manifesto to summarize what we wanted *we're {not} having a baby!* to be about. We wanted it to represent our dual interest in joyfully claiming our choice and demystifying the childfree life. Inspired by some of our own experiences in sharing our choice with others, we also wanted to push back, in as good-natured a way as possible, against the myths we'd encountered that some believe about people like ourselves.

In the manifesto, we explain that "we {are} a family, we {do} lead rich and meaningful lives, we're {not} selfish, we {don't} hate kids . . . we think {some} are cool, and we're {not} missing out . . . we {chose} something else!"[46] Today, we know these things to be true not just because one brave couple had the courage to share their experience on national television over four decades ago but also thanks to the social scientists who've conducted hundreds of studies in the decades since and to the thousands of childfree people who have spoken their own truths loudly and proudly. But while we've come a long way since Marcia Drut-Davis's horrific experience, we still have much further to go. We each have the right to make the choice that feels best for our own families and fertility. And we share the responsibility of supporting others in making the choice that's right for them.

A few years ago I found myself taking an extended break from my day job. Amy was well into her research on the childfree and we spent a lot of time talking about her work, the existing literature on the topic, and our choice.

There'd been an upswell of interest in the childfree choice, so the timing was right to start our blog, *we're {not} having a baby!* As the more technical of the two, and having time on my hands, I took on the project of setting up the blog and corresponding social media. We blogged and posted and commented and engaged. We got happy and angry and sad and excited. We helped some people, annoyed others, and even offended a few.

A good balance, I think.

And so began my foray into the childfree movement.

I spent hours, days, and weeks on our site and others, and one thing was glaringly clear—there are a lot more women talking about this issue than men.

Like way more.

On our own Facebook page, 84 percent of followers are women. That only leaves 16 percent as men or other. And men engage on the page much less than women.

I think there are good reasons for this. After all, when it comes to having children, women bear more costs than men. This includes obvious up-front things like the discomfort, inconvenience, and pain of pregnancy and childbirth, up to and including irreparable damage to the body and even the risk of death. Also, women (still) do a disproportionate amount of the child-rearing as compared to men. And, of course, women experience significantly more societal pressure to have children than men do; it is their destiny!

So women are directly and indirectly stigmatized when they don't have or want children. Men, not so much. Or at least not as much.

One day perhaps females won't be the only sex that can give birth. Ideally, sooner rather than later, men and/or robots will do more to share the burden of childbearing and child-rearing. And, hopefully, one of these days—for the love of Pete . . . don't we have bigger things to worry about?—women who do not want children will stop receiving shit for the decision not to have them. But today it is shit they receive. Some men who don't want kids are given a hard time for it, too. But not nearly as much as women.

Given these imbalances, it's understandable that more women than men are vocal about their choice to be childfree.

Of course, none of this means that men have no interest or stake in the childfree choice. Minimally, all men should support the women in our lives to make the decision that is right for them. We should understand the issues they face in society, biased as it is so heavily toward procreation without thought. We need to do this even if we childfree guys aren't on the receiving end of the same level of abuse, stereotypes, and stigma that the childfree women in our lives face.

THE LONGER SHORT STICK

Even if childfree men don't receive as short a short stick as childfree women, it doesn't mean we are immune from misunderstandings about who we are or why we've made our choice. We share many of the challenges Amy mentions: workplace issues, accusations of self-ishness, worries that we'll die alone, and so on. Though we may face these challenges less often or to a lesser degree, they are as real for childfree men as they are for childfree women.

And—lucky us!—there are even a few challenges that are more commonly experienced by men than by women. "Who will carry on the family name?" is one many men hear. Or what about proving your virility through offspring? And "leaving a legacy"—that's one the childfree men I've met mention. All of these, we're told, are the "manly" reasons to have kids.

Though most of these don't happen to be issues I've faced per-sonally, I haven't been completely immune. I have experienced the offhand comments and questions from family, friends, colleagues, acquaintances, and complete strangers that have raised my eyebrows and sometimes my blood pressure.

The most common questions I've faced have been some variant of "When are you going to have kids?" These questions are not so much memorable themselves; they're memorable because of the ef-fect my answer has on the asker. My response has varied over time. Early on, it was "We're probably not . . ." but it evolved to a more solid "Never!" as I became convinced Amy wasn't going to change her mind about not having kids. In any case, my answer is always accompanied by a huge grin.

This approach often causes consternation.

> . . . not having children?
> . . . so happy about it?
> What? Who? How?

I enjoy responding in a way that surprises people. Instead of me being on the defensive or falsely apologetic in some way, I get to show how happy I am with a choice that often confounds others. But the experience of being childfree in a world where most people become parents isn't always a fun one.

THE CASE OF PARENTHOOD AND FRIENDSHIP

Despite the relatively easy go I've had compared to the childfree women I know, one thing that really has affected me as a childfree man is experiencing the loss of close friends as they disappeared into parenthood. The list of friends I've lost this way isn't trivial. But men's friendships are rarely talked about, and discussing the hurt caused by the loss of those connections certainly isn't considered "manly."

There was the couple who lived in the heart of a city who gave us never-ending shit for living in the suburbs . . . who then promptly moved to the burbs as soon as they got pregnant. There was the colleague who accidentally knocked up another colleague, the first of a long list of bad decisions including marrying the woman only because of the pregnancy, then fathering more kids in short order.

Like many other friends, after kids, these folks' lives changed to revolve almost entirely around their roles as parents. They acquired new friends with kids of their own. And as the only childfree couple remaining, Amy and I were locked out.

Of all the friends I've lost to parenthood, one stings the most.

My best friend—let's call him Joe—was a confirmed bachelor for the longest time. We spent a lot of our free time together . . . coffee shops, bars, and each other's homes. We brewed beer together, sometimes with explosive results. We both loved to cook and drink Scotch, so gatherings featuring both happened often. He was always there for me and I'd like to think I was there for him.

Another bonus was that Joe and Amy were close. It's not always true that your guy friends get along well with your wife. But Joe and

Amy did, so when Joe met a woman and they got serious, we easily added her to the friendship. The four of us traveled together extensively—trips to the family cabin in Wisconsin, Scotch drinking in Scotland, a dog show in New York, steaks in Chicago, to name just a few.

And then everything changed. Joe and his wife adopted a child.

Joe and his wife are exactly the kind of people you want parenting. They are great parents and they are raising a great kid, a kid whom I like a lot. We knew they'd excel at parenthood, which is why we didn't hesitate when they asked us to give a character reference to the adoption agency.

But I was horribly naive about how the addition of a third party would affect my and Joe's friendship. Before fatherhood, Joe was the guy who took care of people. He showed up to help you move or build that deck or, in my case, pick up, acclimate, and put away shipments of marine fish and coral from the Philippines or Hawaii at 2:00 A.M. With the adoption, suddenly that formidable caring side had a singular target. Joe's son became the center of his world and there was little time or energy for anyone else.

I watched as this tough, self-sufficient, former linebacker and wrestler, woodworker, international traveler, Scotch and sushi connoisseur, technical guru, and all-around Renaissance man pushed everything aside for this one thing . . . parenthood.

I don't regret that character reference—I love seeing Joe happy and he is raising a happy, good kid. But I do miss him. And I wonder if he misses who he used to be.

Joe and I are still friends and always will be, but he's made clear that we won't be seeing much of each other until his boy gets older and moves out. For now, our friendship is fully on Joe's terms.

The shift in my friendship with Joe—and with others—after they become parents has been one of the most difficult things for me about being childfree. I'm happy for Joe and for others who wanted to be dads, are good at it, and enjoy the role. But what happens when their kids leave the nest? From media reports, you'd think only women's friendships are affected when one of them becomes a parent. But I can attest that it's a challenge for men, too.

MY CHILDFREE STORY

Because pretty much all of society's machinery primes us to be parents, every person who decides against parenthood must work their own special path to that conclusion. But we rarely hear men's perspectives on the decision or their experiences making it.

I grew up knowing that I'd have kids one day. The path was obvious: grow up, date, get married, have kids, and be a dad. Preferably in that order. No steps optional.

This is, after all, how it works. Or so I believed.

I first questioned this path at around age nine when I realized that kids are a *lot* of work. My mom was a stay-at-home mom who did all our laundry, cleaned constantly, put three meals on the table every day, and had a side gig as a custom seamstress. My dad didn't make a lot of money as a fundamentalist minister and he spent most of his time at the church or at church-related activities.

I watched my parents deal unsuccessfully with angry, petulant, self-centered tweens and teens—it was me and four older sisters—who had seemingly endless needs and demands for time, food, money, laundry, and so on. They loved us but certainly never seemed to enjoy us.

I remember thinking, "Who does this to themselves?"

Yes, I know. "Such a deep thinker at only nine!" "Wise beyond his years."

I figured I must be missing something. People put themselves through so much effort and heartache while giving up so much freedom and time, ergo there must be more to the story. I chalked it up to not understanding *yet*, to being young. I thought, "When I'm more mature I'll get it, and when I get it, then I'll want kids."

Time rolled on. I grew up. I dated. I got married. It never happened, though. Amy and I would touch base every year or so. After establishing the general ground rules, it went something like this:

LANCE: "You want kids yet?"
AMY: "No . . . do you?"
LANCE: "No."
AMY: "Nice chat!"
LANCE: "Talk to you next year!"

In the end, that magic moment never occurred. I never wanted kids. And neither did Amy.

It's not that I never saw an upside. I do see how meaningful kids can be to parents who really want them, and who can and do care for them. I have the utmost respect for the good parents that I see, and I even enjoy being around some kids. Sometimes.

But I've never wanted kids because I see very clearly the downsides and for me the cons outweigh the pros.

Now I'm in my forties. I've been married for twenty-three years. I love my life as it is, childfree. Funny thing . . . I almost wrote "I couldn't imagine having kids," but that is completely wrong. I can easily imagine having kids. I can see clearly from friends and family what that would mean for my life. That is why I'm so happy about my decision not to have them. For me, it works.

I've never really understood why we talk about childfree as a choice but we don't describe parenthood in the same way. In today's world, people can choose to become parents. Or not. And while the stakes in today's world may be higher for women, the choice to become a parent is one we should all understand is a choice, one that comes with consequences whatever our gender.

It seems to me that we've constructed a world in which the (historically) uncontrollable outcome of having children, which is driven (mercilessly) by the desire to have sex, is considered the socially desirable outcome, pretty much at any cost.

To me this is like saying the (historically) uncontrollable outcome of dying, which is driven by our desire to dive deeply underwater and stay there for an extended period of time, is the desirable outcome.

But we've got scuba gear and submarines and bathyscaphes now. You—yes, you!—can dive deeply underwater and stay there for an extended period of time, get this, *without even dying!* We've all, even the Pope as far as I can tell, adjusted to this new, exciting reality.

Now we need to adjust to the reality we live in when it comes to procreation.

Simply put, we can, and should, *choose* to have children {or not}. And that's okay.

ACKNOWLEDGMENTS

Thank you to my partner in life and love, Lance, for taking this adventure with me. Lance did all of the heavy lifting in getting our blog, *we're {not} having a baby!*, off the ground. Anything you find there that's designed well or particularly witty is thanks to Lance. Our family may be small but it is mighty and of our own design, built from years of sometimes grueling, often joyful, and always-worth-it hard work and dedication.

My parents have been my number one supporters for my entire life, even as they came to understand that I wouldn't be gifting them with grandchildren. I owe my sister, Kathy, a debt of gratitude for taking the pressure off me by having two fantastic kids of her own and for never pressuring me, once she knew my intentions. One area where my own experience doesn't resonate with that of many other childfree people is in the stories they share about being chastised by family members for their choice. I know how fortunate I am to have a family that supports me, and for that I am exceedingly grateful.

The most outstanding team of professionals guided this first-timer through the process of writing a book of this sort. Stephanie Tade took a chance on an unknown. Colleen Martell has been a much-needed source of encouragement throughout the process. I knew from the second I first Skyped with them that I was in if they'd have me. And Stephanie Kelly, I could see from our very first conversation, got it. She got this childfree thing, she got the big picture, she got the small struggles, she got when I needed a nudge, she got when I needed some space. I've never before had the pleasure of working with someone so skilled at pushing me beyond my comfort zone while being so reassuring and kind the whole time. I wish all writers the chance to work with such pros.

To Alyssa Hunter and Amy Ronnkvist, my original writing buddies, thank you for your support, friendship, feedback, and encouragement. And to Andrea Irwin, who performed the role of snark checker when I worried my tone might be too defensive. Gail Bolson-Magnuson and Laura Carlson provided feedback and information that were also a big help.

I've been incredibly lucky to work with amazing students on this research. Molly Hunt wrote a fantastic thesis, which I cite throughout the book, and I enjoyed our many chats about research and the childfree choice. Mahala Stewart was transcriptionist extraordinaire and has turned into a wonderful sociologist and a favorite collaborator. Amy Greenleaf created a fantastic independent study and became a co-author on a paper as a result. Robert Jackson helped with interviews and transcripts and in the process helped me broaden my thinking about the project. Nicole Golden Bouchard performed the unsung labor of background research and asked thoughtful and challenging questions; I can't wait to vote her into office! And there are countless others (Alyssa Radmore, Linda Fogg, Ellee Petersen, Jamie Pelletier, Matt Leavitt, Jeremy Beaulieu, Heather McLaughlin, Jason Houle, Dawn Norris, Chris Whitcomb, Torie Lebreton—I could go on) who have been inspirations in their own ways. I may not have children of my own, but my students help me understand my own stake in our collective future.

The University of Maine and my colleagues in the Sociology Department have provided support and encouragement on the project for many years. In particular, Stephen Marks encouraged the launch of the project, and his writing on families provided the initial starting place for the work. Laurie Cartier helped with transcriptions. The National Council on Family Relations' Feminism and Family Studies section provided funding that helped me begin the interviews and the endorsement that confirmed for me that the project was worthy.

Penelope La Montagne offered her beautiful home at a steal so that I could have much-needed space and solitude to write and edit. Laura Carroll provided the introduction that made that possible. Maxine Trump and Therese Shechter, fabulous filmmakers and cool-cat collaborators, became fast friends. They're both on my list of who I want to be when I grow up. Karen Malone Wright and Laura LaVoie continue to provide the only place I've known as an adult where I can be certain I won't be asked, "So how many kids do you have?" Thank you, all!

Many writers and academics whom I admire took the time to offer their advice and share their expertise as I worked to expand my reach beyond the ivory tower. Rebecca Traister, Lauren Sandler, Meghan Daum, Melanie Notkin, Lisa Wade, Pepper Schwartz, and Stephanie Coontz all took the time to respond to my plea for advice despite the fact that they'd either never met me or had only ever done so very briefly. Tammy Coia and Linda George Brown provided the chance to try out new ways of writing in a nurturing environment. Mentors and public sociologists Doug Hartmann and Chris Uggen were instrumental in shaping my ideas about the purpose of sociology and instilling in me the belief, to borrow from Chris, "that good science can light the way to a more just and peaceful world." I'm also grateful to writer and Loft Literary Center instructor Ashley Shelby and the fine folks at the OpEd Project and the Alan Alda Center for Communicating Science, all of whom provided training and encouragement that helped me attempt the leap from the safety of my ivory tower.

ACKNOWLEDGMENTS

Of course the project never would have been possible without the fifty women and twenty men who took the time to share their stories and reflections with me and the many people—parents and childfree—who've weighed in via our blog and social media pages. Thank you for sharing yourself and your stories with me. I hope I've done you proud.

INTRODUCTION

1. Lorber, Judith. 1994. *Paradoxes of Gender*. New Haven: Yale University Press.
2. https://www.newscientist.com/article/2107219-exclusive-worlds-first-baby-born-with-new-3-parent-technique/.
3. Hunt, Mary K. 2015. *On the Childfree, Religion, and Stigma Consciousness*. Sociology Honors College Thesis, University of Maine.
4. Hollingsworth, Leta. 1916. "Social Devices for Impelling Women to Bear and Rear Children." *American Journal of Sociology* 22(1): 19–29; Veevers, Jean E. 1974. "Voluntary Childlessness and Social Policy: An Alternative View." *The Family Coordinator* 23(4): 397–406; Houseknecht, Sharon K. 1979. "Timing of the Decision to Remain Voluntarily Childless: Evidence for Continuous Socialization." *Psychology of Women Quarterly* 4(1): 81–96; Park, Kristin. 2005. "Choosing Childlessness: Weber's Typology of Action and Motives of the Voluntary Childless." *Sociological Inquiry* 75(3): 372–402; Koropeckyj-Cox, Tanya, Zeynep Copur, Victor Romano, and Susan Cody-Rydzewski. 2018. "University Students' Perceptions of Parents and Childless or Childfree Couples." *Journal of Family Issues* 39(1): 155–179; Gillespie, Rosemary. 2003. "Childfree and Feminine: Understanding the Gender Identity of Voluntarily Childless Women." *Gender & Society* 17(1): 122–136; Dennis, Kimya. 2018. "No, we are NOT all the same: Being of African diaspora and childfree-by-choice." Presented at the Annual Meeting of the Southern Sociological Society, New Orleans, LA; Volsch, Shelly, and Peter Gray. 2016. "'Dog Moms' Use Authoritative Parenting Styles." *Human-Animal Interaction Bulletin* 4(2): 1–16; Long, Brooke L., and Fritz W. Yarrison. 2016. "What Does It Mean to Be Childless? Exploring Meaning Structures of Parents and Childless Individuals." Presented at the Annual Meeting of the American Sociological Association, Seattle, WA; Ayers, Gillian. 2013. *"I Could Be a Father, but I Could Never Be a Mother": Values and Meanings of Women's Voluntary Childlessness in Southern Alberta*.

Master's Thesis, Department of Sociology, University of Lethbridge; Settle, Braelin, and Krista Brumley. 2014. "'It's the Choices You Make That Get You There': Decision-Making Pathways of Childfree Women." *Michigan Family Review* 18(1): 1–22; Laurent-Simpson, Andrea. 2017. "'They Make Me Not Wanna Have a Child': Effects of Companion Animals on Fertility Intentions of the Childfree." *Sociological Inquiry* 87(4): 586–607; Healey, Jenna. 2016. "Rejecting Reproduction: The National Organization for Non-Parents and Childfree Activism in 1970s America." *Journal of Women's History* 28(1): 131–156.

5. Carroll, Laura. 2000. *Families of Two: Interviews with Happily Married Couples without Children by Choice.* Bloomington, IN: Xlibris; see also Carroll, Laura. 2012. *The Baby Matrix: Why Freeing Our Minds from Outmoded Thinking about Parenthood & Reproduction Will Create a Better World.* LiveTrue Books.

6. Scott, Laura S. 2009. *Two Is Enough: A Couple's Guide to Living Childless by Choice.* Berkeley, CA: Seal Press; Scott, Laura S. 2012. *The Childless by Choice Project, documentary film.*

7. Drut-Davis, Marcia. 2013. *Confessions of a Childfree Woman: A Life Spent Swimming against the Mainstream.* Amazon Digital Services.

8. *To Kid or Not to Kid: The Movie,* by Maxine Trump; *My So-Called Selfish Life,* film by Therese Shechter.

9. Tugend, Alina. 2016. "Childless Women to Marketers: We Buy Things Too." *New York Times,* July 9. https://www.nytimes.com/2016/07/10/business/childless -women-to-marketers-we-buy-things-too.html?mcubz=0.

10. Devries Global Public Relations. 2014. "Shades of Otherhood: Marketing to Women without Children." White paper. http://melanienotkin.com/portfolio /shades-of-otherhood-marketing-to-women-without-children/.

11. Tugend, Alina. 2016. "Childless Women to Marketers: We Buy Things Too." *New York Times,* July 9. https://www.nytimes.com/2016/07/10/business/childless -women-to-marketers-we-buy-things-too.html?mcubz=0.

12. Stein, Jill. "Why America Needs a Woman President This Mother's Day." https: //www.jill2016.com/_a_women_president_mothers_day.

13. Castle, Stephen. 2016. "Contest for British Premier Flares over Claims on Motherhood." *New York Times,* July 9. https://www.nytimes.com/2016/07/10/world /europe/contest-for-british-premier-flares-over-claims-on-motherhood.html?_r=1.

CHAPTER 1

1. Peck, Ellen. 1972. "Obituary: Motherhood." *New York Times,* May 13, p. 31.

2. Healey, Jenna. 2016. "Rejecting Reproduction: The National Organization for

NOTES

Non-Parents and Childfree Activism in 1970s America." *Journal of Women's History* 28(1): 131–156.

3. *Time*. 1972. "Down with Kids." Vol. 100, Issue 1, p. 37.

4. Sandler, Lauren. 2013. "None Is Enough." *Time*, August 12.

5. Richie, Cristina. 2014. "The Augustinian Legacy of Procreative Marriage: Contemporary Implications and Alternatives." *Feminist Theology* 23(1): 18–36.

6. Blake, Judith. 1979. "Is Zero Preferred? American Attitudes toward Childlessness in the 1970s." *Journal of Marriage and the Family* 41(2): 245–257; Heaton, Tim B., Cardell K. Jacobson, and Xuan Ning Fu. 1992. "Religiosity of Married Couples and Childlessness." *Review of Religious Research* 33: 244–255; Seccombe, Karen. 1991. "Assessing the Costs and Benefits of Children: Gender Comparisons among Childfree Husbands and Wives." *Journal of Marriage and the Family* 53(1): 191–202.

7. Richie, Cristina. 2013. "Disrupting the Meaning of Marriage? Childfree, Infertile and Gay Unions in Evangelical and Catholic Theologies of Marriage." *Theology & Sexuality* 13(2): 123–142.

8. Hunt, Mary K. 2015. *On the Childfree, Religion, and Stigma Consciousness*. Sociology Honors College Thesis, University of Maine.

9. United States Conference of Catholic Bishops. 2009. "Marriage: Love and Life in the Divine Plan. A Pastoral Letter of the United States Conference of Catholic Bishops." Washington, DC: United States Conference of Catholic Bishops.

10. Hunt, Mary K. 2015. *On the Childfree, Religion, and Stigma Consciousness*. Sociology Honors College Thesis, University of Maine; see also Hollinger, Dennis P. 2009. *The Meaning of Sex: Christian Ethics and the Moral Life*. Grand Rapids: Baker.

11. Richie, Cristina. 2014. "The Augustinian Legacy of Procreative Marriage: Contemporary Implications and Alternatives." *Feminist Theology* 23(1): 18–36.

12. Llewllyn, Dawn. 2016. "Maternal Silences: Motherhood and Voluntary Childlessness in Contemporary Christianity." *Religion & Gender* 6(1): 64–79.

13. Mintz, Steven. 2004. *Huck's Raft: A History of American Childhood*. Cambridge: Harvard University Press.

14. Coontz, Stephanie. 1992. *The Way We Never Were: American Families and the Nostalgia Trap*. New York: Basic Books.

15. Coontz, Stephanie. 2005. *Marriage, a History: How Love Conquered Marriage*. New York: Penguin.

16. Hernandez, Donald J., with David E. Myers. 1993. *America's Children: Resources from Family, Government, and the Economy*. New York: Russell Sage.

17. Coontz, Stephanie. 2005. *Marriage, a History: How Love Conquered Marriage.* New York: Penguin.

18. Doug Owram. Quoted in Coontz, 2005, p. 229.

19. Galton, Francis. 1883. *Inquiries into the Human Faculty.* New York: MacMillan. Quoted in Roberts, Dorothy. 1997. *Killing the Black Body: Race, Reproduction, and the Meaning of Liberty.* New York: Random House.

20. Roberts, Dorothy. 1997. *Killing the Black Body: Race, Reproduction, and the Meaning of Liberty.* New York: Random House; see also Kluchin, Rebecca M. 2009. *Fit to Be Tied: Sterilization and Reproductive Rights in America.* New Brunswick, NJ: Rutgers University Press.

21. May, Elaine Tyler. 1995. *Barren in the Promised Land: Childless Americans and the Pursuit of Happiness.* Cambridge: Harvard University Press.

22. Roosevelt, Theodore. 1903. "Sixth Annual Message to Congress." December 3. Quoted in May, Elaine Tyler. 1995. *Barren in the Promised Land: Childless Americans and the Pursuit of Happiness.* Cambridge: Harvard University Press.

23. Letter from Henry Fairfield Osborn to Major Leonard Darwin. December 5, 1921. Henry Fairfield Osborn Papers, Archives of the American Museum of Natural History. As cited in Baker, Graham J. 2014. "Christianity and Eugenics: The Place of Religion in the British Eugenics Education Society and the American Eugenics Society, c. 1907–1940." *Social History of Medicine* 27(2): 280–302.

24. Selden, Steven. 2005. "Transforming Better Babies into Fitter Families: Archival Resources and the History of the American Eugenics Movement, 1908–1930." *Proceedings of the American Philosophical Society* 149(2): 199–225.

25. Library of Congress. "Topics in Chronicling America: The Early American Eugenics Movement." https://www.loc.gov/rr/news/topics/eugenics.html.

26. Gerais, Reem. 2017. "Better Babies Contests in the United States (1908–1916)." *The Embryo Project Encyclopedia.* Tempe: Arizona State University, School of Life Sciences, Center for Biology and Society. https://embryo.asu.edu/pages/better -babies-contests-united-states-1908–1916.

27. Kibbe, Tina M. 2012. *In "Fitness" and in Health: Eugenics, Public Health, and Marriage in the United States.* State University of New York at Buffalo, ProQuest Dissertations Publishing.

28. Stern, Alexandra Minna. 2002. "Making Better Babies: Public Health and Race Betterment in Indiana, 1920–1935." *American Journal of Public Health* 92(5): 742–752.

29. "The Best of Better Babies." *Woman's Home Companion* 41 (May 1914): 26. As cited in Kibbe, Tina M. 2012. *In "Fitness" and in Health: Eugenics, Public Health, and*

Marriage in the United States. State University of New York at Buffalo, ProQuest Dissertations Publishing.

30. Kibbe, Tina M. 2012. *In "Fitness" and in Health: Eugenics, Public Health, and Marriage in the United States.* State University of New York at Buffalo, ProQuest Dissertations Publishing.

31. Selden, Steven. 2005. "Transforming Better Babies into Fitter Families: Archival Resources and the History of the American Eugenics Movement, 1908–1930." *Proceedings of the American Philosophical Society* 149(2): 199–225.

32. Rydell, Robert W. 1993. *World of Fairs: The Century-of-Progress Expositions.* Chicago: The University of Chicago Press.

33. http://www.worldometers.info/world-population/.

34. Popenoe, Paul. 1936. "Motivation of Childless Marriages." *Journal of Heredity* 27(112): 469–472.

35. Gillespie, Rosemary. 2003. "Childfree and Feminine: Understanding the Gender Identity of Voluntarily Childless Women." *Gender & Society* 17(1): 122–136; see also Davis, Angela Y. 1983. *Women, Race & Class.* New York: Random House.

36. Roberts, Dorothy. 1997. *Killing the Black Body: Race, Reproduction, and the Meaning of Liberty.* New York: Random House; also discussed in May, Elaine Tyler. 1995. *Barren in the Promised Land: Childless Americans and the Pursuit of Happiness.* Cambridge: Harvard University Press.

37. Kluchin, Rebecca M. 2009. *Fit to Be Tied: Sterilization and Reproductive Rights in America.* New Brunswick, NJ: Rutgers University Press, p. 99.

38. Kluchin, Rebecca M. 2009. *Fit to Be Tied: Sterilization and Reproductive Rights in America.* New Brunswick, NJ: Rutgers University Press.

39. May, Elaine Tyler. 1995. *Barren in the Promised Land: Childless Americans and the Pursuit of Happiness.* Cambridge: Harvard University Press.

40. Marks, Lara V. 2001. *Sexual Chemistry: A History of the Contraceptive Pill.* New Haven: Yale University Press.

41. Planned Parenthood Federation of America. 2015. *The Birth Control Pill: A History.* https://www.plannedparenthood.org/files/1514/3518/7100/Pill_History_FactSheet.pdf.

42. Hartmann, Betsy. 2016. *Reproductive Rights and Wrongs: The Global Politics of Population Control. 3rd edition.* Chicago: Haymarket Books.

43. Krase, Kathryn. 2014. "History of Forced Sterilization and Current U.S. Abuses." *Our Bodies, Ourselves website.* https://www.ourbodiesourselves.org/health-info/forced-sterilization/.

44. García, Ana María. 1982. *La operación.* Film.

45. Johnson, Corey G. 2013. "Female Inmates Sterilized in California Prisons without Approval." *Reveal*, July 7. https://www.revealnews.org/article/female-inmates -sterilized-in-california-prisons-without-approval/.

46. May, Elaine Tyler. 1995. *Barren in the Promised Land: Childless Americans and the Pursuit of Happiness*. Cambridge: Harvard University Press.

47. Hoover, J. Edgar. 1956. "The Twin Enemies of Freedom: Crime and Communism." Address before the 28th Annual Convention of the National Council of Catholic Women, Chicago, November 9. As quoted in May, Elaine Tyler. 1995. *Barren in the Promised Land: Childless Americans and the Pursuit of Happiness*. Cambridge: Harvard University Press.

48. Sterling, Evelina Weidman. 2013. *From No Hope to Fertile Dreams: Procreative Technologies, Popular Media, and the Culture of Infertility*. Doctoral dissertation, Georgia State University.

49. Marsh, Margaret, and Wanda Ronner. 1996. *The Empty Cradle: Infertility in America from Colonial Times to the Present*. Baltimore: Johns Hopkins University Press.

50. Rorvik, David. 1974. "The Embryo Sweepstakes." *New York Times*, September 15.

51. Greil, Arthur L. 1993. "Infertility: Social and Demographic Aspects." In *Encyclopedia of Childbearing: Critical Perspectives*, edited by Barbara Katz Rothman. Phoenix: Oryx Press, pp. 202–203.

52. https://www.sciencemuseum.org.uk/see-and-do/ivf-6-million-babies-later.

53. Haberman, Clyde. 2018. "Scientists Can Design 'Better' Babies. Should They?" *New York Times*, June 10.

54. Kanazawa, Satoshi. 2014. "Intelligence and Childlessness." *Social Science Research* 48: 157–170.

55. Peck, Ellen. 1971. *The Baby Trap*. New York: Pinnacle Books.

56. Healey, Jenna. 2016. "Rejecting Reproduction: The National Organization for Non-Parents and Childfree Activism in 1970s America." *Journal of Women's History* 28(1): 131–156.

57. Kluchin, Rebecca M. 2009. *Fit to Be Tied: Sterilization and Reproductive Rights in America*. New Brunswick, NJ: Rutgers University Press.

58. Healey, Jenna. 2016. "Rejecting Reproduction: The National Organization for Non-Parents and Childfree Activism in 1970s America." *Journal of Women's History* 28(1): 131–156.

59. Healey, Jenna. 2016. "Rejecting Reproduction: The National Organization for Non-Parents and Childfree Activism in 1970s America." *Journal of Women's History* 28(1): 131–156.

60. Gillespie, Rosemary. 2003. "Childfree and Feminine: Understanding the Gender

Identity of Voluntarily Childless Women." *Gender & Society* 17(1): 122–136; see also Campbell, Elaine. 1985. *The Childless Marriage: An Exploratory Study of Couples Who Do Not Want Children.* London: Tavistock; Weigle, Marta. 1982. *Spiders and Spinsters: Women and Mythology.* Albuquerque: University of New Mexico Press.

61. Dykstra, Pearl A., and Gunhild O. Hagestad. 2007. "Roads Less Taken: Developing a Nuanced View of Older Adults without Children." *Journal of Family Issues* 29(10): 1275–1310.

62. Bolick, Kate. 2015. *Spinster: Making a Life of One's Own.* New York: Crown Publishing; Traister, Rebecca. 2016. *All the Single Ladies: Unmarried Women and the Rise of an Independent Nation.* New York: Simon & Schuster.

63. Bartlett, Jane. 1996. *Will You Be Mother: Women Who Choose to Say No.* London: Virago Press; Campbell, Elaine. 1985. *The Childless Marriage: An Exploratory Study of Couples Who Do Not Want Children.* London: Tavistock; Gillespie, Rosemary. 2000. "When No Means No: Disbelief, Disregard, and Deviance as Discourses of Voluntary Childlessness." *Women's Studies International Forum* 23(2): 223–234; Ireland, Mardy S. 1993. *Reconceiving Women: Separating Motherhood from Female Identity.* New York: Guilford Press; McAllister, Fiona, with Lynda Clarke. 1998. *Choosing Childlessness.* London: Family Policy Studies Centre.

64. Friedan, Betty. 1963. *The Feminine Mystique.* New York: Norton.

65. May, Elaine Tyler. 1995. *Barren in the Promised Land: Childless Americans and the Pursuit of Happiness.* Cambridge: Harvard University Press.

66. National Center for Education Statistics. 1999. "Table 187: College Enrollment Rates of High School Graduates, by Sex: 1960 to 1998." *Digest of Education Statistics.* https://nces.ed.gov/programs/digest/d99/d99t187.asp.

67. http://history.house.gov/Exhibitions-and-Publications/WIC/Historical-Essays /Changing-Guard/Introduction/.

68. Faludi, Susan. 1991. *Backlash: The Undeclared War against American Women.* New York: Crown.

69. Van Assendelft, Laura A., and Jeffrey D. Schultz. 1999. *Encyclopedia of Women in American Politics.* Phoenix: Oryx Press; Republican Platform 2016. https://prod -cdn-static.gop.com/media/documents/DRAFT_12_FINAL[1]-ben_146887 2234.pdf.

70. McGinn, Daniel. 2006. "Marriage by the Numbers." *Newsweek*, June 4. http: //www.newsweek.com/marriage-numbers-110797.

71. United States Census Bureau. 2016. "Historical Table 1: Percent Childless and Births per 1,000 Women in the Last 12 Months: CPS, Selected Years, 1976–

2016." *Historical Time Series Tables.* https://www.census.gov/data/tables/time
-series/demo/fertility/his-cps.html#par_list.

72. Desilver, Drew. 2014. "Chart of the Week: The Great Baby Recession." *FactTank: News in the Numbers,* July 25. Pew Research Center. http://www.pewresearch.org /fact-tank/2014/07/25/chart-of-the-week-the-great-baby-recession/.

73. Patten, Eileen, and Gretchen Livingston. 2016. "Why Is the Teen Birth Rate Falling?" *FactTank: News in the Numbers,* April 29. Pew Research Center. http ://www.pewresearch.org/fact-tank/2016/04/29/why-is-the-teen-birth-rate -falling/.

74. Last, Jonathan V. 2013. "*Time* Magazine, 'The Childfree Life,' and Me." *The Weekly Standard,* August 9. http://www.weeklystandard.com/time-magazine-the -childfree-life-and-me/article/745867.

75. Coleman, David. 2013. Review of *What to Expect When No One's Expecting: America's Coming Demographic Disaster* by Jonathan V. Last. *Population and Development Review* 39(4): 711–714.

76. Aniston, Jennifer. 2016. "For the Record." *Huffington Post,* July 12. https ://www.huffingtonpost.com/entry/for-the-record_us_57855586e4b03fc3ee4e626f.

CHAPTER 2

1. Siegel, Harry. 2013. "Why the Choice to Be Childless Is Bad for America." *Newsweek,* February 19. http://www.newsweek.com/why-choice-be-childless-bad -america-63335.

2. Rhiannon, Lucy Cosslett, and Holly Baxter. 2013. "Why Is the Happily Childless Woman Seen as the Unicorn of Society?" *NewStatesman,* July 3. https://www .newstatesman.com/lifestyle/2013/07/why-happily-childless-woman-seen -unicorn-society.

3. National Center for Health Statistics. 2018. "Quarterly Provisional Estimates for Selected Birth Indicators, 2015–Quarter 4, 2017." Centers for Disease Control and Prevention. https://www.cdc.gov/nchs/nvss/vsrr/natality.htm.

4. Arnett, J. J. 2000. "Emerging Adulthood: A Theory of Development from the Late Teens through the Twenties." *American Psychologist* 55(5): 469–480.

5. Healey, Jenna. 2014. "Babies in Your 30s? Don't Worry, Your Great-Grandma Did It Too." *The Conversation,* December 19. https://theconversation.com/babies -in-your-30s-dont-worry-your-great-grandma-did-it-too-34273.

6. United States Census Bureau. 2017. *Historical Marriage Tables.* https://www .census.gov/data/tables/time-series/demo/families/marital.html.

7. Fry, Richard. 2016. "For First Time in Modern Era, Living with Parents Edges

Out Other Living Arrangements for 18- to 34-Year-Olds." *Social & Demographic Trends*, May 24. Pew Research Center. http://www.pewsocialtrends.org/2016/05/24/for-first-time-in-modern-era-living-with-parents-edges-out-other-living-arrangements-for-18-to-34-year-olds/.

8. Sullivan, Oriel, and Scott Coltrane. 2008. "Men's Changing Contribution to Housework and Childcare." *Brief Reports, Online Symposia*, April 25. Council on Contemporary Families. https://contemporaryfamilies.org/mens-changing-contribution-to-housework-and-childcare-brief-report/.

9. Livingston, Gretchen. 2011. "In a Down Economy, Fewer Births." *Social & Demographic Trends*, October 12. Pew Research Center. http://www.pewsocialtrends.org/2011/10/12/in-a-down-economy-fewer-births/.

10. Douthat, Ross. 2012. "More Babies, Please." *New York Times*, December 1. http://www.nytimes.com/2012/12/02/opinion/sunday/douthat-the-birthrate-and-americas-future.html?_r=0.

11. Trillingsgaard, Tea, and Diom Sommer. 2018. "Associations between Older Maternal Age, Use of Sanctions, and Children's Socio-Emotional Development through 7, 11, and 15 Years." *European Journal of Developmental Psychology* 15(2): 141–155.

12. Sun, Fangui et al. 2015. "Extended Maternal Age at Birth of Last Child and Women's Longevity in the Long Life Family Study." *Menopause* 22(1): 26–31.

13. Rackin, Heather M., and Christina M. Gibson-Davis. 2017. "Low-Income Childless Young Adults' Marriage and Fertility Frameworks." *Journal of Marriage and Family* 79: 1096–1110.

14. CDC National Center for Health Statistics. 2017. "Births: Final Data for 2015." *National Vital Statistics Reports* 66(1).

15. Patten, Eileen, and Gretchen Livingston. 2016. "Why Is the Teen Birth Rate Falling?" *FactTank: News in the Numbers*, April 29. Pew Research Center. http://www.pewresearch.org/fact-tank/2016/04/29/why-is-the-teen-birth-rate-falling/.

16. Livingston, Gretchen. 2011. "In a Down Economy, Fewer Births." *Social & Demographic Trends*, October 12. Pew Research Center. http://www.pewsocialtrends.org/2011/10/12/in-a-down-economy-fewer-births/.

17. Kearney, Melissa S., and Phillip B. Levine. 2015. "Media Influences on Social Outcomes: The Impact of MTV's *16 and Pregnant* on Teen Childbearing." Working Paper 19795, National Bureau of Economic Research. Cambridge, MA.

18. Patten, Eileen, and Gretchen Livingston. 2016. "Why Is the Teen Birth Rate Falling?" *FactTank: News in the Numbers*, April 29. Pew Research Center. http

://www.pewresearch.org/fact-tank/2016/04/29/why-is-the-teen-birth-rate
-falling/.

19. Stone, Lyman. 2018. "American Women Are Having Fewer Children than They'd Like." *New York Times, The Upshot,* February 13.

20. Rowland, Donald T. 2007. "Historical Trends in Childlessness." *Journal of Family Issues* 28(10): 1311–1337.

21. The World Bank. 2017. "Fertility Rate, Total (Births per Woman)." http://data .worldbank.org/indicator/SP.DYN.TFRT.IN?end=2015&locations= US&start=1972.

22. Steed, Charley. 2018. "UNO Report: U.S. Fertility Rates Fall to New Lows, NE Rates Remain Relatively High." University of Nebraska, Omaha. https://www .unomaha.edu/news/2015/01/fertility.php.

23. Jones, Jo. 2008. *Adoption Experiences of Women and Men and Demand for Children to Adopt by Women 18–44 Years of Age in the United States, 2002.* Vital Statistics Series 23, Number 27. Hyattsville, MD: National Center for Health Statistics.

24. "A Portrait of Stepfamilies." 2011. *Social & Demographic Trends,* January 13. Pew Research Center. http://www.pewsocialtrends.org/2011/01/13/a-portrait-of-step families/#fn-6955-1.

25. Clarke, Victoria, Nikki Hayfield, Sonja Ellis, and Gareth Terry. Forthcoming. "Lived Experiences of Childfree Lesbians in the UK: A Qualitative Exploration." *Journal of Family Issues.*

26. Dye, Jane Lawler. 2008. "Fertility of American Women: 2006." Washington, DC: U.S. Census Bureau.

27. Dye, Jane Lawler. 2008. "Fertility of American Women: 2006." Washington, DC: U.S. Census Bureau; Osborne, Ruth S. 2003. *"Percentage of Childless Women 40 to 44 Years Old Increases Since 1976, Census Bureau Reports."* U.S. Census Bureau Press Release.

28. Biddlecom, Ann, and Steven Martin. 2006. "Childless in America." *Contexts* 5: 54; Paul, Pamela. 2001. "Childless by Choice." *American Demographics* 23: 45–50.

29. Though some research indicates that about half of women without children have made the choice not to have kids, while the other half are involuntarily childless.

30. Biddlecom, Ann, and Steven Martin. 2006. "Childless in America." *Contexts* 5: 54; Crispell, Diane. 1993. "Planning No Family, Now or Ever." *American Demographics* 15: 23–24.

31. DeOllos, Ione Y., and Carolyn A. Kapinus. 2002. "Aging Childless Individuals and Couples: Suggestions for New Directions in Research." *Sociological Inquiry* 72:

72–80; Woodfull, Lucy. 2015. "If You Wanted to Use the Sidewalk, You Should Have Had Two Babies Like Me." *Reductress* 19(1): Oct 1.

32. Agrillo, Christian, and Cristian Nelini. 2008. "Childfree by Choice: A Review." *Journal of Cultural Geography* 25: 347–363; Baber, Kristine M., and Albert S. Dreyer. 1986. "Gender-Role Orientations in Older Child-Free and Expectant Couples." *Sex Roles* 14: 501–512; Houseknecht, Sharon K. 1987. "Voluntary Childlessness." In *Handbook of Marriage and Family*, edited by Marvin B. Sussman and Suzanne K. Steinmetz. New York: Plenum Press; Heaton, Tim B., Cardell K. Jacobson, and Xuan Ning Fu. 1992. "Religiosity of Married Couples and Childlessness." *Review of Religious Research* 33: 244–255.

33. Hunt, Mary K. 2015. "On the Childfree, Religion, and Stigma Consciousness." Sociology Honors College Thesis, University of Maine.

34. Lipka, Michael. 2016. "10 Facts about Atheists." *FactTank: News in the Numbers*, June 1. Pew Research Center. http://www.pewresearch.org/fact-tank/2016/06/01/10-facts-about-atheists/.

35. "Americans Express Increasingly Warm Feelings toward Religious Groups." 2017. *Religion & Public Life*, February 15. Pew Research Center. http://www.pewforum.org/2017/02/15/americans-express-increasingly-warm-feelings-toward-religious-groups/?utm_content=buffer210e3&utm_medium=social&utm_source=twitter.com&utm_campaign=buffer#views-of-religious-groups-vary-widely-by-religious-affiliation-partisanship.

36. U.S. Department of Agriculture. 2014. "Parents Projected to Spend $245,340 to Raise a Child Born in 2013, according to USDA Report." https://www.usda.gov/media/press-releases/2014/08/18/parents-projected-spend-245340-raise-child-born-2013-according-usda.

37. Blackstone, Amy, and Mahala Stewart. 2016. "'There's More Thinking to Decide': How the Childfree Decide Not to Parent." *The Family Journal* 24(3): 296–303.

38. Lunneborg, Patricia. 1999. *Chosen Lives of Childfree Men*. Westport, CT: Bergin & Garvey.

39. Gerson, Kathleen. 1994. *No Man's Land: Men's Changing Commitments to Family and Work*. New York: Basic Books.

40. Livingston, Gretchen. 2015. "Childlessness Falls, Family Size Grows among Highly Educated Women." *Social & Demographic Trends*, May 7. Pew Research Center.

41. Russo, Nancy Felipe. 1976. "The Motherhood Mandate." *Journal of Social Issues*, 32 (3): 143–153.

42. Sandler, Lauren. 2013. *One and Only: The Freedom of Having an Only Child, and the Joy of Being One*. New York: Simon & Schuster.

43. Gao, George. 2015. "Americans' Ideal Family Size Is Smaller than It Used to Be." *FactTank: News in the Numbers*, May 8. Pew Research Center. http ://www.pewresearch.org/fact-tank/2015/05/08/ideal-size-of-the-american -family/.

44. Dally, Ann. 1983. *Inventing Motherhood: The Consequences of an Ideal*. New York: Schocken.

45. Roth-Johnson, Danielle. 2010. "Environments and Mothering." In *Encyclopedia of Motherhood*, edited by Andrea O'Reilly. Thousand Oaks: Sage.

46. May, Elaine Tyler. 1995. *Barren in the Promised Land: Childless Americans and the Pursuit of Happiness*. Cambridge: Harvard University Press.

47. Wolf, Joan B. 2007. "Is Breast Really Best? Risk and Total Motherhood in the National Breastfeeding Awareness Campaign." *Journal of Health Politics, Policy and Law* 32(4): 595–636; Trevino, Marcella Bush. 2010. "History of Motherhood: 1000 to 1500." In *Encyclopedia of Motherhood*, edited by Andrea O'Reilly. Thousand Oaks: Sage.

48. Wolf, Joan B. 2007. "Is Breast Really Best? Risk and Total Motherhood in the National Breastfeeding Awareness Campaign." *Journal of Health Politics, Policy and Law* 32(4): 595–636.

49. I explore this idea further in chapter 3.

50. Shapiro, Gilla. 2014. "Voluntary Childlessness: A Critical Review of the Literature." *Studies in the Maternal* 6 (1): 1–15.

51. Peck, Ellen, and Judith Senderowitz, eds. 1974. *Pronatalism: The Myth of Mom & Apple Pie*. New York: Crowell; May, Elaine Tyler. 1995. *Barren in the Promised Land: Childless Americans and the Pursuit of Happiness*. Cambridge: Harvard University Press; Carroll, Laura. 2012. *The Baby Matrix*. LiveTrue Books.

52. Holton, Sara, Jane Fisher, and Heather Rowe. 2009. "Attitudes toward Women and Motherhood: Their Role in Australian Women's Childbearing Behaviour." *Sex Roles* 61: 677–687.

53. United Nations. 2011. "World Fertility Policies 2011." UN.org. Retrieved December 15, 2012. http://www.un.org/esa/population/publications/worldfertilitypolicies 2011/wfpolicies2011.html.

54. For example, see Bahrampour, Tara. 2012. "U.S. Birthrate Plummets to Its Lowest Level since 1920." *Washington Post*, November 29. Retrieved December 17, 2012. http://articles.washingtonpost.com/2012–11–29/local/35585758_1_birthrate -immigrant-women-population-growth; Matthews, Steve. 2012. "Americans

Having Fewer Babies Crimping Consumer Spending." *Bloomberg Business Week,* August 21. Retrieved December 17, 2012. http://www.businessweek.com /news/2012–08–21/americans-having-fewer-babies-crimping-consumer -spending; Sanburn, Josh. 2012. "Why the Falling U.S. Birth Rates Are So Troubling." *Time,* October 4. Retrieved December 17, 2012. http://business .time.com/2012/10/04/why-the-falling-u-s-birth-rates-are-so-troubling/.

55. King, Leslie. 2002. "Demographic Trends, Pronatalism, and Nationalist Ideologies in the Late Twentieth Century." *Ethnic and Racial Studies* 25(3): 367–389.

56. Hong Fincher, Leta. 2018. "China Dropped Its One-Child Policy. So Why Aren't Chinese Women Having More Babies?" *New York Times,* February 20; see also Hong Fincher, Leta. 2016. *Leftover Women: The Resurgence of Gender Inequality in China.* London: Zed Books.

57. Kurdi, Edina. 2014. "Women's Non-Parenting Intentions in Contemporary UK." Presented at the British Sociological Association annual conference at University of Leeds, April 23–25.

58. Trueman, Tony. 2014. "Many Couples Need Just One Conversation to Decide Not to Have Children." Press Release from the British Sociological Association, April 25.

59. Though the exact origins of the term *childfree* are uncertain, it is possible that the National Organization for Non-Parents (NON), founded by Ellen Peck and Shirley Radl in 1972, was among the first to use it.

60. Morell, Carolyn Mackelcan. 1994. *Unwomanly Conduct: The Challenges of Intentional Childlessness.* New York: Routledge.

61. Daum, Meghan. 2016. *Selfish, Shallow, and Self-Absorbed: Sixteen Writers on the Decision Not to Have Kids.* New York: Picador.

62. McQuillan, Julia et al. 2012. "Does the Reason Matter? Variations in Childlessness Concerns among U.S. Women." *Journal of Marriage and Family* 74(5): 1166–1181.

63. It is worth noting that the article itself was an empathetic and smart exploration of the childfree experience. In our interview with its author, Lauren Sandler, for our blog, Lance and I learned that neither the cover nor the title was chosen by Sandler herself.

64. May, Elaine Tyler. 1995. *Barren in the Promised Land: Childless Americans and the Pursuit of Happiness.* Cambridge: Harvard University Press, pp. 208–209.

CHAPTER 3

1. Douthat, Ross. 2012. "More Babies, Please." *New York Times,* December 1.

http://www.nytimes.com/2012/12/02/opinion/sunday/douthat-the-birthrate-and
-americas-future.html.

2. Blackstone, Amy. 2012. "Childless and Loving It: Not Being a Parent Has Advantages for Families and Kids." *Bangor Daily News*, July 11.

3. Ashburn-Nardo, Leslie. 2017. "Parenthood as a Moral Imperative? Moral Outrage and the Stigmatization of Voluntarily Childfree Women and Men." *Sex Roles* 76(5–6): 393–401.

4. Caron, Sandra, and Ruth L. Wynn. 1992. "The Intent to Parent among Young, Unmarried College Graduates." *Families in Society* 73: 480–487.

5. Edin, Kathryn, and Maria Kefalas. 2011. *Promises I Can Keep: Why Poor Women Put Motherhood before Marriage*. Berkeley: University of California Press.

6. Gerson, Kathleen. 1994. *No Man's Land: Men's Changing Commitments to Family and Work*. New York: Basic Books.

7. Livingston, Gretchen, and D'Vera Cohn. 2010. "The New Demography of American Motherhood." *Social & Demographic Trends*, May 6. Pew Research Center.

8. Blackstone, Amy, and Mahala Stewart. 2012. "Choosing to Be Childfree: Research on the Decision Not to Parent." *Sociology Compass* 6(9): 718–727.

9. McMichael, Anthony J. 2002. "Population, Environment, Disease, and Survival: Past Patterns, Uncertain Futures." *Public Health* 359: 1145–1148.

10. Dunlap, Riley E., and Andrew K. Jorgenson. 2012. "Environmental Problems." In *The Wiley-Blackwell Encyclopedia of Globalization*, first edition, edited by George Ritzer. Blackwell Publishing.

11. Jorgenson, Andrew K., and Brett Clark. 2009. "The Economy, Military, and Ecologically Unequal Exchange Relationships in Comparative Perspective: A Panel Study of the Ecological Footprints of Nations, 1975–2000." *Social Problems* 56(4): 621–646.

12. Reed, Robert. 2012. *Challenging Stereotypes of the Childless in Pronatalist Society*. Doctoral Dissertation, Texas Woman's University.

13. Blume, Lesley M. M. 2018. "Sarah Paulson's American Success Story." *Town & Country*, January 2. http://www.townandcountrymag.com/leisure/arts-and-culture/a14426831/sarah-paulson-interview-the-post/.

14. Hunt, Mary K. 2015. *On the Childfree, Religion, and Stigma Consciousness*. Sociology Honors College Thesis, University of Maine.

15. Department of Labor Statistics. 2016. "Volunteering in the United States, 2015." United States Department of Labor. https://www.bls.gov/news.release/volun.nr0.htm.

16. Haskell, Meg. 2017. "Why Some Mainers Choose to Be Child-Free." *Bangor*

Daily News, March 31. https://bangordailynews.com/2017/03/30/next/why-some -mainers-choose-to-be-child-free/?ref=moreInstate.

17. Wenger, Clare G., Pearl A. Dykstra, Tuula Melkas, and Kees C. P. M. Knip-scheer. 2007. "Social Embeddedness and Late-Life Parenthood: Community Activity, Close Ties, and Support Networks." *Journal of Family Issues* 28(11): 1419–1456.

18. Albertini, Marco, and Martin Kohli. 2009. "What Childless Older People Give: Is the Generational Link Broken?" *Ageing & Society* 29(8): 1261–1274.

19. Thomas, Patricia A. 2011. "Trajectories of Social Engagement and Limitations in Late Life." *Journal of Health and Social Behavior* 52(4): 430–443.

20. McMullin, Julie Ann, and Victor W. Marshall. 1996. "Friends, Family, Stress, and Well-Being: Does Childlessness Make a Difference?" *Canadian Journal on Aging* 15(3): 355–373.

21. DeVries Global. 2014. "Shades of Otherhood: Marketing to Women without Children." White paper. http://savvyauntie.com/customimages/shadesofotherhood _WHITE%20PAPER_42914.pdf.

22. Shandwick, Weber, and Savvy Auntie. 2012. *Digital Women Influencers Study: The Power of PANK, Engaging New Digital Influencers.* https://www.webershandwick .com/uploads/news/files/2012_PANKs_ExecutiveSummary.pdf.

23. Daum, Meghan. 2016. *Selfish, Shallow, and Self-Absorbed: Sixteen Writers on the Decision Not to Have Kids.* New York: Picador.

24. Daum, Meghan. 2014. "Difference Maker: The Childless, the Parentless, and the Central Sadness." *The New Yorker*, September 29. http://www.newyorker.com /magazine/2014/09/29/difference-maker.

25. https://www.youtube.com/watch?v=HB3xM93rXbY.

26. Hays, Sharon. 1998. *The Cultural Contradictions of Motherhood.* New Haven: Yale University Press.

27. Sullivan, Oriel, and Scott Coltrane. 2008. "Men's Changing Contribution to Housework and Childcare." *Brief Reports, Online Symposia*, April 25. Council on Contemporary Families. https://contemporaryfamilies.org/mens-changing-contri bution-to-housework-and-childcare-brief-report/.

28. Adecco. 2014. *Adecco Way to Work Survey: Attitudes and Perceptions of American Youth.* https://www.adeccousa.com/about-adecco-staffing/newsroom/press-releases /way-to-work-attitude-perception-2014/.

29. http://rh-us.mediaroom.com/2016–08–16-Mom-To-Employer-Do-You-Mind -If-I-Sit-In-On-My-Sons-Interview.

30. Rizzo, Kathryn M., Holly H. Schiffrin, and Miriam Liss. 2013. "Insight into the

Parenthood Paradox: Mental Health Outcomes of Intensive Mothering." *Journal of Child and Family Studies* 22(5): 614–620.

31. Experts Respond to "Men's Changing Contributions to Housework and Childcare." https://contemporaryfamilies.org/mens-changing-contributions-to-household-childcare-commentaries/.

32. Sandler, Lauren. 2013. *One and Only: The Freedom of Having an Only Child, and the Joy of Being One.* New York: Simon & Schuster.

33. Sandler, Lauren. 2013. "The Childfree Life." *Time*, August 12. http://content.time.com/time/subscriber/article/0,33009,2148636,00.html.

34. http://werenothavingababy.com/childfree/lauren-sandler-interview/.

35. http://www.pewresearch.org/fact-tank/2015/05/08/ideal-size-of-the-american-family/.

36. Mueller, Karla A., and Janice D. Yoder. 1999. "Stigmatization of Non-Normative Family Size Status." *Sex Roles* 41(11/12): 901–919.

37. LeMoyne, Terri, and Tom Buchanan. 2011. "Does 'Hovering' Matter? Helicopter Parenting and Its Effect on Well-Being." *Sociological Spectrum* 31(4): 399–418.

38. Burkett, Elinor. 2002. *The Baby Boon: How Family-Friendly America Cheats the Childless.* New York: Free Press.

39. Fuller, Sylvia, and Lynn Prince Cooke. 2018. "Workplace Variation in Fatherhood Wage Premiums: Do Formalization and Performance Matter?" *Work, Employment, and Society.* DOI: http://dx.doi.org/10.1177/0950017018764534.

40. Budig, Michelle J. 2014. *The Fatherhood Bonus and the Motherhood Penalty: Parenthood and the Gender Gap in Pay.* Washington, DC: Third Way; see also Kleven, Henrik, Camille Landais, and Jakob Egholt Sogaard. 2018. "Children and Gender Inequality: Evidence from Denmark." National Bureau of Economic Research Working Paper No. 24219.

41. Hochschild, Arlie, and Anne Machung. 2012. *The Second Shift: Working Families and the Revolution at Home.* New York: Penguin.

42. Correll, Shelly, Stephen Benard, and In Paik. 2007. "Getting a Job: Is There a Motherhood Penalty?" *American Journal of Sociology* 112(5): 1297–1339; see also Budig, Michelle. 2014. *The Fatherhood Bonus and the Motherhood Penalty: Parenthood and the Gender Gap in Pay.* Washington, DC: Third Way.

43. Bush, Michael C., and The Great Place to Work Research Team. 2018. *A Great Place to Work for All: Better for Business, Better for People, Better for the World.* Oakland, CA: Berret-Koehler Publishers.

44. http://www.huffingtonpost.com/2012/08/24/maternal-mortality-rate-infographic_n_1827427.html.

45. https://www.nichd.nih.gov/health/topics/preeclampsia/conditioninfo/risk.

46. Kneer, Lee, Ethan Colliver, Man Hung, Michelle Pepper, and Stuart Willick. 2010. "Epidemiology of Roller Derby Injuries." *Medicine & Science in Sports & Exercise* 42(5): 474.

47. Haar, Jarrod M. 2013. "Testing a New Measure of Work-Life Balance: A Study of Parent and Non-Parent Employees from New Zealand." *The International Journal of Human Resource Management* 24(17): 3305–3324.

48. Keeney, Jessica, Elizabeth M. Boyd, Ruchi Sinha, Alyssa F. Westring, and Ann Marie Ryan. 2013. "From 'Work-Family' to 'Work-Life': Broadening Our Conceptualization and Measurement." *Journal of Vocational Behavior* 82(3): 221–237.

49. Gallup. 2013. "State of the American Workplace." Report.

50. Slaughter, Anne-Marie. 2015. *Unfinished Business: Women, Men, Work, Family.* New York: Random House.

51. While parental status is not a protected class, pregnant women are protected from discrimination.

52. Flynn, Gillian. 1996. "Backlash: Why Single Employees Are Angry." *Personnel Journal* 75(9): September issue.

53. O'Connor, Lindsey Trimble, and Erin A. Cech. 2018. "Not Just a Mothers' Problem: The Consequences of Perceived Workplace Flexibility Bias for All Workers." *Sociological Perspectives Online*, April 13.

54. Kane, Rosalie A. 1996. "Toward Understanding Legacy: A Wish List." *Generations* 20(3): 5–9.

55. https://www.thenotmom.com/faq.

56. http://www.owla.co.za.

57. www.demandabolition.org.

58. http://www.ellentv.com/tags/EllensOrganizations/.

59. http://www.ellentv.com/kids/.

60. http://yum-o.org/.

61. Hitchens, Christopher. 1995. *The Missionary Position: Mother Teresa in Theory and Practice.* London: Verso.

62. https://www.nunsonthebusmovie.com/.

63. Rubenstein, Robert L. 1996. "Childlessness, Legacy, and Generativity." *Generations* 20(3): 58–60.

64. Maslow, Abraham H. 1943. "A Theory of Human Motivation." *Psychology Review* 50(4): 370–396.

65. Kirnan, Jean Powell, Julie Ann Alfieri, Jennifer DeNicolis Bragger, and Robert Sean Harris. 2009. "An Investigation of Stereotype Threat in Employment Tests."

Journal of Applied Social Psychology 39(2): 359–388; Wout, Daryl A., Margaret J. Shih, James S. Jackson, and Robert M. Sellers. 2009. "Targets as Perceivers: How People Determine When They Will Be Negatively Stereotyped." *Journal of Personality and Social Psychology* 96(2): 349–362; Rydell, Robert J., Allen R. McConnell, and Sian L. Beilock. 2009. "Multiple Social Identities and Stereotype Threat: Imbalance, Accessibility, and Working Memory." *Journal of Personality and Social Psychology* 96(5): 949–966.

66. Ganong, Lawrence H., Marilyn Coleman, and Dennis Mapes. 1990. "A Meta-Analytic Review of Family Structure Stereotypes." *Journal of Marriage and Family* 52(2): 287–297.

67. Pierce, C., J. Carew, D. Pierce-Gonzalez, D. Willis. 1978. "An Experiment in Racism: TV Commercials." In *Television and Education*, edited by C. Pierce. Beverly Hills: Sage, pp. 62–88.

68. Sue, Derald Wing. 2010. *Microaggressions in Everyday Life: Race, Gender, and Sexual Orientation*. Hoboken, NJ: Wiley.

CHAPTER 4

1. Shapiro, Gilla. 2014. "Voluntary Childlessness: A Critical Review of the Literature." *Studies in the Maternal* 6(1): 1–15.

2. Morell, Carolyn Mackelcan. 1994. *Unwomanly Conduct: The Challenges of Intentional Childlessness*. New York: Routledge.

3. Peck, Ellen. 1971. *The Baby Trap*. New York: Pinnacle Books.

4. Peck, Ellen, and Judith Senderowitz, eds. 1974. *Pronatalism: The Myth of Mom & Apple Pie*. New York: Crowell.

5. Blake, Judith. 1974. "Coercive Pronatalism and American Population Policy." *Pronatalism: The Myth of Mom & Apple Pie*, edited by Ellen Peck and Judith Senderowitz. New York: Crowell, pp. 29–67.

6. Vicedo-Castello, Maria Margarita. 2005. *The Maternal Instinct: Mother Love and the Search for Human Nature*. Doctoral Dissertation, Department for the History of Science, Harvard University, Cambridge, MA.

7. O'Reilly, Andrea. 2010. *Encyclopedia of Motherhood*. Los Angeles: Sage.

8. Livingston, Gretchen. 2015. "Childlessness Falls, Family Size Grows among Highly Educated Women." *Social & Demographic Trends*, May 7. Pew Research Center.

9. Badinter, Elisabeth. 1981. *Mother Love: Myth and Reality: Motherhood in Modern History*. New York: Macmillan; Dally, Ann. 1983. *Inventing Motherhood: The Consequences of an Ideal*. New York: Schocken Books; Roth-Johnson, Danielle. 2010.

"Environments and Mothering." In *Encyclopedia of Motherhood*, edited by Andrea O'Reilly. Los Angeles: Sage.

10. Edmond, Yanique, Suzanne Randolph, and Guylaine Richard. 2007. "The Lakou System: A Cultural, Ecological Analysis of Mothering in Rural Haiti." *The Journal of Pan African Studies* 2(1): 19–32.

11. Lieblich, Amia. 2010. "A Century of Childhood, Parenting, and Family Life in the Kibbutz." *The Journal of Israeli History* 29(1): 1–24.

12. Pinker, Steven. 2002. *The Blank Slate: The Modern Denial of Human Nature*. New York: Penguin.

13. Hollingsworth, Leta S. 1916. "Social Devices for Impelling Women to Bear and Rear Children." *American Journal of Sociology* 22(1): 19–29.

14. Leyser, Ophra. 2010. "Infertility." In *Encyclopedia of Motherhood*, edited by Andrea O'Reilly. Los Angeles: Sage.

15. Blakemore, Judith E. Owen, and Renee E. Centers. 2005. "Characteristics of Boys' and Girls' Toys." *Sex Roles* 53(9/10): 619–633; see also "Who's in the Picture? Gender Stereotypes and Toy Catalogues." 2017. A report by Let Toys Be Toys.

16. Martin, Carol Lynn. 1990. "Attitudes and Expectations about Children with Nontraditional and Traditional Gender Roles." *Sex Roles* 22(3/4): 151–166.

17. Ruddick, Sara. 1995. *Maternal Thinking: Toward a Politics of Peace*. Boston: Beacon Press; see also Kinser, Amber E. 2010. "Feminist Theory and Mothering." In *Encyclopedia of Motherhood*, edited by Andrea O'Reilly. Los Angeles: Sage.

18. Cain, Madelyn. 2001. *The Childless Revolution*. New York: Perseus; Casey, Terri. 1998. *Pride and Joy: The Lives and Passions of Women without Children*. Hillsboro: Beyond Words Publishing; Gandolfo, Enza. 2005. "A Less Woman? Fictional Representations of the Childless Woman." In *Motherhood: Power and Oppression*, edited by Andrea O'Reilly, Marie Porter, and Patricia Short. Toronto: Women's Press; Lisle, Laurie. 1999. *Without Child: Challenging the Stigma of Childlessness*. New York: Routledge; Morell, Carolyn Mackelcan. 1994. *Unwomanly Conduct: The Challenges of Intentional Childlessness*. New York: Routledge.

19. Chodorow, Nancy J. 1978. *The Reproduction of Mothering: Psychoanalysis and the Sociology of Gender*. Berkeley: University of California Press.

20. Badinter, Elisabeth. 1981. *Mother Love: Myth and Reality: Motherhood in Modern History*. New York: Macmillan.

21. Nicolson, Paula. 1999. "The Myth of Maternal Instinct: Feminism, Evolution and the Case of Postnatal Depression." *Psychology, Evolution & Gender* 1(2): 161–181; Blackstone, Amy. 2017. "There Is No Maternal Instinct." *Huffington Post*, May 10.

22. Keyes, Destiny. 2017. "I Don't Want Kids and That Doesn't Make Me Less of a Woman." *Odyssey*, January 9.

23. Williams, Mary Elizabeth. 2015. "Kim Cattrall Is Right about Childless Women: 'It Sounds Like You're Less, Because You Haven't Had a Child.'" *Salon*, September 16.

24. Oja, Tanya Elise. 2008. *Considering Childlessness: An Argument for the Extrication of Childbearing and Motherhood from the Concept of Womanhood.* Master's Thesis, Queen's University, Kingston, Ontario.

25. Rich, Adrienne. 1978. "Motherhood: The Contemporary Emergency and the Quantum Leap." Reprinted in Rich, Adrienne. 1980. *On Lies, Secrets, and Silence.* London: Virago.

26. https://www.lauracarroll.com/qa-with-kimya-dennis-on-her-childfree -research/.

27. Mezey, Nancy J. 2008. *New Choices, New Families: How Lesbians Decide about Motherhood.* Baltimore: Johns Hopkins University Press.

28. Mezey, Nancy J. 2013. "How Lesbians and Gay Men Decide to Become Parents or Remain Childfree." *LGBT-Parent Families: Innovations in Research and Implications for Practice*, edited by Abbie E. Goldberg and Katherine R. Allen. New York: Springer, pp. 59–70.

29. Berkowitz, Dana, and William Marsiglio. 2007. "Gay Men: Negotiating Procreative, Father, and Family Identities." *Journal of Marriage and Family* 69(2): 366–381; Gato, Jorge, Sara Santos, and Anne-Marie Fontaine. 2017. "To Have or Not to Have Children? That Is the Question. Factors Influencing Parental Decisions among Lesbians and Gay Men." *Sexuality Research and Social Policy* 14: 310–323; Riskind, Rachel G., Charlotte J. Patterson, and Brian A. Nosek. 2013. "Childless Lesbian and Gay Adults' Self-Efficacy about Achieving Parenthood." *Couple and Family Psychology: Research and Practice* 2(3): 222–235.

30. http://www.nytimes.com/2012/08/10/us/gay-couples-face-pressure-to-have -children.html.

31. Attridge, Nicole. 2018. *Inconceivable: An Exploratory Study of South African Childfree Lesbian Couples.* Master's Thesis in Psychology, Stellenbosch University, South Africa.

32. Clarke, Victoria, Nikki Hayfield, Sonja Ellis, and Gareth Terry. Forthcoming. "Lived Experiences of Childfree Lesbians in the UK: A Qualitative Exploration." *Journal of Family Issues*.

33. Gates, Gary J., M. V. Lee Badgett, Jennifer Ehrle Macomber, and Kay Chambers.

2007. *Adoption and Foster Care by Gay and Lesbian Parents in the United States.* Washington, DC: The Urban Institute.

34. McCabe, Katherine, and J. E. Sumerau. 2018. "Reproductive Vocabularies: Interrogating Intersections of Reproduction, Sexualities, and Religion among U.S. Cisgender College Women." *Sex Roles* 78: 352–366.

35. Kazyak, Emily, Nicholas Park, Julia McQuillan, and Arthur L. Greil. 2016. "Attitudes toward Motherhood among Sexual Minority Women in the United States." *Journal of Family Issues* 37(13): 1771–1796.

36. Sullivan, Oriel, and Scott Coltrane. 2008. "Men's Changing Contribution to Housework and Childcare." *Brief Reports, Online Symposia*, April 25. Council on Contemporary Families. https://contemporaryfamilies.org/mens-changing-contri bution-to-housework-and-childcare-brief-report/.

37. Hochschild, Arlie, with Anne Machung. 1989. *The Second Shift: Working Parents and the Revolution at Home.* New York: Viking.

38. http://www.nytimes.com/1989/06/25/books/she-minds-the-child-he-minds -the-dog.html?pagewanted=all.

39. https://www.bls.gov/tus/tables/a6_1115.pdf; see also Parker, Kim, and Wendy Wang. 2013. "Modern Parenthood." *Social & Demographic Trends*, March 14. Pew Research Center.

40. http://www.asanet.org/press-center/press-releases/americans-think-sex-should -determine-chores-straight-couples-masculinity-and-femininity-same-sex.

41. Cowan, Carolyn Pape et al. 1985. "Transitions to Parenthood: His, Hers, and Theirs." *Journal of Family Issues* 6(4): 451–481.

42. Faludi, Susan. 1991. *Backlash: The Undeclared War against American Women.* New York: Crown; Hays, Sharon. 1998. *The Cultural Contradictions of Motherhood.* New Haven: Yale University Press; see also Green, Fiona Joy. 2010. "Intensive Mothering," in *Encyclopedia of Motherhood*, edited by Andrea O'Reilly. Los Angeles: Sage.

43. Sullivan, Oriel, and Scott Coltrane. 2008. "Men's Changing Contribution to Housework and Childcare." *Brief Reports, Online Symposia*, April 25. Council on Contemporary Families. https://contemporaryfamilies.org/mens-changing-contri bution-to-housework-and-childcare-brief-report/.

44. McLanahan, Sara, and Julia Adams. 1989. "The Effects of Children on Adults' Psychological Well-Being: 1957–1976." *Social Forces* 68(1): 124–146.

45. Hird, Myra J. 2003. "Vacant Wombs: Feminist Challenges to Psychoanalytic Theories of Childless Women." *Feminist Review* 75(1): 5–19.

46. Gillespie, Rosemary. 2003. "Childfree and Feminine: Understanding the Gender Identity of Voluntarily Childless Women." *Gender & Society* 17(1): 122–136.

47. https://www.dailymail.co.uk/news/article-3590832/I-never-wanted-baby-Yesterday-dream-came-true-NHS-sterilised-hell-trolls.html.

48. http://www.nzherald.co.nz/lifestyle/news/article.cfm?c_id=6&objectid=11639668.

49. May, Elaine Tyler. 1995. *Barren in the Promised Land: Childless Americans and the Pursuit of Happiness*. Cambridge: Harvard University Press.

50. http://www.chicagotribune.com/sns-health-men-choosing-vasectomies-story.html.

51. Terry, Gareth, and Virginia Braun. 2012. "Sticking My Finger Up at Evolution: Unconventionality, Selfishness, and Choice in the Talk of Men Who Have Had 'Preemptive' Vasectomies." *Men and Masculinities* 15(3): 207–229.

52. Wetherell, Margaret, and Nigel Edley. 1999. "Negotiating Hegemonic Masculinity: Imaginary Positions and Psycho-Discursive Practices." *Feminism & Psychology* 9(3): 335–356.

53. Terry, Gareth, and Virginia Braun. 2011. "'It's Kind of Me Taking Responsibility for These Things': Men, Vasectomy, and 'Contraceptive Economies.'" *Feminism & Psychology* 21(4): 477–495.

54. Bertotti, Andrea M. 2013. "Gendered Divisions of Fertility Work: Socioeconomic Predictors of Female Versus Male Sterilization." *Journal of Marriage and Family*. 75(1): 13–25.

55. https://childfreeafrican.com/about/.

56. Rubin, Susan E., Giselle Campos, and Susan Markens. 2012. "Primary Care Physicians' Concerns May Affect Adolescents' Access to Intrauterine Contraception." *Journal of Primary Care & Community Health* 4(3): 216–219.

57. Avison, Margaret, and Adrian Furnham. 2015. "Personality and Voluntary Childlessness." *Journal of Population Research* 32(1): 45–67; Newton, Nicky J., and Abigail J. Stewart. 2013. "The Road Not Taken: Women's Life Paths and Gender-Linked Personality Traits." *Journal of Research in Personality* 47(4): 306–316.

58. Callan, Victor J. 1986. "Single Women, Voluntary Childlessness and Perceptions about Life and Marriage." *Journal of Biosocial Science* 18(4): 479–487.

59. Bram, Susan. 1984. "Voluntarily Childless Women: Traditional or Nontraditional?" *Sex Roles* 10(3–4): 195–206.

60. McAllister, Fiona, with Lynda Clarke. 1998. *Choosing Childlessness*. London: Family Policy Studies Centre.

61. Graham, Melissa, Erin Hill, Julia Shelly, and Ann Taket. 2013. "Why Are

Childless Women Childless? Findings from an Exploratory Study in Victoria, Australia." *Journal of Social Exclusion* 4(1): 70–89; Holton, Sara, Jane Fisher, and Heather Rowe. 2009. "Attitudes toward Women and Motherhood: Their Role in Australian Women's Childbearing Behavior." *Sex Roles* 61(9–10): 677–687.

CHAPTER 5

1. Coontz, Stephanie. 1992. *The Way We Never Were: American Families and the Nostalgia Trap*. New York: Basic Books.

2. https://www.census.gov/prod/2013pubs/p20–570.pdf.

3. U.S. Census. 2012.

4. Weston, Kath. 1991. *Families We Choose: Lesbians, Gays, Kinship*. New York: Columbia University Press; Powell, Brian, Catherine Bolzendahl, Claudia Geist, and Lala Carr Steelman. 2010. *Counted Out: Same-Sex Relations and Americans' Definitions of Family*. New York: Russell Sage Foundation.

5. Indeed, sociologist Brian Powell and colleagues found in 2010 that Americans believe parenthood is the most important factor in determining what counts as family.

6. Oswald, Ramona Faith, Libby Balter Blume, and Stephen R. Marks. 2005. "Decentering Heteronormativity: A Model for Family Studies." *Sourcebook of Family Theory and Research*, edited by Vern L. Bengtson, Alan C. Acock, Katherine R. Allen, Peggy Dilworth-Anderson, and David M. Klein. Thousand Oaks, CA: Sage, pp. 143–154.

7. May, Elaine Tyler. 1997. *Barren in the Promised Land: Childless Americans and the Pursuit of Happiness*. Cambridge: Harvard University Press; Russo, Nancy Felipe. 1979. "Overview: Sex Roles, Fertility and the Motherhood Mandate." *Psychology of Women Quarterly* 4: 7–15; Veevers, Jean E. 1974. "Voluntary Childlessness and Social Policy: An Alternative View." *The Family Coordinator* 23: 397–406.

8. Henslin, James M. 2010. *Sociology: A Down-to-Earth Approach, Core Concepts*. 4th edition. Boston: Pearson; Horwitz, Steven. 2005. "The Functions of the Family in the Great Society." *Cambridge Journal of Economics* 29: 669–684; Kramer, Laura. 2011. *The Sociology of Gender: A Brief Introduction*. New York: Oxford University Press.

9. Copur, Zeynep, and Tanya Koropeckyj-Cox. 2010. "University Students' Perceptions of Childless Couples and Parents in Ankara, Turkey." *Journal of Family Issues* 31: 1481–1506; Park, Kristin. 2002. "Stigma Management among the Voluntarily Childless." *Sociological Perspectives* 45: 21–45.

10. Angeles, Luis. 2010. "Children and Life Satisfaction." *Journal of Happiness*

Studies 11: 523–538; Hansen, Thomas. 2012. "Parenthood and Happiness: A Review of Folk Theories versus Empirical Evidence." *Social Indicators Research* 108: 29–64; Hoffenaar, Peter Johannes, Frank van Balen, and Jo Hermanns. 2010. "The Impact of Having a Baby on the Level and Content of Women's Well-Being." *Social Indicators Research* 97: 279–295; Stanca, Luca. 2012. "Suffer the Little Children: Measuring the Effect of Parenthood on Well-Being Worldwide." *Journal of Economic Behavior & Organization* 81: 742–750; Twenge, Jean M., W. Keith Campbell, and Craig A. Foster. 2003. "Parenthood and Marital Satisfaction: A Meta-Analytic Review." *Journal of Marriage and Family* 65: 574–583.

11. DeOllos, Ione Y., and Carolyn A. Kapinus. 2002. "Aging Childless Individuals and Couples: Suggestions for New Directions in Research." *Sociological Inquiry* 72: 72–80.

12. Gillespie, Rosemary. 2003. "Childfree and Feminine: Understanding the Identity of Voluntarily Childless Women." *Gender & Society* 17(1): 122–136.

13. Giddens, Anthony. 1992. *The Transformation of Intimacy: Sexuality, Love & Eroticism in Modern Societies*. Stanford, CA: Stanford University Press.

14. Meghan Daum interview on *Pregnant Pause* podcast, episode 4a, "The Central Sadness w/Meghan Daum." https://cms.megaphone.fm/channel/PSM7314629533?selected=PSM4393347499.

15. Houseknecht, Sharon K. 1987. "Voluntary Childlessness." *Handbook of Marriage and the Family*, edited by Marvin B. Sussman and Suzanne K. Steinmetz. New York: Plenum Press, pp. 369–395.

16. Aron, Arthur, Christina C. Norman, Elaine N. Aaron, Colin McKenna, and Richard E. Heyman. 2000. "Couples' Shared Participation in Novel and Arousing Activities and Experienced Relationship Quality." *Journal of Personality and Social Psychology* 78(2): 273–284.

17. Johnson, Heather A., Ramon B. Zabriskie, and Brian Hill. 2006. "The Contribution of Couple Leisure Involvement, Leisure Time, and Leisure Satisfaction to Marital Satisfaction." *Marriage & Family Review* 40(1): 69–91.

18. U.S. Travel Association. 2013. "Travel Strengthens Relationships and Ignites Romance." Research Report, Washington, DC.

19. Aron, Arthur, Christina C. Norman, Elaine N. Aaron, Colin McKenna, and Richard E. Heyman. 2000. "Couples' Shared Participation in Novel and Arousing Activities and Experienced Relationship Quality." *Journal of Personality and Social Psychology* 78(2): 273–284.

20. Crawford, Duane W., and Ted L. Huston. 1993. "The Impact of the Transition to

Parenthood on Marital Leisure." *Personality and Social Psychology Bulletin* 19(1): 39–46.

21. Macvarish, Jan. 2006. "What Is 'the Problem' of Singleness?" *Sociological Research Online* 11(3): 1–8.

22. Reynolds, Jill, and Margaret Wetherell. 2003. "The Discursive Climate of Singleness: The Consequences for Women's Negotiation of a Single Identity." *Feminism & Psychology* 13(4): 489–510.

23. DePaulo, Bella. 2016. *Single, No Children: Who Is Your Family?* Amazon Digital Services: DoubleDoor Books.

24. Addie, Elizabeth, and Charlotte Brownlow. 2014. "Deficit and Asset Identity Constructions of Single Women without Children Living in Australia: An Analysis of Discourse." *Feminism & Psychology* 24(4): 423–439.

25. Kramer, Laura. 2011. *The Sociology of Gender: A Brief Introduction*. New York: Oxford University Press.

26. Laslett, Barbara, and Johanna Brenner. 1989. "Gender and Social Reproduction: Historical Perspectives." *Annual Review of Sociology* 15: 381–404.

27. Owens, Nicole, and Liz Grauerholz. 2018. "Interspecies Parenting: How Pet Parents Construct Their Roles." *Humanity & Society* 42: 1–24; see also Basten, Stuart. 2009. "Pets and the 'Need to Nurture.'" The Future of Human Reproduction: Working Paper #3. St. John's College, Oxford, and Vienna Institute of Demography.

28. Serpell, James. 1996. *In the Company of Animals: A Study of Human-Animal Relationships*. Cambridge: Cambridge University Press; Mathes, Eugene W., and Donna J. Deuger. 1982. "Jealousy, a Creation of Human Culture?" *Psychological Reports* 51: 351–354.

29. Rehn, Therese, Ragen T. S. McGowan, and Linda J. Keeling. 2013. "Evaluating the Strange Situation Procedure (SSP) to Assess the Bond between Dogs and Humans." *PLoS ONE* 8: e56938.

30. Greenebaum, Jessica. 2004. "It's a Dog's Life: Elevating Status from Pet to 'Fur Baby' at Yappy Hour." *Society & Animals* 12: 117–135.

31. Eggum, Arne. 1984. *Edvard Munch: Paintings, Sketches, and Studies*. New York: Clarkson Potter.

32. Hodgson, Kate et al. 2015. "Pets' Impact on Your Patients' Health: Leveraging Benefits and Mitigating Risk." *Journal of the American Board of Family Medicine* 28(4): 526–534.

33. Herzog, Harold. 2011. "The Impact of Pets on Human Health and Psychological Well-Being." *Current Directions in Psychological Science* 20(4): 236–239.

34. McConnell, Allen R., Christina M. Brown, Tonya M. Shoda, Laura E. Stayton, and Colleen E. Martin. 2011. "Friends with Benefits: On the Positive Consequences of Pet Ownership." *Journal of Personality and Social Psychology* 101(6): 1239–1252.

35. Casciotti, Dana, and Diana Zuckerman. "The Benefits of Pets for Human Health." National Center for Health Research nonprofit organization. http ://center4research.org/healthy-living-prevention/pets-and-health-the-impact-of -companion-animals/.

36. Newman, Lareen. 2008. "How Parenthood Experiences Influence Desire for More Children in Australia: A Qualitative Study." *Journal of Population Research* 25(1): 1–27; see also Margolis, Rachel, and Mikko Myrskylä. 2015. "Parental Well-Being Surrounding First Birth as a Determinant of Further Parity Progression." *Demography* 52: 1147–1166.

37. Basten, Stuart. 2009. "Pets and the 'Need to Nurture.'" The Future of Human Reproduction: Working Paper #3. St. John's College, Oxford, and Vienna Institute of Demography; see also Laurent-Simpson, Andrea. 2017. "'They Make Me Not Wanna Have a Child': Effects of Companion Animals on Fertility Intentions of the Childfree." *Sociological Inquiry* 87(4): 586–607.

38. Owens, Nicole, and Liz Grauerholz. 2018. "Interspecies Parenting: How Pet Parents Construct Their Roles." *Humanity & Society* 42: 1–24.

39. Gillespie, Dair L., Ann Leffler, and Elinor Lerner. 2002. "If It Weren't for My Hobby, I'd Have a Life: Dog Sport, Serious Leisure, and Boundary Negotiations." *Leisure Studies* 21: 285–304.

40. Volsche, Shelly, and Peter Gray. 2016. "'Dog Moms' Use Authoritative Parenting Styles." *Human-Animal Interaction Bulletin* 4(2): 1–16.

41. Prato-Previde, Emanuela, Gaia Fallani, and Paolo Valsecchi. 2006. "Gender Differences in Owners Interacting with Pet Dogs: An Observational Study." *Ethology: International Journal of Behavioral Biology* 112(1): 64–73.

42. http://asecher.com/the-not-moms/.

43. Gillespie, Dair L., Ann Leffler, and Elinor Lerner. 2002. "If It Weren't for My Hobby, I'd Have a Life: Dog Sport, Serious Leisure, and Boundary Negotiations." *Leisure Studies* 21: 285–304; Greenebaum, Jessica. 2004. "It's a Dog's Life: Elevating Status from Pet to 'Fur Baby' at Yappy Hour." *Society & Animals* 12: 117–135.

44. Henderson, Steve. 2013. "Spending on Pets: 'Tails' from the Consumer Expenditure Survey." *Beyond the Numbers: Prices & Spending*, Vol. 2, No. 16 (U.S.

Bureau of Labor Statistics). https://www.bls.gov/opub/btn/volume-2/spending-on
-pets.htm.

45. http://www.etonline.com/news/171968_kim_cattrall_explains_why_the_term
_childless_is_offensive/.

46. Bird, Chloe E. 1999. "Gender, Household Labor, and Psychological Distress:
The Impact of the Amount and Division of Housework." *Journal of Health and
Social Behavior* 40(1): 32–45; Craig, Lyn, and Abigail Powell. 2018. "Shares of
Housework between Mothers, Fathers, and Young People: Routine and Non-
Routine Housework, Doing Housework for Oneself and Others." *Social Indica-
tors Research* 136(1): 269–281; Hochschild, Arlie, and Anne Machung. 1989,
2003. *The Second Shift*. New York: Penguin; Horne, Rebecca M., Matthew D.
Johnson, Nancy L. Galambos, and Harvey J. Krahn. 2017. "Time, Money, or
Gender? Predictors of the Division of Household Labour across Life States." *Sex
Roles Online First*, September 26, pp. 1–15; Lachance-Grzela, Mylene. 2010.
"Why Do Women Do the Lion's Share of Housework? A Decade of Research."
Sex Roles 63(11–12): 767–780.

47. Charmes, Jacques. 2015. "Time Use across the World: Findings of a World Com-
pilation of Time Use Surveys." Background paper for Human Development Report 2015. United Nations Development Programme, Human Development
Report Office, New York.

48. United Nations Development Programme. 2016. Human Development Report
2016: Human Development for Everyone. Washington, DC: Communications
Development Incorporated.

49. Endendijk, Joyce J., Belle Derkes, and Judi Mesman. 2018. "Does Parenthood
Change Implicit Gender-Role Stereotypes and Behaviors?" *Journal of Marriage
and Family* 80(1): 61–79.

50. Barnes, Medora W. 2015. "Gender Differentiation in Paid and Unpaid Work during the Transition to Parenthood." *Sociology Compass* 9(5): 348–364.

51. Baxter, Janeen, Belinda Hewitt, and Michele Haynes. 2008. "Life Course Transitions and Housework: Marriage, Parenthood, and Time on Housework." *Journal
of Marriage and Family* 70(2): 259–272.

52. Callan, Victor. 1986. "Single Women, Voluntary Childlessness and Perceptions
about Life and Marriage." *Journal of Biosocial Science* 18: 479–487.

53. Abma, Joyce C., and Gladys M. Martinez. 2006. "Childlessness among Older
Women in the United States: Trends and Profiles." *Journal of Marriage and Family*
68: 1045–1056; Baber, Kristine M., and Albert S. Dreyer. 1986. "Gender-Role

Orientations in Older Child-Free and Expectant Couples." *Sex Roles* 14: 501–512; Bram, Susan. 1984. "Voluntarily Childless Women: Traditional or Nontraditional?" *Sex Roles* 10: 195–206; Callan, Victor J. 1986. "Single Women, Voluntary Childlessness and Perceptions about Life and Marriage." *Journal of Biosocial Science* 18: 479–487; Houseknecht, Sharon K. 1982. "Voluntary Childlessness in the 1980s: A Significant Increase?" *Alternatives to Traditional Family Living*: 51–69.

54. Baber, Kristine M., and Albert S. Dreyer. 1986. "Gender-Role Orientations in Older Child-Free and Expectant Couples." *Sex Roles* 14(9/10): 501–512.

55. Callan, Victor. 1986. "Single Women, Voluntary Childlessness and Perceptions about Life and Marriage." *Journal of Biosocial Science* 18: 479–487.

56. Coontz, Stephanie. 2005. *Marriage, a History: How Love Conquered Marriage*. New York: Penguin.

57. Bachu, Amara. 1999. "Is Childlessness among American Women on the Rise?" Population Division Working Paper No. 37. Washington, DC: U.S. Bureau of the Census; Chandra, Anjani, Gladys M. Martinez, William D. Mosher, Joyce C. Abma, and Jo Jones. 2005. "Fertility, Family Planning, and Reproductive Health of U.S. Women: Data from the 2002 National Survey of Family Growth." Division of Vital Statistics, Series 23, Number 25. Hyattsville, MD: U.S. Department of Health and Human Services, Centers for Disease Control and Prevention; Hagestad, Gunhild O., and Vaughn R. Call. 2007. "Pathways to Childlessness: A Life Course Perspective." *Journal of Family Issues* 28: 1338–1361; Mattessich, Paul W. 1979. "Childlessness and Its Correlates in Historical Perspective: A Research Note." *Journal of Family History* 4: 299–307.

58. Bachu, Amara. 1999. "Is Childlessness among American Women on the Rise?" Population Division Working Paper No. 37. Washington, DC: U.S. Bureau of the Census.

59. Wood, Glenice J., and Janice Newton. 2006. "Childlessness and Women Managers: 'Choice,' Context, and Discourses." *Gender, Work and Organization* 13: 338–358.

60. Keizer, Renske, Pearl A. Dykstra, and Anne-Rigt Poortman. 2010. "Life Outcomes of Childless Men and Fathers." *European Sociological Review* 26(1): 1–15; Budig, Michelle J. 2014. *The Fatherhood Bonus and the Motherhood Penalty: Parenthood and the Gender Pay Gap*. Washington, DC: Third Way.

61. Shea, Molly. 2018. "Baby Birthday Parties Have Infested Brooklyn's Bar Scene." *New York Post*, February 27.

62. http://www.cso.ie/en/media/csoie/census/documents/census2011profile5/Profile
_5_Households_and_Families_full_doc_sig_amended.pdf.

CHAPTER 6

1. Clinton, Hillary Rodham. 1996. *It Takes a Village: And Other Lessons Children Teach Us*. New York: Simon & Schuster.

2. Collins, Patricia Hill. 1990. *Black Feminist Thought: Knowledge, Consciousness, and the Politics of Empowerment*. Boston: Unwin Hyman.

3. Pollet, Thomas V., and Robin I. Dunbar. 2008. "Childlessness Predicts Helping of Nieces and Nephews in United States, 1910." *Journal of Biosocial Science* 40(5): 761–770.

4. Reid, Megan, and Andrew Golub. 2018. "Low-Income Black Men's Kin Work: Cohabiting Stepfamilies." *Journal of Family Issues* 39(4): 960–984.

5. Glass, Amy. 2014. "I Look Down on Young Women with Husbands and Kids and I'm Not Sorry." *Thought Catalogue*, January 16.

6. Jeub, Chris. 2014. "We Look Down on Child Free Ideology and We're Not Sorry." www.chrisjeub.com.

7. Graham, Melissa, Carly Smith, and Margaret Shield. 2015. "Women's Attitudes towards Children and Motherhood: A Predictor of Future Childlessness?" *Journal of Social Inclusion* 6(2): 5–18.

8. McQuillan, Julia, Arthur L. Greil, Karina M. Shreffler, and Veronica Tichenor. 2008. "The Importance of Motherhood among Women in the Contemporary United States." *Gender & Society* 22(4): 477–496.

9. Callan, Victor. 1982. "How Do Australians Value Children? A Review and Research Update Using the Perceptions of Parents and Voluntarily Childless Adults." *Australian & New Zealand Journal of Sociology* 18(3): 384–398.

10. Seccombe, Karen. 1991. "Assessing the Costs and Benefits of Children: Gender Comparisons among Childfree Husbands and Wives." *Journal of Marriage and the Family* 53(1): 191–202; Blackstone, Amy, and Mahala Dyer Stewart. 2016. "'There's More Thinking to Decide': How the Childfree Decide Not to Parent." *The Family Journal* 24: 296–303.

11. Cohany, Sharon R., and Emy Sok. 2007. "Trends in Labor Force Participation of Married Mothers of Infants." *Monthly Labor Review* 130(2): 9–16.

12. Hochschild, Arlie, and Anne Machung. 1989, 2003. *The Second Shift*. New York: Penguin.

13. Matysiak, Anna, Letizia Mencarini, and Daniel Vignoli. 2016. "Work-Family

Conflict Moderates the Relationship between Childbearing and Subjective Well-Being." *European Journal of Population* 32(3): 355–379.

14. http://www.salon.com/2015/10/07/im_a_baby_hater_and_im_not_sorry/.

15. Houseknecht, Sharon. 1987. "Voluntary Childlessness." *Handbook of Marriage and Family*, edited by Marvin B. Sussman and Suzanne K. Steinmetz. New York: Plenum Press, pp. 369–395.

16. Melanie Notkin, a childless-by-circumstance author and marketer, coined and trademarked the term PANK. As the founder of lifestyle brand Savvy Auntie, "for cool aunts, great-aunts, godmothers, and all women who love kids," Notkin was among the first to call attention to the reality that not being a mother does not mean one does not enjoy children. Though much of her work centers on calling attention to women without children as a viable market segment, Notkin's market research highlights the significant role that non-mothers play in children's lives.

17. Sotirin, Patty, and Laura L. Ellingson. 2007. "Rearticulating the Aunt: Feminist Alternatives of Family, Care, and Kinship in Popular Performances in Aunting." *Cultural Studies <-> Critical Methodologies* 7(4): 442–459.

18. May, Elaine Tyler. 1995. *Barren in the Promised Land: Childless Americans and the Pursuit of Happiness*. Cambridge: Harvard University Press.

19. May, Elaine Tyler. 1995. *Barren in the Promised Land: Childless Americans and the Pursuit of Happiness*. Cambridge: Harvard University Press, p. 205.

20. DeVries Global. 2014. *Shades of Otherhood: Marketing to Women without Children*. White paper.

21. Milardo, Robert. 2005. "Generative Uncle and Nephew Relations." *Journal of Marriage and Family* 67(5): 1226–1236.

22. Ellingson, Laura L., and Patricia J. Sotirin. 2006. "Exploring Young Adults' Perspectives on Communication with Aunts." *Journal of Social and Personal Relationships* 23(3): 483–501.

23. Burton, Linda M., and Cecily R. Hardaway. 2012. "Low-Income Mothers as 'Othermothers' to Their Romantic Partners' Children: Women's Coparenting in Multiple Partner Fertility Relationships." *Family Process* 51(3): 343–359; Case, Karen. 1997. "African American Othermothering in the Urban Elementary School." *The Urban Review* 29(1): 25–39.

24. Ellingson, Laura L., and Patricia J. Sotirin. 2006. "Exploring Young Adults' Perspectives on Communication with Aunts." *Journal of Social and Personal Relationships* 23(3): 483–501.

25. Ellingson, Laura L., and Patricia J. Sotirin. 2006. "Exploring Young Adults'

Perspectives on Communication with Aunts." *Journal of Social and Personal Relationships* 23(3): 491.

26. Ellingson, Laura L., and Patricia J. Sotirin. 2006. "Exploring Young Adults' Perspectives on Communication with Aunts." *Journal of Social and Personal Relationships* 23(3): 483–501.

27. https://www.webershandwick.com/uploads/news/files/2012_PANKs_Executive Summary.pdf.

28. Tanskanen, Antti O. 2014. "Childlessness and Investment in Nieces, Nephews, Aunts, and Uncles in Finland." *Journal of Biosocial Science* 47(3): 402–406.

29. Pollet, Thomas V., Toon Kuppens, and Robin I. M. Dunbar. 2006. "When Nieces and Nephews Become Important: Differences between Childless Women and Mothers in Relationships with Nieces and Nephews." *Journal of Cultural and Evolutionary Psychology* 4(2): 83–93.

30. https://www.nysun.com/opinion/why-i-let-my-9-year-old-ride-subway-alone /73976./

31. Skenazy, Lenore. 2010. *Free-Range Kids: How to Raise Safe, Self-Reliant Children (without Going Nuts with Worry)*. San Francisco: Jossey-Bass.

32. https://www.nytimes.com/2018/07/27/opinion/sunday/motherhood-in-the-age -of-fear.html?smid=fb-nytimes&smtyp=cur.

33. https://le.utah.gov/~2018/bills/static/SB0065.html.

34. Baldwin Grossman, Jean, Nancy Resch, and Joseph P. Tierney. 2000. "Making a Difference: An Impact Study of Big Brothers/Big Sisters." Re-issue of 1995 Study. Public/Private Ventures.

35. Valenti, Jessica. 2012. *Why Have Kids? A New Mom Explores the Truth about Parenting and Happiness*. New York: Houghton Mifflin Harcourt, p. 166.

36. Milardo, Robert M. 2009. *The Forgotten Kin: Aunts and Uncles*. Cambridge: Cambridge University Press.

CHAPTER 7

1. Houseknecht, Sharon. 1987. "Voluntary Childlessness." *Handbook of Marriage and Family*, edited by Marvin B. Sussman and Suzanne K. Steinmetz. New York: Plenum Press, pp. 369–395.

2. Blackstone, Amy, and Mahala Stewart. 2012. "Choosing to Be Childfree: Research on the Decision Not to Parent." *Sociology Compass* 6: 718–727; Copur, Zeynep, and Tanya Koropeckyj-Cox. 2010. "University Students' Perceptions of Childless Couples and Parents in Ankara, Turkey." *Journal of Family Issues* 31: 1481–1506; Koropeckyj-Cox, Tanya, Victor Romano, and Amanda Moras. 2007.

"Through the Lenses of Gender, Race, and Class: Students' Perceptions of Childless/Childfree Individuals and Couples." *Sex Roles* 56: 415–428; Park, Kristin. 2002. "Stigma Management among the Voluntarily Childless." *Sociological Perspectives* 45: 21–45; Veevers, Jean E. 1973. "Voluntary Childlessness: A Neglected Area of Family Study." *The Family Coordinator* 22: 199–205.

3. Dykstra, Pearl A., and Gunhild O. Hagestad. 2007. "Road Less Taken: Developing a Nuanced View of Older Adults without Children." *Journal of Family Issues* 28(10): 1275–1310.

4. http://time.com/2814527/pope-francis-dogs-cats-pets/.

5. http://werenothavingababy.com/childfree/funnywoman-jen-kirkman-is-not-having-a-baby-i-can-barely-take-care-of-myself/.

6. Morell, Carolyn. 1994. *Unwomanly Conduct: The Challenges of Intentional Childlessness*. New York: Routledge.

7. Hank, Karsten, and Michael Wagner. 2013. "Parenthood, Marital Status, and Well-Being Later in Life: Evidence from SHARE." *Social Indicators Research* 114: 639–653.

8. Wenger, G. Clare. 2001. "Ageing without Children: Rural Wales." *Journal of Cross-Cultural Gerontology* 16(1): 79–109.

9. DePaulo, Bella. 2006. *Singled Out: How Singles Are Stereotyped, Stigmatized, and Ignored, and Still Live Happily Ever After*. New York: St. Martin's Press; Klinenberg, Eric. 2012. *Going Solo: The Extraordinary Rise and Surprising Appeal of Living Alone*. New York: Penguin; Traister, Rebecca. 2016. *All the Single Ladies: Unmarried Women and the Rise of an Independent Nation*. New York: Simon & Schuster.

10. https://www.youtube.com/watch?v=lyZysfafOAs.

11. DeLyser, Gail. 2012. "At Midlife, Intentionally Childfree Women and Their Experiences of Regret." *Clinical Social Work Journal* 40: 66–74.

12. Connidis, Ingrid Arnet, and Julie A. McMullin. 1999. "Permanent Childlessness: Perceived Advantages and Disadvantages among Older Persons." *Canadian Journal on Aging* 18(4): 447–465.

13. Jeffries, Sherryl, and Candace Konnert. 2002. "Regret and Psychological Well-Being among Voluntarily and Involuntarily Childless Women and Mothers." *International Journal of Aging and Human Development* 54(2): 89–106.

14. http://money.cnn.com/2015/11/25/news/economy/friendsgiving-on-the-rise/index.html.

15. Weston, Kath. 1991. *Families We Choose: Lesbians, Gays, Kinship*. New York: Columbia University Press.

16. Kendig, Hal, Pearl A. Dykstra, Ruben I. van Gaalen, and Tuula Melkas. 2007. "Health of Aging Parents and Childless Individuals." *Journal of Family Issues* 28(11): 1457–1486.

17. Włodarczyk, Piotr, and Artur Ziółkowski. 2009. "Having Children and Physical Activity Level and Other Types of Pro-Health Behaviour of Women from the Perspective of the Theory of Planned Behaviour." *Baltic Journal of Health and Physical Activity* 1(2): 143–149.

18. Modig, Karin, Mats Talbäck, and Anders Ahlbom. 2017. "Payback Time? Influence of Having Children on Mortality in Old Age." *Journal of Epidemiology & Community Health* 71(5): 424–430.

19. It should be noted that the study cited did not distinguish childfree from childless. It is possible that an absence of children affects life expectancy differently depending on whether that absence was chosen.

20. Nelson, Margaret K. 2013. "Fictive Kin, Families We Choose, and Voluntary Kin: What Does the Discourse Tell Us?" *Journal of Family Theory & Review* 5(4): 259–281; Roberto, Karen A., and Rosemary Blieszner. 2015. "Diverse Family Structures and the Care of Older Persons." *Canadian Journal on Aging* 34(3): 305–320; Weston, Kath. 1991. *Families We Choose: Lesbians, Gays, Kinship*. New York: Columbia University Press.

21. Croghan, Catherine F., Rajean P. Moone, and Andrea M. Olson. 2014. "Friends, Family, and Caregiving among Midlife and Older Lesbian, Gay, Bisexual, and Transgender Adults." *Journal of Homosexuality* 61(1): 79–102.

22. Muraco, Anna, and Karen Fredriksen-Goldsen. 2011. "'That's What Friends Do': Informal Caregiving for Chronically Ill Midlife and Older Lesbian, Gay, and Bisexual Adults." *Journal of Social and Personal Relationships* 28(8): 1073–1092.

23. Dykstra, Pearl A., and Michael Wagner. 2007. "Pathways to Childlessness and Late-Life Outcomes." *Journal of Family Issues* 28(11): 1487–1517.

24. Connidis, Ingrid Arnet, and Julie A. McMullin. 1994. "Social Support in Older Age: Assessing the Impact of Marital and Parent Status." *Canadian Journal on Aging* 13(4): 510–527.

25. Wenger, Clare G., Pearl A. Dykstra, Tuula Melkas, and Kees C. P. M. Knipscheer. 2007. "Social Embeddedness and Late-Life Parenthood: Community Activity, Close Ties, and Support Networks." *Journal of Family Issues* 28(11): 1419–1456.

26. Klinenberg, Eric. 2012. *Going Solo: The Extraordinary Rise and Surprising Appeal of Living Alone*. New York: Penguin.

27. Cornwell, Benjamin, Edward Laumann, and L. Philip Shumm. 2008. "The Social Connectedness of Older Adults: A National Profile." *American Sociological Review* 73: 185–203.

28. Wenger, G. Clare. 2009. "Childlessness at the End of Life: Evidence from Rural Wales." *Ageing & Society* 29(8): 1243–1259.

29. "Grandparents Investing in Grandchildren: The MetLife Study on How Grandparents Share Their Time, Values, and Money." 2012. Report released by Generations United and MetLife Mature Market Institute. http://gu.org/LinkClick .aspx?fileticket=E-Cw0qhYz4U%3D&tabid=157&mid=606.

30. Callan, Victor. 1982. "How Do Australians Value Children? A Review and Research Update Using the Perceptions of Parents and Voluntarily Childless Adults." *The Australian & New Zealand Journal of Sociology* 18(3): 384–398.

31. Rauhala, Emily. 2018. "He Was One of Millions of Chinese Seniors Growing Old Alone. So He Put Himself Up for Adoption." *Washington Post*, May 1. https:// www.washingtonpost.com/world/asia_pacific/he-was-one-of-millions -of-chinese-seniors-growing-old-alone-so-he-put-himself-up-for-adoption /2018/05/01/53749264–3d6a-11e8–912d-16c9e9b37800_story.html?utm _term=.fad434511642.

32. Hatton, Celia. 2013. "New China Law Says Children 'Must Visit Parents.'" BBC News, July 1. http://www.bbc.com/news/world-asia-china-23124345.

33. Kim, Leland. 2012. "Loneliness Linked to Serious Health Problems and Death among Elderly." UCSF News Center, June 18. https://www.ucsf.edu/news /2012/06/12184/loneliness-linked-serious-health-problems-and-death-among -elderly.

34. http://www.apa.org/news/press/releases/2017/08/lonely-die.aspx.

35. Perissinotto, Carla M., Irena Stijacic Cenzer, and Kenneth E. Covinsky. 2012. "Loneliness in Older Persons: A Predictor of Functional Decline and Death." *Archives of Internal Medicine* 172(14): 1078–1083.

36. Courtin, Emilie, and Martin Knapp. 2017. "Social Isolation, Loneliness and Health in Old Age: A Scoping Review." *Health & Social Care in the Community* 25(3): 799–812.

37. Kitzmüller, Gabriele, Anne Clancy, Mojtaba Vaismoradi, Charlotte Wegener, and Terese Bondas. 2018. "'Trapped in an Empty Waiting Room'—The Existential Human Core of Loneliness in Old Age: A Meta-Synthesis." *Qualitative Health Research* 28(2): 213–230.

38. Klinenberg, Eric. 2012. *Going Solo: The Extraordinary Rise and Surprising Appeal of Living Alone*. New York: Penguin.

39. Callan, Victor. 1982. "How Do Australians Value Children? A Review and Research Update Using the Perceptions of Parents and Voluntarily Childless Adults." *The Australian & New Zealand Journal of Sociology* 18(3): 384–398.

40. http://www.pewsocialtrends.org/2015/05/21/4-caring-for-aging-parents/.

41. http://www.pewresearch.org/fact-tank/2015/11/18/5-facts-about-family-caregivers/.

42. Blake, Lucy. 2017. "Parents and Children Who Are Estranged in Adulthood: A Review and Discussion of the Literature." *Journal of Family Theory & Review* 9(4): 521–536.

43. Bland, Becca. 2014. "Stand Alone: The Prevalence of Family Estrangement." Report of Stand Alone, United Kingdom.

44. http://www.pewsocialtrends.org/2015/05/21/5-helping-adult-children/.

45. http://www.travelandleisure.com/parenting/mother-retirement-home-take-care-of-son.

46. Walsemann, Katrina M., and Jennifer A. Ailshire. 2017. "A New Midlife Crisis? An Examination of Parents Who Borrow to Pay for Their Children's College Education." Presented at Population Association of America Annual Meeting, Chicago.

47. Scholz, John Karl, and Ananth, Seshadri. 2007. "Children and Household Wealth." Michigan Retirement Research Center Research Paper No. WP 2007–158.

48. http://www.pewresearch.org/fact-tank/2013/02/11/most-say-adult-children-should-give-financial-help-to-parents-in-need/.

49. Klinenberg, Eric. 2012. *Going Solo: The Extraordinary Rise and Surprising Appeal of Living Alone.* New York: Penguin.

50. Connidis, Ingrid Arnet, and Julie A. McMullin. 1994. "Social Support in Older Age: Assessing the Impact of Marital and Parent Status." *Canadian Journal on Aging* 13(4): 510–527.

51. Daatland, Svein Olav. 1990. "'What Are Families For?': On Family Solidarity and Preference for Help." *Ageing & Society* 10(1): 1–15.

52. Rubin-Terrado, Marilyn Ann. 1994. *Social Supports and Life Satisfaction of Older Childless Women and Mothers Living in Nursing Homes.* Doctoral Dissertation in Human Development and Social Policy, Northwestern University.

53. Zhang, Zhenmei, and Mark D. Hayward. 2001. "Childlessness and the Psychological Well-Being of Older Persons." *Journal of Gerontology: Social Sciences* 56B(5): S311–S320.

54. Scholz, John Karl, and Ananth Seshadri. 2007. "Children and Household Wealth." Michigan Retirement Research Center Research Paper No. WP 2007–158.

55. Lugauer, Steven, Jinlan Ni, and Zhichao Yin. 2015. "Micro-Data Evidence on Family Size and Chinese Household Savings Rates." Working Paper Series, University of Notre Dame, Department of Economics; Plotnick, Robert D. 2009. "Childlessness and the Economic Well-Being of Older Americans." *Journal of Gerontology: Social Sciences* 64B(6): 767–776.

56. Blanchard, Janice. 2013–2014. "Aging in Community: The Communitarian Alternative to Aging in Place, Alone." *Journal of the American Society on Aging* 37(4): 6–13.

57. https://www.washingtonpost.com/local/a-new-generation-of-golden-girls-embrace
-communal-living-as-they-get-older/2014/06/15/b3a67b30-edb3–11e3–9b2d
-114aded544be_story.html?utm_term=.2bf4e17ff8ac; https://goldengirlsnetwork
.com/.

58. http://www.cohousing.org/aging.

59. Coele, Michele. 2014. "Co-Housing and Intergenerational Exchange: Exchange of Housing Equity for Personal Care Assistance in Intentional Communities." *Working with Older People* 18(2): 75–81.

60. http://littlebrotherssf.org/.

61. "All in Together: Creating Places Where Young and Old Can Thrive." 2018. Report released by The Eisner Foundation and Generations United. http:
//gu.org/RESOURCES/PublicationLibrary/AllInTogether.aspx.

62. According to AARP, 11.6 percent of women aged eighty to eighty-four in 2010 were non-mothers; by 2030 that number is expected to increase to 16 percent. Redfoot, Donald, Lynn Feinberg, and Ari Houser. 2013. "The Aging of the Baby Boom and the Growing Care Gap: A Look at Future Declines in the Availability of Family Caregivers." *Insight on the Issues* 85: 1–12.

63. Rodman, Margaret Critchlow. 2013. "Co-Caring in Senior Cohousing: A Canadian Model for Social Sustainability." *Social Sciences Directory* 2(4): 106–113.

64. https://www.realtor.com/news/trends/seniors-seeking-roommates/.

65. Zhang, Zhenmei, and Mark D. Hayward. 2001. "Childlessness and the Psychological Well-Being of Older Persons." *Journal of Gerontology: Social Sciences* 56B(5): S311–S320.

66. Cowan, Carolyn Pape et al. 1985. "Transitions to Parenthood: His, Hers, and Theirs." *Journal of Family Issues* 6(4): 451–481; Johnson, Matthew D. 2016. *Great Myths of Intimate Relationships: Dating, Sex, and Marriage*. West Sussex: Wiley-Blackwell; Karney, Benjamin R., and Thomas N. Bradbury. 1995. "The Longitudinal Course of Marital Quality and Stability: A Review of Theory, Method, and

Research." *Psychological Bulletin* 118(1): 3–34; White, Lynn K., and Alan Booth. 1985. "The Transition to Parenthood and Marital Quality." *Journal of Family Issues* 6(4): 435–449.

67. Bures, Regina M., Tanya Koropeckyj-Cox, and Michael Lee. 2009. "Childlessness, Parenthood, and Depressive Symptoms among Middle-Aged and Older Adults." *Journal of Family Issues* 30(5): 670–687.

68. Simon, Robin W., and Leda Nath. 2004. "Gender and Emotion in the United States: Do Men and Women Differ Significantly in Self-Reports of Feelings and Expressive Behavior?" *American Journal of Sociology* 109(5): 1137–1176.

69. Kahneman, Daniel, Alan B. Krueger, David A. Schkade, Norbert Schwartz, and Arthur A. Stone. 2004. "A Survey Method for Characterizing Daily Life Experience: The Day Reconstruction Method." *Science* 306: 1776–1780.

70. Twenge, Jean M., W. Keith Campbell, and Craig A. Foster. 2003. "Parenthood and Marital Satisfaction: A Meta-Analytic Review." *Journal of Marriage and Family* 65: 574–583.

71. Glass, Jennifer, Robin W. Simon, and Matthew A. Andersson. 2016. "Parenthood and Happiness: Effects of Work-Family Reconciliation Policies in 22 OECD Countries." *American Journal of Sociology* 122(3): 886–929; Nugent, Colleen N., and Lindsey I. Black. 2016. "Sleep Duration, Quality of Sleep, and Use of Sleep Medication, by Sex and Family Type, 2013–2014." NCHS Data Brief, No. 230.

72. Simon, Robin W. 2008. "The Joys of Parenthood, Reconsidered." *Contexts* 7(2): 40–45.

73. Myrskylä, Mikko, and Rachel Margolis. 2012. "Happiness: Before and After Kids." Max Planck Institute for Demographic Research. Working Paper.

74. Nelson, S. Katherine, Kostadin Kushlev, Tammy English, Elizabeth W. Dunn, and Sonia Lyubomirsky. 2013. "In Defense of Parenthood: Children Are Associated with More Joy than Misery." *Psychological Science* 24(1): 3–10.

75. Bhargava, Saurabh, Karim S. Kassam, and George Loewenstein. 2014. "A Reassessment of the Defense of Parenthood." *Psychological Science* 25(1): 299–302.

76. Cheng, Sheung-Tak, Trista Wai Sze Chan, Geoff H. K. Li, and Edward M. F. Leung. 2014. "Childlessness and Subjective Well-Being in Chinese Widowed Persons." *Journals of Gerontology, Series B: Psychological Sciences and Social Sciences* 69(1): 48–52.

77. Evenson, Ranae J., and Robin W. Simon. 2005. "Clarifying the Relationship between Parenthood and Depression." *Journal of Health and Social Behavior* 46(4): 341–358.

78. Cetre, Stephanie, Andrew E. Clark, and Claudia Senik. 2016. "Happy People Have Children: Choice and Self-Selection into Parenthood." *European Journal of Population* 32: 445–473.

79. Margolis, Rachel, and Mikko Myrskylä. 2011. "A Global Perspective on Happiness and Fertility." *Population and Development Review* 37(1): 29–56.

80. Glass, Jennifer, Robin W. Simon, and Matthew A. Andersson. 2016. "Parenthood and Happiness: Effects of Work-Family Reconciliation Policies in 22 OECD Countries." *American Journal of Sociology* 122(3): 886–929.

81. McLanahan, Sara, and Julia Adams. 1987. "Parenthood and Psychological Well-Being." *Annual Review of Sociology* 13: 237–257.

82. Glenn, Norval D., and Sara McLanahan. 1981. "The Effects of Offspring on the Psychological Well-Being of Older Adults." *Journal of Marriage and Family* 43(2): 409–421.

83. Simon, Robin W. 2008. "The Joys of Parenthood, Reconsidered." *Contexts* 7(2): 40–45.

84. Blackstone, Amy. 2014. "Doing Family without Having Kids." *Sociology Compass* 8: 52–62; DeOllos, Ione Y., and Carolyn A. Kapinus. 2002. "Aging Childless Individuals and Couples: Suggestions for New Directions in Research." *Sociological Inquiry* 72: 72–80; Houseknecht, Sharon K. 1987. "Voluntary Childlessness." *Handbook of Marriage and the Family*, edited by Marvin B. Sussman and Suzanne K. Steinmetz. New York: Plenum Press, pp. 369–395; Tomczak, Lisa M. 2012. *Childfree or Voluntarily Childless? The Lived Experience of Women Choosing Non-Motherhood*. Master's Thesis, Northern Arizona University. Ann Arbor: ProQuest; Veevers, Jean E. 1980. *Childless by Choice*. Toronto: Butterworths.

85. Cowan, Carolyn Pape et al. 1985. "Transitions to Parenthood: His, Hers, and Theirs." *Journal of Family Issues* 6(4): 451–481.

86. Renne, Karen S. 1970. "Correlates of Dissatisfaction in Marriage." *Journal of Marriage and the Family* 32(1): 54–67.

87. Belsky, Jay, Graham B. Spanier, and Michael Rovine. 1983. "Stability and Change in Marriage across the Transition to Parenthood." *Journal of Marriage and Family* 45(3): 567–577.

88. Somers, Marsha D. 1993. "A Comparison of Voluntarily Childfree Adults and Parents." *Journal of Marriage and the Family* 55: 643–650.

89. Twenge, Jean M., W. Keith Campbell, and Craig A. Foster. 2003. "Parenthood and Marital Satisfaction: A Meta-Analytic Review." *Journal of Marriage and Family* 65: 574–583.

90. Chong, Alexandra, and Kristin D. Mickelson. 2016. "Perceived Fairness and

Relationship Satisfaction during the Transition to Parenthood: 'The Mediating Role of Spousal Support." *Journal of Family Issues* 37(1): 3–28.

91. Burman, Bonnie, and Diane de Anda. 1986. "Parenthood and Nonparenthood: A Comparison of Intentional Families." *Lifestyles* 8: 69–84; Cowan, Carolyn Pape et al. 1985. "Transitions to Parenthood: His, Hers, and Theirs." *Journal of Family Issues* 6(4): 451–481; Dew, Jeffrey, and W. Bradford Wilcox. 2011. "If Momma Ain't Happy: Explaining Declines in Marital Satisfaction among New Mothers." *Journal of Marriage and Family* 73(1): 1–12; Feldman, Harold. 1971. "The Effects of Children on the Family." *Family Issues of Employed Women in Europe and America*, edited by Andrée Michel. Leiden, The Netherlands: E. J. Brill, pp. 107–125; Houseknecht, Sharon K. 1979. "Childlessness and Marital Adjustment." *Journal of Marriage and the Family* 41(2): 259–265; White, Lynn K., and Alan Booth. 1985. "The Transition to Parenthood and Marital Quality." *Journal of Family Issues* 6(4): 435–449.

92. Zagura, Michelle. 2012. *Parental Status, Spousal Behaviors and Marital Satisfaction*. Master's Thesis, SUNY-Albany. Ann Arbor: ProQuest.

93. Hansen, Thomas. 2012. "Parenthood and Happiness: A Review of Folk Theories versus Empirical Evidence." *Social Indicators Research* 108: 29–64.

94. Angeles, Luis. 2010. "Children and Life Satisfaction." *Journal of Happiness Studies* 11: 523–538.

95. Bien, Agnieszka, Ewa Rzonca, Grazyna Iwanowicz-Palus, Urszula Lecyk, and Iwona Bojar. 2017. "Quality of Life and Satisfaction with Life of Women Who Are Childless by Choice." *Annals of Agricultural and Environmental Medicine* 24(2): 250–253; Dykstra, Pearl A., and Michael Wagner. 2007. "Pathways to Childlessness and Late-Life Outcomes." *Journal of Family Issues* 28(11): 1487–1517; Koropeckyj-Cox, Tanya. 1998. "Loneliness and Depression in Middle and Old Age: Are the Childless More Vulnerable?" *Journal of Gerontology: Social Sciences* 53B(6): S303-S312.

96. Rubin-Terrado, Marilyn Ann. 1994. *Social Supports and Life Satisfaction of Older Childless Women and Mothers Living in Nursing Homes*. Doctoral Dissertation in Human Development and Social Policy, Northwestern University.

97. Vikstrom, Josefin et al. 2011. "The Influences of Childlessness on the Psychological Well-Being and Social Network of the Oldest Old." *BMC Geriatrics* 11:78.

CHAPTER 8

1. As quoted in Healey, Jenna. 2016. "Rejecting Reproduction: The National

Organization for Non-Parents and Childfree Activism in 1970s America." *Journal of Women's History* 28(1): 131–156.

2. Drut-Davis, Marcia. 2013. *Confessions of a Childfree Woman: A Life Spent Swimming against the Mainstream*. Amazon Digital Services.

3. http://www.childfreereflections.com/wp-content/uploads/2013/11/Marcia _Drut-Davis_Exclusive_Interview_NPR.mp3.

4. https://internationalchildfreeday.com/winner-announcement/.

5. http://werenothavingababy.com/childfree/childfree-1974–2013-marcia-drut -davis/.

6. http://werenothavingababy.com/childfree/childfree-choice-circumstance/.

7. https://nypost.com/2016/09/28/these-women-think-having-a-dog-car-or-job -is-the-same-as-having-a-kid/.

8. Leavesley, J. H. 1980. "Brief History of Vasectomy." *Family Planning Information Service* 1(5): 2–3.

9. Shih, Grace, David K. Turok, and Willie J. Parker. 2011. "Vasectomy: The Other (Better) Form of Sterilization." *Contraception* 83(4): 310–315.

10. Bartz, Deborah, and James Greenberg. 2008. "Sterilization in the United States." *Reviews in Obstetrics & Gynecology* 1(1): 23–32.

11. http://www.malehealthcenter.com/c_vasectomy.html.

12. https://www.brookings.edu/blog/social-mobility-memos/2016/10/14/whats -stopping-american-men-from-getting-vasectomies/.

13. United Nations, Department of Economic and Social Affairs, Population Division. 2015. *Trends in Contraceptive Use Worldwide 2015* (ST/ESA/SER.A /349); Joshi, Ritu, Suvarna Khadilkar, and Madhuri Patel. 2015. "Global Trends in Use of Long-Acting Reversible and Permanent Methods of Contraception: Seeking a Balance." *International Journal of Gynecology and Obstetrics* 131: S60-S63.

14. Shattuck, Dominick, Brian Perry, Catherine Packer, and Dawn Chin Quee. 2016. "A Review of 10 Years of Vasectomy Programming and Research in Low-Resource Settings." *Global Health: Science and Practice* 4(4): 647–660.

15. https://www.mayoclinic.org/tests-procedures/vasectomy/about/pac-20384580.

16. Amor, Cathy et al. 2008. "Men's Experiences of Vasectomy: A Grounded Theory Study." *Sexual and Relationship Therapy* 23(3): 235–245.

17. Terry, Gareth, and Virginia Braun. 2013. "'We Have Friends, for Example, and He Will *Not* Get a Vasectomy': Imagining the Self in Relation to Others When Talking about Sterilization." *Health Psychology* 32(1): 100–109.

18. Cragun, Ryan T., and J. E. Sumerau. 2017. "Losing Manhood Like a Man: A Collaborative Autoethnographic Examination of Masculinities and the Experience of a Vasectomy." *Men and Masculinities* 20(1): 98–116.

19. https://www.cnn.com/2014/11/07/health/world-vasectomy-day/index.html.

20. http://www.worldvasectomyday.org/what-is-wvd/.

21. https://www.devex.com/news/opinion-world-vasectomy-day-how-to-engage -men-in-family-planning-efforts-91537.

22. http://www.worldvasectomyday.org/what-is-wvd/.

23. United Nations, Department of Economic and Social Affairs, Population Division. 2015. *Trends in Contraceptive Use Worldwide 2015* (ST/ESA/SER.A/349).

24. http://people.com/bodies/male-birth-control-study-ends-mood-swings/; https:// www.theatlantic.com/health/archive/2016/11/the-different-stakes-of -male-and-female-birth-control/506120/; https://www.salon.com/2016/10/31/men -cant-handle-side-effects-from-hormonal-birth-control-that-women-deal -with-every-day/; https://broadly.vice.com/en_us/article/59mpgq/men-abandon -groundbreaking-study-on-male-birth-control-citing-mood-changes; https://www .cosmopolitan.com/health-fitness/a8038748/male-birth-control-study-stopped/.

25. Behre, Hermann M. et al. 2016. "Efficacy and Safety of an Injectable Combination Hormonal Contraceptive for Men." *Journal of Clinical Endocrinology & Metabolism* 101(12): 4779–4788.

26. Liao, Pamela Verma, and Janet Dollin. 2012. "Half a Century of the Oral Contraceptive Pill: Historical Review and View to the Future." *Canadian Family Physician* 58: e757-e760.

27. http://www.independent.co.uk/voices/male-contraceptive-injection-successful -trial-halted-a7384601.html.

28. https://www.endocrine.org/news-room/2018/dimethandrolone-undecanoate -shows-promise-as-a-male-birth-control-pill.

29. http://www.un.org/en/development/desa/population/publications/pdf/family /trendsContraceptiveUse2015Report.pdf.

30. Christopher, F. Scott. 1995. "Adolescent Pregnancy Prevention." *Family Relations* 44(4): 384–391; Kirby, Douglas B. 2008. "The Impact of Abstinence and Comprehensive Sex and STD/HIV Education Programs on Adolescent Behavior." *Sexuality Research & Social Policy* 5(3): 18–27.

31. Jozkowski, Kristen N., and Brandon L. Crawford. 2016. "The Status of Reproductive and Sexual Health in Southern USA: Policy Recommendations for Improving Health Outcomes." *Sexuality Research and Social Policy* 13(3): 252–262.

32. Potera, Carol. 2008. "Comprehensive Sex Education Reduces Teen Pregnancies." *American Journal of Nursing* 108(7): 18.

33. Marr, Chuck, and Bryann DaSilva. 2016. *Childless Adults Are Lone Group Taxed into Poverty.* Washington, DC: Center on Budget and Policy Priorities.

34. https://www.thebalance.com/state-inheritance-tax-chart-3505460.

35. https://static01.nyt.com/images/2016/07/10/business/10NOTMOM2 /10NOTMOM2-blog427.jpg.

36. Saatchi & Saatchi. 2016. *Moms & Marketing.* http://saatchi.com/en-us/news /saatchi-saatchi-global-study-finds-more-than-half-of-moms-feel-advertisers -arent-speaking-to-them/.

37. Tugend, Alina. 2016. "Childless Women to Marketers: We Buy Things Too." *New York Times,* July 9. https://www.nytimes.com/2016/07/10/business/childless-women -to-marketers-we-buy-things-too.html?mcubz=0.

38. Elder, Katie, and Jess Retrum. 2012. Framework for Isolation in Adults over 50. Report from AARP Foundation. https://www.aarp.org/content/dam/aarp/aarp _foundation/2012_PDFs/AARP-Foundation-Isolation-Framework-Report.pdf.

39. "All in Together: Creating Places Where Young and Old Can Thrive." 2018. Report released by The Eisner Foundation and Generations United. http://gu.org /RESOURCES/PublicationLibrary/AllInTogether.aspx.

40. Marks, Gene. 2017. "A Restaurant Sees a 50% Increase in Sales after Banning Children." *Inc.,* April 6. https://www.inc.com/gene-marks/a-restaurant-sees-a -50-increase-in-sales-after-banning-children.html.

41. Radl, Shirley Rogers. 1973. *Mother's Day Is Over.* New York: Charterhouse.

42. Donath, Orna. 2015. "Regretting Motherhood: A Sociopolitical Analysis." *Signs: Journal of Women in Culture and Society* 40(2): 343–367; see also Donath, Orna. 2017. *Regretting Motherhood: A Study.* Berkeley: North Atlantic Books.

43. Mackenzie, Jean. 2018. "The Mothers Who Regret Having Children." *BBC News,* April 3. http://www.bbc.com/news/education-43555736; Selinger-Morris, Samantha. 2016. "Scratching Beneath the Surface of Motherhood Regret." *ABC News (Australia),* July 15. http://www.abc.net.au/news/2016–07–16/motherhood -regret-scratching-beneath-the-surface/7588594; Marsh, Stefanie. 2017. "'It's the Breaking of a Taboo': The Parents Who Regret Having Children." *Guardian,* February 11. https://www.theguardian.com/lifeandstyle/2017/feb/11/breaking -taboo-parents-who-regret-having-children; Treleaven, Sarah. 2016. "Inside the Growing Movement of Women Who Wish They'd Never Had Kids." *Marie Claire,* September 30. https://www.yahoo.com/lifestyle/inside-growing-move ment-women-wish-172948984.html.

44. Burns, Judith. 2018. "It's Not Just Women Who Sometimes Regret Parenthood.'" *BBC News*, April 18. http://www.bbc.com/news/education-43703221.

45. Santoro, Alessia. 2018. "Mom Throws a 'Balls Voyage' Party for Her Husband's Vasectomy and LOL, We're Done." *Popsugar*, February 25. https://www.popsugar .com/moms/Mom-Throws-Balls-Voyage-Party-Husband-Vasectomy-44448408.

46. http://werenothavingababy.com/wnhab-childfree-manifesto/.

ABOUT THE AUTHOR

Dr. Amy Blackstone is a professor in sociology at the Margaret Chase Smith Policy Center at the University of Maine, where she studies childlessness and the childfree choice, workplace harassment, and civic engagement. Her work has been published in a variety of peer-reviewed journals, including *American Sociological Review*, *Law & Society Review*, *Sociology Compass*, and *Gender & Society*. Professor Blackstone's research has been featured by various media outlets, including the *Katie* show, public radio, *Washington Post*, BuzzFeed, *USA Today*, *New York Magazine*, *Huffington Post*, and other local and national venues. *Childfree by Choice* is her first book.